Praise for *Creative Construction*

"I really loved this book. Larger companies have so many opportunities to innovate both in technology and business models. The problem isn't scale, but with management practice and mindset; how do we think about, manage, or be smart about it? While it is hard to strike the balance between short-term needs and committing resources to bigger, but unknown changes, it is critical. Gary P. Pisano addresses many issues that can help improve support and strategy for change."

—Ed Catmull, president of Pixar and
Walt Disney Animation Studios, author of *Creativity, Inc.*

"Innovation is the heart of economic progress. *Creative Construction* provides the intellectual framework to understand it, and describes the leadership, strategy, culture, and skills for it to occur in well-resourced large organizations. Along the way, these ideas are beautifully brought to life by examples from the earliest days of the Industrial Revolution to the current era of the FAANGs—Facebook, Amazon, Apple, Netflix, Google."

—Conor Kehoe, McKinsey & Company

"Finally, a book that speaks to me and, actually, any leader in a business that has been around for more than a few years on how we can creatively use our scale for innovation. The next time you hear people opining that innovation is the province of the nimble startup, have them sit down and start reading *Creative Construction.*"

—Joseph Hinrichs, president of global operations,
Ford Motor Company

"In this highly engaging book, Pisano's starting point is the uncomfortable truth that innovation is difficult—sometimes very difficult—to achieve and sustain. Pisano is equally compelling and clear in explaining how companies can evolve their understanding of and approach to innovation, and come to see it not as something ethereal, random, or near-magical, but as the natural outcome of a set of efforts focused on culture, organization, and the bringing together of mindsets and ideas in creative ways. Any entrepreneur or company executive who wants to build a vibrant, innovation-driven business will profit from Pisano's lucid exposition and enjoy his accessible and humorous prose."

—Noubar Afeyan, PhD and chief executive officer,
Flagship Pioneering

"This is not just another book focusing on technical innovation. While Pisano shows concrete examples of innovation in business models, he systematically approaches the fundamental concept of business innovation in the real world. If you are an executive, or a rising leader seeking innovation in your business, Pisano's book offers significant and practical insight for your future strategy and its implementation."

—Michimasa Fujino, president and CEO,
Honda Aircraft Company

"Refreshingly practical in its emphasis on the very difficult 'how-to' of creating value through innovation, while staying grounded in the larger theoretical considerations of strategy, organization and leadership."

—Vicki L Sato, advisor to life science companies and retired
president, Vertex Pharmaceuticals

CREATIVE
CONSTRUCTION

CREATIVE CONSTRUCTION

THE DNA OF
SUSTAINED INNOVATION

GARY P. PISANO

PUBLICAFFAIRS

NEW YORK

PublicAffairs
Hachette Book Group
1290 Avenue of the Americas, New York, NY 10104
www.publicaffairsbooks.com
@Public_Affairs

Printed in the United States of America

First Edition: January 2019

Published by PublicAffairs, an imprint of Perseus Books, LLC, a subsidiary of Hachette Book Group, Inc. The PublicAffairs name and logo is a trademark of the Hachette Book Group.

The publisher is not responsible for websites (or their content) that are not owned by the publisher.

Library of Congress Cataloging-in-Publication Data

Names: Pisano, Gary P., author.
Title: Creative construction : the DNA of sustained innovation / Gary P. Pisano.
Description: New York City : PublicAffairs, an imprint of Perseus Books, a subsidiary
    of Hachette Book Group, [2019] | Includes bibliographical references and index.
Identifiers: LCCN 2018027780 (print) | LCCN 2018044029 (ebook) |
    ISBN 9781610398763 (e-book) | ISBN 9781610398770 (hardcover)
Subjects: LCSH: Technological innovations. | Strategic planning.
Classification: LCC HD45 (ebook) | LCC HD45 .P543 2019 (print) |
    DDC 658.4/063—dc23
LC record available at https://lccn.loc.gov/2018027780

ISBNs: 978-1-61039-877-0 (hardcover); 978-1-61039-876-3 (e-book)

LSC-C

10 9 8 7 6 5 4 3 2 1

To Alice
For never letting me take myself too seriously

Contents

Preface and Acknowledgments   ix

INTRODUCTION
Innovation's Catch-22   1

PART I: CREATING AN INNOVATION STRATEGY   **19**

1 BEGINNING THE JOURNEY
The Discipline and Focus of an Innovation Strategy   21

2 NAVIGATING THE ROUTE
Creating Your Innovation Portfolio   37

3 WHATEVER HAPPENED TO BLOCKBUSTER?
Competing Through Business Model Innovation   57

4 IS THE PARTY REALLY OVER?
Why You Should Not Always Eat Your Own Lunch   85

PART II: DESIGNING THE INNOVATION SYSTEM   **109**

5 VENTURING OUTSIDE YOUR HOME COURT
Search: Discovering Novel Problems and Solutions   111

6 SYNTHESIS
Bringing the Pieces Together   129

7 WHEN TO HOLD 'EM AND WHEN TO FOLD 'EM
Uncertainty, Ambiguity, and the Art and Science
of Selecting Projects   153

PART III: BUILDING THE CULTURE   **179**

8 THE PARADOX OF INNOVATIVE CULTURES
Why It's Not All Fun and Games   181

9 LEADERS AS CULTURAL ARCHITECTS
Reengineering the Cultural DNA of an Enterprise   197

10 BECOMING A CREATIVE CONSTRUCTIVE LEADER   217

Notes   225
Bibliography   241
Index   253

Preface and Acknowledgments

Larger enterprises are rarely viewed as fountains of innovation. Over the past several decades, a barrage of writings, news stories, and lectures has conditioned us to accept as a "law" that scale stifles innovation. As enterprises grow, the narrative goes, they inevitably suffer organizational sclerosis and become feeble shadows of their once-dominant former selves. They are helpless in the wake of "disruptive" innovation attacks by nimble, entrepreneurial firms. It is a depressing story that, unfortunately, has unfolded many times. And yet it does not have to be this way.

Creative Construction challenges the dogma that, as enterprises grow, they inevitably lose their capacity for transformative innovation. Over my thirty-year career, I have worked with companies across the full-size spectrum—from the tiniest start-ups to the largest corporations on the planet. Sure enough, I have seen many large enterprises whose inertia, bureaucracy, myopia, and culture left them too paralyzed to undertake anything but the most incremental innovation. Even when they tried to rejuvenate themselves through some type of "innovation initiative," I saw more failures than successes. These cases seemed to confirm the prevailing hypothesis that large scale and innovation don't mix. As I peered further, however, I began to realize that the root cause of such malaise and the reason so many innovation initiatives fail have more to do with management practice and leadership than with organizational scale per se. Yes, organizational size complicates innovation and can make it hard to sustain or renew innovation capabilities. But, the more I looked (and the more I compared experiences with small start-ups), the more I believed that scale *if properly exploited* could actually be an advantage, not a liability, for innovation.

The hypothesis that larger enterprises can become highly innovative started me on a decade-long journey of research, case writing, and consulting to better understand which management practices enable companies to sustain their innovative capabilities even as they grow quite large.

I also dug deeply into decades of academic literature on the drivers of innovation performance. My research and experience along with the work of other scholars led me to conclude that company growth and size do *not* need to spell the end of an organization's innovative days. Innovative performance is rooted in a combination of *strategy, organizational systems, and culture,* all of which are shaped by leadership. *Creative Construction* explores how leaders of both growing and large established enterprises can develop strategies, design systems, and build cultures required for sustained innovation performance.

Many management books promise simple solutions to complex problems. Unfortunately, at least when it comes to innovation, I do not believe such a recipe or formula exists. Innovation is *hard.* It is not only hard to come up with a commercially successful innovation, but it is even harder to build an organization capable of creating such innovations time and again. There is no magic elixir or single best model for building a durably innovative enterprise. Different enterprises have followed different approaches. Thus, I offer no simple blueprints for instant innovation success. Instead, I wrote *Creative Construction* for thoughtful practitioners seeking well-grounded principles and frameworks that can help them find the paths that work best for *their* organizations. Innovation is and always will be a difficult journey. My hope is that this book inspires and prepares you to lead this journey.

Although I have spent my entire career as an academic at the Harvard Business School, I have also engaged heavily in the world of practice as a consultant, as a company cofounder, and as a board member of several enterprises. Having my feet in the worlds of both practice and academia has shaped how I see the problems explored in this book. I have written *Creative Construction* to bridge these two worlds. While drawing from my own and others' scholarly research on innovation (references are provided in the endnotes for the interested reader), I have tried to write in an accessible style. My hope was to create a book that has the expected *rigor* of scholarly work without its typical *mortis*.

A project like this would not have been possible without the help and support of many different organizations and individuals. I am grateful for the generous financial support provided by the Harvard Business School to pursue the research underpinning this book. Many of the examples used in the book are from case studies I wrote thanks to the funding of the Harvard Business School. These examples are acknowledged in the references.

In addition to academic research and case writing, my work has benefitted from extensive consulting experience with a broad range of companies throughout the world and across many industries, including the pharmaceutical and life sciences industry, specialty chemicals, medical devices, manufacturing, financial services, consumer products, electronics, and telecommunications. Such experience has exposed me to the real challenges faced by practitioners operating in complex organizations. Through my consulting, I have been better able to understand how hypothesized solutions to problems actually work in practice. The feedback I received from numerous clients has been enormously valuable to me. In various parts of this book, I use examples drawn from my consulting experience. Where those examples may contain proprietary or sensitive information, I do not name the companies unless I have received explicit permission from the individuals and companies involved.

Many company examples in the book are based on publicly available information. Some of those examples include companies with which I also happened to have consulted or been associated in some capacity. In keeping with Harvard Business School's conflict of interest policies, and my own personal beliefs in transparency, the companies referenced in the book for whom I have consulted, served as a director, or have a financial interest exceeding $10,000 include the following: Johnson & Johnson, Genentech (a wholly owned subsidiary of the Roche Group), Corning Corporation, Becton Dickinson, GlaxoSmithKline, Microsoft, Teradyne, and Flagship Pioneering (a significant investor in Axcella Health, where I serve on the board of directors).

I am deeply grateful to my colleagues at Harvard Business School, who have been enormous sources of intellectual stimulation. In particular, I want to thank my mentors, Kent Bowen, Kim Clark, Bob Hayes, and Steve Wheelwright, whose intellectual fingerprints are all over this book. My understanding of the issues explored here also benefitted immeasurably from collaboration and teaching with Amy Edmondson, Willy Shih, and Vicki Sato. I also want to thank Dean Nitin Nohria of the Harvard Business School for his friendship and support over the course of my career.

I am grateful to Andrea Kates for a number of conversation that really got me thinking seriously about the problems of innovating at scale and for her insightful comments on an early outline. I would especially like to thank Bill Kozy for his helpful comments on the proposal and for countless conversations over the years that shaped this book in profound ways.

I am indebted to Eric von Hippel of MIT, who has inspired my work since we met in the early 1980s and who generously provided detailed comments and suggestions on several chapters. I want to thank my good friend, collaborator, and colleague Francesca Gino for her comments on specific chapters and for the many conversations we have shared about the topics covered in this book.

I am deeply indebted to John Mahaney, my editor at Hachette Book Group. From our first conversation about the book proposal, John has been incredibly supportive and is everything an author could ask for in an editor. I also want to thank my agent, Danny Stern, and his team at Stern & Associates for support and guidance on this project from the beginning.

My longtime collaborator, Sharon Pick, worked behind the scenes once again, reading and editing drafts and providing very helpful comments. This is now the third book I have written with Sharon's help, and I grow ever more grateful to her with each one. Jesse Shulman, my research assistant at Harvard Business School, did a terrific job conducting extensive and diligent background research. I am especially thankful to Sophie Bick, who did a first-rate job in preparing the manuscript for publication.

Finally, I want to sincerely thank my wife, Alice. I know full well the sacrifices you have borne for the sake of my work, particularly in the past year. You accommodated my incessant travel and my countless sudden urges to write (regardless of the chaos our two young children might be wreaking at the moment!). Your patience and endless support make me realize how lucky I am to have you by my side. This work is as much yours as it is mine.

Concord, Massachusetts
April 3, 2018

INTRODUCTION
Innovation's Catch-22

One of the many unforgettable scenes in Joseph Heller's *Catch-22* culminates in Yossarian's insight that "Orr would be crazy to fly more missions and sane if he didn't, but if he was sane he had to fly them. If he flew them he was crazy and didn't have to; but if he didn't want to he was sane and had to. Yossarian was moved very deeply by the absolute simplicity of this clause of Catch-22 and let out a respectful whistle. 'That's some catch, that Catch-22.'"

Yossarian would perhaps also be deeply moved by the paradox of innovation, one that comes with its own special catch. Innovation spawns growth, and growth by definition leads to scale, but scale seems to make the task of innovation more difficult. Even worse, the imperative to innovate keeps escalating because competition is dynamic. Rivals and new entrants eventually imitate what you have or come up with something even better. The more you succeed at innovation, the more you need to keep innovating, but the harder the task becomes. It is like those cardiac stress tests where the medical technician turns up the speed of the treadmill every time you get comfortable. You might be forgiven for thinking the technician is trying to kill you. Fortunately, the technician (usually) knows enough to stop the test before you have a heart attack. But competition does not work this way. No one is turning down the dial. In fact, competitors really do want to kill you!

Companies innovate to grow. It is hard to think of many companies in the past hundred years that achieved significant scale without being an innovator. Industrial giants of the twentieth century—DuPont, RCA, Ford, General Electric, Disney, Johnson & Johnson, McDonald's, IBM, Walmart, Kodak, Intel, Microsoft—and those of the twenty-first century—Apple, Google, Amazon, Facebook—were all innovators of

1

either technology or business models. Innovate and you grow. This is the promise. It's why in 2017 US companies invested about $365 billion on R&D. Globally, corporate R&D expenditures topped $700 billion in 2017, according to the most recent estimates.[1] It's why venture capitalists invested $155 billion in 2017.[2] And why every company CEO talks about the imperative to innovate and why business school executive programs on innovation are oversubscribed. Like all promises, though, this one comes with a catch.

The idea that successful innovators sow the seeds of their own destruction was originally posed more than seventy years ago. The great Austrian economist Joseph Schumpeter described a process he termed "creative destruction" whereby existing "economic structures" (which included existing enterprises) could be destroyed by either technological innovation or organizational innovation.[3] Writing in 1939, Schumpeter was particularly astute in recognizing that established successful enterprises were vulnerable to the "gales of creative destruction":

> Most new firms are founded with an idea and for a definite purpose. The life goes out of them when that idea or purpose has been fulfilled or has become obsolete or even if, without having become obsolete, it has ceased to be new. That is the fundamental reason why firms do not exist forever. Many of them are, of course, failures from the start.... [O]thers die a "natural" death, as men die of old age. And the "natural" cause, in the case of firms, is precisely their inability to keep up the pace in innovating which they themselves had been instrumental in setting in the time of their vigor.[4]

Beginning in the 1980s, a set of scholarly studies began to unearth the underlying reasons why once-successful innovators might ultimately be swept away by the winds of creative destruction.[5] As the autopsies piled up—Xerox, RCA, Polaroid, Kodak, Wang, DEC, Nokia, RIM, Sun Microsystems, AT&T, Yahoo, and many others—a depressing picture emerged. Large established enterprises not only appeared to be incapable of leading any type of revolution; they could not even respond to attacks by new entrants. Their organizational pathologies included inertia and growing bureaucratization, loss of tolerance for risk, fears about cannibalizing existing products, ingrained processes for R&D, commitment to existing technologies and assets, religious adherence to current business models, an overreliance on flawed financial metrics, and leadership myopia. When it comes to innovation, large enterprises looked like patients suffering from multiple deadly maladies.

The thesis that large corporations cannot succeed at transformative innovation has been repeated so often by so many that—like some law of nature—it is no longer questioned. This is not just an academic issue but also one that influences management practice. Even leaders of many larger enterprises seem to have surrendered to the "fact" that they cannot grow organically through innovation but instead must buy innovation through acquisitions. Investors and analysts also believe it. They pressure larger enterprises to cut back on riskier, long-term research projects to free up cash for stock buybacks and dividends. The highly influential investment bank Morgan Stanley, for instance, issued an analyst report in January 2010 recommending that pharmaceutical companies dramatically slash internal research spending and instead focus on in-licensing development drugs from external sources.[6] Citing the industry's poor track record of R&D productivity, the report argued that buying innovation from the outside offered a better return on investment. The implicit assumption in this report is that larger companies are inherently less capable of innovation than are smaller biotechnology companies.

Transformative innovation inside a large enterprise is viewed as a complete waste of shareholder money. Better to return the money to shareholders, who can give it to venture capitalists to invest in start-ups. When I told a longtime venture capitalist friend of mine that I was writing a book on innovation in large enterprises, he smiled wryly and said, "At least it will be a short book. They can't."

Large organizations are said to lack the DNA for innovation. This genetic metaphor is powerful because for natural species (like us humans), capabilities are deeply rooted in DNA. DNA explains why a cheetah runs faster than an elephant. And, in natural species, DNA is essentially immutable for the individual. Growing up in Westwood, Massachusetts, I dreamed of playing for the Boston Celtics. Unfortunately, my DNA (or, more precisely, the DNA I inherited from my parents) endowed me with neither great height nor much athletic prowess. And, no matter how many hours I practiced in the driveway, there was nothing I could do to change my DNA. This is where the metaphor breaks down. Natural laws, like those associated with genetics, govern *natural* phenomena. Organizations, of course, are not natural phenomena; they are completely man-made, designed and run by people. "Organizational DNA" is not immutable. Unlike you or me, organizations *can* manipulate their own DNA. *Through systematically creating an innovation strategy, designing an innovation system, and building an innovation culture,* organizations develop the capability for transformative innovation regardless of scale. If larger enterprises seem incapable of transformative innovation, it is because we design them and run them to be that way. *Creative Construction* examines how we can design and run them differently in order to better succeed at innovation.

Small Is Beautiful Does Not Mean Big Is Ugly

There is no doubt that entrepreneurial firms are a potent source of transformative innovation. Entrepreneurial firms have revolutionized countless industries, from software and semiconductors to beer and biotechnology. Whenever you see an industry transformed, you usually do not have to look far to see an Intel, an Apple, a Microsoft, a Genentech, a Netscape, an Amazon, a Google, a Netflix, or an Uber. Yes, many (many!) start-ups die. We only get to celebrate the few big winners, but as an organizational species, entrepreneurial firms are spectacularly successful innovators. When it comes to innovation, small *can be* beautiful.

Does this mean, though, that big must therefore be ugly when it comes to innovation? I spend a lot of time in both entrepreneurial firms and very big companies as researcher and advisor. And, at first glance, the answer would seem to be yes. Instead of the creative focus, energy, and youthful enthusiasm of the start-up, I too often find endless hours of meetings, labyrinths of procedures and policies, and decision making mangled by byzantine organizational matrices. Whereas the start-up wants to be a Formula 1 race car (fast, agile, not very reliable, and sometimes pretty dangerous), the large enterprise emulates a freight train—predictable, boring, and rigid.

You may have made the same observation or even experienced the difference directly by moving from a big corporation to a start-up or working in a start-up acquired by a big corporation. You might have worked in a successful start-up that, thanks to its success, became relatively large. I have come across many instances where the transition from Formula 1 race car to freight train happened relatively fast in the life of a company. One day, it was a nimble, hungry start-up aspiring to revolutionize an industry; a few years later, after it had $1 billion in annual revenue, it was a freight train barreling down a single track. But this observation raises a few questions. Is this state of organizational affairs inevitable? Are the innovation-stifling characteristics we commonly see in a larger organization inherent to its large scale, or are they simply the artifacts of conscious or unconscious design choices made by its leaders? Are successful young companies really doomed to become lumbering freight trains if they are fortunate enough to grow? *Must big be ugly when it comes to innovation?*

Despite our perception about smallness and beauty and bigness and ugliness, it may be surprising that statistical evidence relating company size and innovation paints a far more nuanced picture.[7] Big does not always mean ugly. Scale alone is not an impediment to innovative capacity. My own work on this topic compared the R&D productivity of large pharmaceutical companies to that of biotechnology companies from 1984 to 2004.[8] At the time I performed the study, the conventional wisdom in the industry was that large pharmaceutical companies were less productive at R&D than smaller biotechnology companies (the same logic underpinning the Morgan Stanley analyst report). But my study—which traced the origin of every drug approved over a twenty-year period by the largest twenty pharmaceutical companies and more than 250 biotechnology companies—showed a "statistical dead heat" between the R&D productivity of both types of companies. So much for the hypothesis that big is ugly.

But what about transformational innovation—the type that ushers in waves of creative destruction and leads to upheavals of entire industries? The evidence here is a bit clearer but still not completely without important wrinkles. In general, innovations that disrupt specific industries *tend* to originate from new *entrants*.[9] I stress "tend" because there are important exceptions. Consider, for instance, that Intel revolutionized the semiconductor industry by inventing and commercializing the microprocessor. Intel, however, was already a semiconductor company; it was not a new entrant into the semiconductor industry when it invented and commercialized the microprocessor. Second, I stress "entrants" because there is a big difference between a new firm (a start-up) and a new entrant. Established firms can be new entrants if they diversify from one industry to another. Waves of creative destruction can originate from firms of any size. Large size does not prevent companies from being transformative innovators.

Let's consider some historical and more recent examples. In April 1964, IBM introduced the 360 line of mainframe computers.[10] Prior to that time, every new machine required the development of a unique new operating system and hardware. There was little if any interchangeability between machines, even those made by the same company. This was becoming incredibly costly because everything had to be developed from scratch. It also made maintenance and support a major headache. IBM revolutionized computer architecture by creating common underlying software, like the operating system, and hardware that could be used across multiple machines. Today, we take this concept of modularity and interoperability for granted. In 1964, it was unheard of, and it completely revolutionized the computer industry. It triggered an explosion in demand for mainframes, and it created new markets for peripherals and software development. In 1964, IBM was neither a start-up nor a new entrant into the computer industry. It was already the largest computer company in the world and ranked number 18 on the Fortune 500 that year (its sales of $2 billion would be equivalent to approximately $15.5 billion today after adjusting for inflation).[11] This is a great example of a large, dominant incumbent in an industry disrupting the very industry in which it competed. Most theories of innovation say this is not supposed to happen. But it did.

Let's take another example. In 1982, a team of scientists modified the genetics of a plant cell, an invention that laid the foundation for today's genetically modified crops. Despite the controversy, it is hard to dispute the economic significance of this innovation. GMOs account for the vast majority of soybeans, corn, and cotton produced in the United States and transformed the agricultural seed industry. But this invention did not come from a start-up. It came from a team of scientists working at then-eighty-one-year-old Monsanto Corporation, a behemoth agricultural chemicals company (ranked number 50 on the Fortune 500 in 1982, with sales of $6.9 billion, the equivalent of $17.1 billion today). At the time, Monsanto was not even in the seed business, but today it is the world's largest seed company. This is an example of a large player from one industry transforming itself and another industry through innovation.

There are many other historical examples of large companies succeeding at transformative innovation. Think about 150-year-old Corning, which invented fiber-optic cable and the glass manufacturing processes critical to today's computer, television, and phone displays. And, of course, Bell Labs almost single-handedly drove the transformation of the twentieth century with a series of inventions such as the transistor, the microwave, cellular communications, the laser, satellite communications, digital transmission and switching, solar cells, and the Unix operating system (among many others). Bell's massive size did not seem to impede its capacity for innovation.

Well, then, you may think, "History is fine, but times have changed. The day of the big lab is dead. We live in the age of entrepreneurs." So, let's move closer to the present: Apple. Everyone knows the story of how the iPhone completely redefined the market from mobile phones to mobile communications. It was both a classic Schumpeterian gale—destroying once-mighty incumbents like Nokia, Motorola, and RIM—and a brilliant act of creative construction. In 2007, the year Apple launched the iPhone, the company was no spring chicken: it was thirty years old. And it was no minnow either. Its sales of $24.6 billion put it at number 123 on the Fortune 500.[12]

Amazon is another contemporary example of a huge company invading other industries. There are really two Amazon stories. The first is the classic start-up. This was the story of how Amazon.com brought us into the world of online shopping, at the expense of just about every brick-and-mortar retailer. The second story, though, is one of a still-young but relatively large company, which has continued to succeed at transformational innovation. In 2004, Amazon introduced one of the first cloud-based computing services and launched the cloud computing revolution. This represented a major business model innovation for Amazon, as selling web services is completely different from being an online retail business. Amazon's revenues that year were $5.2 billion, and the company ranked number 342 on the Fortune 500.[13] Amazon might have been young, but it was *not* small by any standard. Today, Amazon is a $178 billion company, and it continues to innovate and experiment with new businesses such as video streaming, content production, drone delivery, groceries, and health care.[14]

Today, we see a number of large companies actively engaged in potentially transformative innovation. Alphabet (formerly known as Google) is a $90 billion enterprise (ranked number 27 on the Fortune 500).[15] It dominates Internet advertising, of course, but it has also been a pioneer in autonomous vehicles. Honda, a giant auto company, is attempting to transform the corporate jet market by developing a low-cost, lightweight jet that can efficiently serve as an "air taxi." It is too early to say whether these businesses will succeed, but they are certainly trying. If large enterprises are not supposed to pursue transformative innovation, it looks like these folks never got the memo.

These examples—and probably many more you can think of—provide something akin to an "existence proof" that scale alone is *not* a showstopper when it comes to transformative innovation. But just because something is possible does not mean it is easy, either. It's not. Innovating at scale takes work—work that is dependent upon thoughtful strategies and significant efforts that are distinct from those that tend to succeed in small enterprises.

The Challenge of Creative Construction

Building an innovative venture from scratch is hard. Many of you can personally attest to the brutally long hours, the harrowing moments when cash is short, and the stress of knowing that just one bad move can spell disaster for the whole enterprise. We celebrate entrepreneurs for good reasons. And yet, as tough as it is to build an innovative company from the ground up, the task of sustaining and rejuvenating an existing organization's innovative capacities—what I call "creative construction"—is even tougher. Whereas entrepreneurship is like building a new house from the ground up (albeit on a tight budget), creative construction is akin to renovating a home while living in it. It takes real creativity to build something new out of something old. Creative construction takes leaders who constantly renew and rebuild their organizations' innovative capabilities. They don't buy the rhetoric that success—and the scale that it produces—must ultimately breed stasis. They don't see their organizations, no matter how large, as immutable blocks of stone. They are not content to decline graciously and to die, as Schumpeter said it, as "old men die of old age."

Creative construction requires a delicate balance of exploiting existing resources and capabilities without becoming imprisoned by them. Johnson & Johnson (J&J) provides insight into why creative construction is so difficult, illustrating the extreme end of both the challenge and the opportunity created by scale. J&J is the world's largest health-care company, with revenues of approximately $75 billion.[16] It is, as of this writing, in the top 100 companies in the world by revenues and in the top 15 by market capitalization.[17] It operates in more than sixty countries around the globe and employs 134,000 people.[18] It spends $10.5 billion in R&D—through more than a dozen different R&D laboratories located throughout the United States, Europe, and Asia and also through more than one hundred external partnerships.[19] The company competes across three major health-care sectors—pharmaceuticals, medical devices, and consumer health products—and operates more than 260 subsidiaries.[20] It sells several thousand brands, and every year it launches more than a hundred new products.

For J&J to maintain its historical rate of top line growth, it must generate about $3 billion–$4 billion of *new* revenue per year. If you consider that some portion of the company's existing revenue base becomes obsolete or declines every year, the net incremental growth target becomes even higher. Over the next ten years, J&J needs to generate about $35 billion in net new revenue. To put this challenge in perspective, there are fewer than 5,000 companies in the whole world today with revenues greater than $1 billion per year.[21] This means that J&J cannot just launch an innovation here and there and expect to grow. It has to generate a continuous stream of innovations over time.

This challenge is tough enough, but it gets worse. (I feel like the medical technician turning up the dial on the treadmill.) J&J does not get to start with a blank slate. It has existing businesses, which generate all its revenue and profits, to support and defend. It cannot take its eye off them while pursuing new opportunities. Although it has a massive reservoir of resources and capabilities, many are honed to the requirements of those existing businesses and may not be suited to the new opportunities it wants to explore. Building new capabilities takes time and investment that must come from the existing businesses generating all the profits.

The challenge gets even tougher when you consider the sheer complexity of an organization like J&J. Complexity is a much bigger problem for innovation than scale alone. Complexity is a function of the number of moving parts—such as different business units, different functions, different geographies, different processes, different technologies, and different people—that must be synchronized. And when you get to be the scale of a J&J, you have *a lot* of moving parts. Complexity makes innovation more difficult because innovation, *by definition*, involves change. In a complex organization, innovation in one part might require carefully synchronized changes across different business units, functions, and geographic markets. Add the common reality that not everyone in the organization may see the benefits of an innovation so positively, and you now have a system with serious frictions. Friction impedes mobility. Lack of mobility means lack of innovation.

An example like J&J also highlights, though, the potential benefits of scale for innovation. Larger enterprises like J&J have massive financial resources to explore new opportunities. They can hedge highly risky technology bets through parallel experimentation in ways that start-ups can only dream of. They can build vast networks of external collaborators to explore a broad array of emerging technologies. They have incredibly deep reservoirs of technical talent and operational skills critical to bringing innovations to market. They have global distribution and a strong brand. They have the infrastructure, know-how, and processes to get an innovative new product into the hands of *millions* of customers around the world almost instantly. They have decades of experience working with regulatory and government authorities. You cannot underestimate how critical such complementary capabilities are to successful innovation. Many start-ups with spectacularly great technologies have failed because they lacked these capabilities.

The example of J&J could be applied to countless other large enterprises that face the dilemma of scale that simultaneously is an incredible strength and an incredible liability with respect to innovation. Jeff Bezos, in his 2015 letter to Amazon shareholders, captures this dilemma succinctly: "Used well, our scale enables us to build services for our customers that we could otherwise never have even contemplated. But also, if we are not vigilant and thoughtful, size could slow us down and diminish our inventiveness."[22]

You do not have to be the size of J&J or Amazon to come face-to-face with this dilemma. The challenge of scale creeps into organizations relatively early in their life cycle. Young companies that have successfully launched their first major products and are growing rapidly face many of these same dilemmas: How much to invest in the existing product versus potentially new platforms? How do we leverage our existing capabilities without letting them hamstring us? How do we preserve our Formula 1 culture as we become a larger, more complex organization? The challenge of innovating at scale is to leverage these real strengths while figuring out ways to circumvent or eliminate the potential weaknesses.

Why Most Innovation Initiatives Fail

If you have worked at a large company, you may have lived through something called an "innovation initiative," a major organizational change effort aimed at creating or rejuvenating an organization's innovative capacities. These initiatives take many different forms, but they usually involve some combination of structural, process, and cultural change. They're a typical response when a company's growth has slowed and the CEO or another senior leader decides that innovation is the key to fixing this problem.

If you have lived through one of these rejuvenation campaigns, you can attest to the hurdles involved. Becoming a reborn innovator is *not* like riding a bicycle. Once the innovation muscle has atrophied, it's not a matter of just a bit of "exercise" to get back in form. You have to rebuild those capabilities from the ground up. You have to create entirely new organizational systems and build a new culture. There is a lot to figure out. How do you find new ideas? How do you stimulate creative thinking? How do you figure out which ideas to pursue and drop? How do you motivate people? How do you get people comfortable with all the uncertainties associated with innovation? This is tough stuff. But now consider that you have to do all this within an existing enterprise with existing systems and processes, current structures, and a deeply ingrained culture. Like any major organizational change effort, innovation initiatives are not necessarily going to garner universal support. Conflicts are inevitable. And now remember that you are going to undertake this massive organizational transformation, all the while keeping your *existing* businesses competitive and your finances healthy.

Throughout my career, I have had a chance to observe many such initiatives unfold. They follow an all too familiar pattern. They are launched with great fanfare and enthusiasm. Senior leadership gives encouraging speeches about how important innovation is to the future of the company. Company communications are laced with talk about innovation. Promises are made about big changes to come. The culture will be more tolerant of failure, less hierarchical, and more open to out of the box thinking. Everyone will be encouraged to contribute innovative ideas. Teams of managers tour exemplar innovators (at least those who are willing to let them visit) and come back intoxicated with ideas about how to make the company more "Silicon Valley–like." Structures—like innovation groups or chief innovation officers—are installed to drive the effort. Optimism reigns. But, after a year or two, things begin to bog down. People start noticing that not much has changed. There are few, if any, new innovative programs under way. The few that do get proposed have a hard time gaining traction. There have also been some costly failures. The CFO is asking about the return on investment. Business unit leaders begin to complain that they are being starved of critical resources needed to upgrade product lines and to fend off intensifying competition. Budgets are tight and tough calls have to be made. The company is feeling earnings pressures, and the once-supportive board is concerned about the lack of progress to date. Senior management is feeling the pressure to deliver an innovation win. Throughout the organization, many of the old behaviors are still alive and well. There is little appetite for risk, and the perception that senior management does not *really* tolerate failures is pervasive. There are complaints that the company's bureaucracy is stifling innovation. Communications about innovation come fewer and further between. Senior leaders who happily associated themselves with the innovation initiative now look nervously for other assignments. As time passes, managers further down the ranks adopt a "this too shall pass" attitude.

Why do so many innovation initiatives follow such a depressing path? Why do so many fail? We first have to acknowledge that any major organizational change—whether focused on innovation, quality, customer service, or something else—is extremely difficult. By some estimates, about 70 percent of organizational change efforts fail.[23] The usual reasons for such failures, such as lack of senior management commitment, middle management resistance, and inability to execute, certainly play their part in stifling innovation initiatives. However, the problems go much deeper. In fact, I have observed a number of cases in my career where senior leadership *was* deeply committed to innovation, where the middle managers *were* enthusiastic about the change, and where extensive attention *was* devoted to execution, and, despite all this, the effort still failed.

Why? Because building a capacity to innovate involves overcoming several specific obstacles. The first is the required time horizon. Building innovation capabilities is a multiyear voyage. It cannot be *this year's* goal. Even once the capabilities are built, it takes *at least* one product development cycle to see any impact from your efforts. Depending on the industry, this can range from a couple of years to more than a decade. This is a long time to sustain the requisite management focus and energy. This is particularly true given that you can expect some degree of management turnover during this period.

A second vexing problem is that inherent trade-offs are demanded by innovation. Any company with existing lines of profitable businesses faces a fundamental strategic dilemma: How much should it invest in existing businesses and existing capabilities versus new (uncertain) businesses and capabilities? How much should it invest in incrementally improving existing products and services versus exploring new technology spaces and new business models? Every dollar that goes into exploring a new space means one less dollar for making an important refinement to an existing product. Too often in the writing on innovation, there is a bias that companies should always be investing in the new wave of "disruptive" innovation, and that investments in existing businesses are myopic at best and suicidal at worst. Such thinking grossly oversimplifies the problem. There is often no simple "right" answer to these choices, just complex trade-offs.

Trade-offs are also inherent in choices made about innovation management practices, and a failure to come to grips with such trade-offs is another reason innovative initiatives fail. Too often, innovation initiatives become a grab bag of widely touted "best practices" such as open innovation, design thinking, rapid prototyping, autonomous decentralized teams, and internal venturing. There is nothing wrong with any of these practices per se, but as I discuss throughout this book, there are no universally "best" innovation practices. *Every* innovation practice has its strengths *and weaknesses*. There are no magic bullets.

As a result, building a capacity to innovate requires making some very difficult organizational and process design choices.

Finally, building innovation capabilities involves profound cultural changes. Just about every behavioral norm that enables a company to succeed with existing products and services—reliability, predictability, disciplined execution of well-defined plans—runs counter to the behaviors required to foster innovation—risk taking, creative exploration, rapid learning and experimentation, comfort with ambiguity, and so on. Going back to the great organizational theorist James March, organizations that tend to be good at "exploiting" existing business tend to struggle with "exploring" new terrain.[24] This is partly due to organizational systems and processes, but more important are the cultural differences between what is required to explore versus what is required to exploit. It's not as easy as saying "banish" the old culture, because that culture is critical to driving performance in the existing businesses (which are, after all, paying the bills). A new culture more oriented toward innovation has to be created while also preserving the culture that supports the existing businesses. Innovation initiatives have to confront this conflict.[25]

The Challenge Is the Opportunity

At this point you might be wondering, Why on earth take on such a challenge? Why should I as a leader take on such a risky organizational transformation? (And, by analogy, why should I continue reading the rest of the book?) The odds surely seem heavily stacked against me. Maybe I should heed the advice of so many others to give up on the idea of building an innovative capacity inside a large organization and instead buy up small companies that are good at innovation. This must be easier, faster, and certainly less risky.

But here's the problem with that strategy: If innovation were easy, everyone could do it, and then innovation could no longer be a source of advantage. Competitive advantage rests on possessing *unique* and *difficult to imitate* skills and capabilities. Apple has done well because there are not many Apples out there. The capability to innovate is a potent source of competitive advantage precisely because it is such a difficult one to foster and sustain.

And this is why acquisitions are no shortcut to innovation nirvana. If you can buy something, so can your competitors. The market for corporate assets is pretty efficient. This means that, on average, you get what you pay for. If a great innovative company that everyone wants to buy is on the market, you are going to pay handsomely for that privilege. In many cases, all you end up doing is transferring some of your shareholders' wealth to the acquired firm's shareholders. There is generally no net gain in shareholder wealth created, and, in fact, large acquisitions tend to destroy value for the acquiring firm.[26] Everyone thinks they can "beat the average" because they believe they are smarter than the average. You do not have to have been a math major to see the fallacy of this logic.

Furthermore, if you acquire an innovative firm (for which you have paid dearly), you will still face the task of trying to keep it an innovative organization. The problem is that enterprises that are not especially innovative have a terrible time managing innovative organizations (almost by definition!). All those obstacles we described above—like competing priorities with existing businesses and different cultures—do not go away just because you acquire an innovative company. Suddenly, that company (now a subsidiary) has to flourish inside an enterprise whose systems and culture are not geared toward innovation. This leads to the common outcome where the acquisition itself destroys the acquired firm's unique innovative capabilities and culture. It does not happen all the time. Some firms are able to protect their new acquisitions from the processes, culture, and strategies that have been suppressing innovation all along. But it's rare. It is much more common for the acquirer to "kill the goose that lays the golden eggs." This does not mean acquisitions cannot be part of your tool kit of innovation tactics. Selective M&A can be extremely valuable, especially if there are unique complementarities between your capabilities and the target firm. We will discuss them later in the book. But M&A alone cannot be your innovation strategy.

Throughout this book, I offer no illusions about how difficult it is to innovate at scale. There are many forces that make it hard to build and maintain a capability to innovate. The journey is fraught with many traps. As a leader, you have to be great at strategy, execution, and culture. You will encounter resistance along the way. I am hoping the frameworks, tools, principles, and examples I provide will make the journey easier for you and your organization. But the journey is not easy. Even with the best equipment, the best guides, the best training, and the best strategy, summiting Mount Everest is no cakewalk. But, imagine trying to take on Everest without these resources! Innovation is a capability that must be built, not bought. It is incredibly hard and very risky. But it creates real value and sustainable advantage, leveraging the strengths of a large company in a way that no small start-up can match. That's exactly why you should be trying to do it. My hope is that this book provides you with motivation and the tools to make this difficult task *easier* for you to accomplish. Building an organization's capacity to innovate involves three essential leadership tasks: (1) creating an innovation strategy, (2) designing an innovation system, and (3) building an innovation culture. It is around these three tasks that *Creative Construction* is organized.

PART I
CREATING AN INNOVATION STRATEGY

An innovation strategy specifies how the company intends to use innovation to create and capture value and clarifies priorities among different types of innovation opportunities. A good innovation strategy serves two critical purposes. First, it helps clarify the trade-offs the company is willing to make between short-term exploitation of existing markets and longer-term exploration of new opportunities.[1] Such clarity is critical because, without it, the temptation in most organizations is to focus on exploitation. It always *seems* more profitable to invest in improving the existing product line than to search for something completely new. In clarifying these trade-offs, a clear innovation strategy sets the stage for effective execution. Second, a good innovation strategy helps to align diverse parts of an organization around common priorities. Such alignment is particularly critical in complex organizations with many moving parts. By driving alignment, a good innovation strategy makes a large organization a less complex place for innovation.

Part I of this book provides frameworks and principles needed to create an effective innovation strategy. It examines the different types of innovations a company might pursue, the trade-offs among them, and how different types of innovation (including business model innovation) can be used as part of a company's overall innovation strategy. Part I also provides insights about how to respond to potentially transformative new technologies that may actually *threaten* your business.

1

BEGINNING THE JOURNEY

The Discipline and Focus of an Innovation Strategy

In Lewis Carroll's *Alice's Adventures in Wonderland,* a lost Alice runs into the Cheshire Cat and asks him, "Where should I go?" The grinning Cheshire Cat responds, "That depends on where you want to end up." We do not normally think of children's books written in the mid-nineteenth century as teaching strategy theory, but in essence the Cheshire Cat was invoking the first principle of strategy: strategy starts with clear understanding of objectives. Many organizations start their innovation journeys much like Alice. They lack a clear sense of their innovation objectives. They do not know where they want to go on their innovation journey. Others have clear objectives but do not put in place the strategy to achieve them. Imagine you were going to take a long and difficult trek through the wilderness to reach the summit of a mountain (your goal is clear). The terrain will shift constantly. Huge rocks, fallen timber, and other obstacles will litter the trails. The trails will not be well marked and will often fork unexpectedly. And your expedition consists of a big group of people, not all of whom share your enthusiasm for the wilderness. You would not even think about setting out on such a journey without a reasonable plan, a good map, and a compass. And yet this is essentially what many leaders do when they try to tackle innovation.

Getting Lost on the Innovation Journey

Earlier in my career, I consulted for a company who had once been a leader in the contact lens market. The company's competitive position was being destroyed by a competitor (a J&J subsidiary, it turns out) that had introduced the world's first disposable contact lens. Because they were thrown away every week (and eventually every day), disposable lenses needed less care and cleaning than conventional lenses, which were generally kept for a year or more. The convenience and cost savings was a highly attractive value proposition to patients. Disposable lenses were eating into not only my client's sales of conventional lenses but also its highly lucrative market for the solutions used to care for and clean lenses. The CEO and other members of the senior team recognized that the company would need to make dramatic changes to its product portfolio and position in order to thrive. The company had not been very innovative for the past decade. Its base technology for lenses was more than twenty years old and could not currently produce a competitive disposable lens. Much of the company's innovation in recent years had focused on incremental process improvements, line extensions, and cosmetic changes (e.g., tinting of lenses). To compete, it needed to innovate—but, to innovate, it needed to transform itself. And this is where the company got lost.

The company faced many complex choices. It had to decide how much to invest in improving its existing base technology (which was still supporting almost 100 percent of the current product portfolio) versus exploring completely new lens technologies. Some within the company's manufacturing and R&D organizations argued that the current process technology—with sufficient investment—could be made quite competitive. The head of marketing wanted see a dramatic attempt to leapfrog the competition with breakthrough technologies that had been percolating in one of the company's smaller European R&D sites. And, even among those who advocated a more aggressive R&D posture, there were big differences in whether the focus should be on disposability or visual acuity and comfort. There were also hard choices to be made about lens-care solutions. Sure, that market was slowly declining but it was still quite lucrative (it generated the vast majority of the company's profits), and there was a view within the business unit that easier-to-use solutions could actually help stave off the decline of the conventional lens market. There was no right decision. Each of these positions—investing more in the existing process, exploring breakthrough lens materials, spending more to support the lens-care products—could be justified on its own. But the company did not have unlimited resources. It needed to figure out where to "place its chips." Each path had broader consequences for the organization. For instance, a decision to go after breakthrough lens technology would require an almost complete overhaul of the company's R&D organiza- tion (which lacked expertise in new materials and alternative process technologies). It would also have implications for the company's lens- care business and its marketing strategy. If the company went after breakthrough technologies, it still needed to figure out a way to keep its current product lines competitive in the short term.

Beyond the vague notion that the company "needed to become in- novative," there was, unfortunately, little agreement about what kinds of innovation might help the company regain its advantage and what capabilities the company needed to build. Everyone had his or her own view on this topic. The futility of this approach became apparent at a senior management retreat held on a hot summer day in Switzerland. The meeting started with the CEO addressing the group about the importance of innovation and his absolute determination to see the company become a leader once again. He spoke clearly about the need for the company to take big risks and move out of its comfort zone. The next presentation, by the head of R&D, laid out the current port- folio of R&D projects. After the CEO's speech, I expected to see some big bets on the board. What was presented, however, was a very long list of projects, almost all of which were incremental improvements in the current process, technical troubleshooting fixes, line extensions, and smaller clinical studies designed to support regulatory filings in a variety of geographic markets. Each of these projects could be fully justified on the basis of return on investment and business need. And, as the head of R&D pointed out, there were many other projects the business units clamored for but that he simply did not have the budget to take on. The disconnect between the CEO's idea of "innovative" and the head of R&D's idea of "innovative" could not have been starker. At this stage, I was not sure whether the uncomfortable feeling in the room was due to the lack of air conditioning or the realization among many in the room that the company had lost its way.

Just like it is easy to get lost in the wilderness, it is easy to get lost on the path to innovation capability. Building an innovation capability means facing many complex and difficult choices. Multiple paths may look equally attractive, but all involve their own trade-offs. You must choose among paths with far less than perfect information. And then you must make sure that everyone is heading in the same direction, with the same destination in mind. To navigate tough choices and trade-offs, you need an *innovation strategy*. That is always true of course but *especially* so for larger enterprises.

In this chapter, I will lay out a conceptual framework for innovation strategy. Then, in Chapter 2, I will describe how you can use this framework to design an innovation strategy that is right for your company.

The Concept of an Innovation Strategy and Why You Need One

A strategy is nothing more than a commitment to a set of coherent, mutually reinforcing policies or behaviors aimed at achieving a specific goal.[1] Do not be intimidated by the concept. We all develop and use strategies. "Hit to Jane's backhand and get to the net" is a strategy you may be using in your Saturday morning tennis game. It does not mean you hit to Jane's backhand and go to the net *every* stroke or even every point. It just means you are looking for that opportunity as much as possible because you believe that exploiting Jane's relatively weak backhand (and getting to the net behind it) gives you the best chance to win (your goal). Similarly, "Eat more vegetables and exercise more" is a wellness strategy you might be pursuing. It does not mean becoming a militant vegetarian and working out like a Navy Seal every day. It just means you start prioritizing vegetables in your diet and exercise in your schedule. It's not that complicated. Strategies define patterns of behavior and priorities. They are not exhaustive to-do lists.

Company strategies do not need to be complicated. Southwest Airlines, arguably the most successful airline over the past four decades, has had a pretty simple strategy: offer convenient (nonstop and frequent), low-cost service between medium-sized cities not typically served by traditional airlines. This strategy framed many of the company's subsequent decisions (e.g., which routes? what type of planes? how to staff? etc.). As a principle, strategies should be simple and clear. They should not require a seventy-five-page PowerPoint presentation. (In fact, seventy-five pages is a pretty good indication that this document does not contain a strategy!) Good strategies promote alignment among diverse groups within an organization, clarify objectives and priorities, and help focus efforts around them. In essence, they act like a map and compass. They provide direction. They also speed up decision making. Without a strategy, every decision has to be debated. Should we advertise more this month or less? Should we open a new store in Midtown Manhattan? Should we enter that partnership? Should we launch that product? A strategy should be clear enough to take certain options off the table and to make others no-brainers. Companies regularly create overall business strategies that specify the type of customers they are seeking, the ways they differentiate themselves, and the key value proposition they offer. They also create strategies for how various functions like R&D, marketing, operations, human resources, and finance will support the overall business strategy.

Surprisingly, though, leaders rarely articulate strategies to align innovation with their business strategy. Too often, as with the contact lens company, leaders start the journey of building a new innovation capability with only a vague sense of what they are trying achieve. They do not grapple with the fundamental question, "Why exactly do we want to innovate?" Instead, they start with generalities like "We must innovate to grow" or "We must innovate to stay ahead of competitors," but these are not strategies. They do not provide any clarity about the specific types of innovation that might help the company achieve its competitive objectives and those that won't.

A robust innovation strategy specifies the kinds of innovation that are important for the company to pursue. It requires being clear about how innovation is supposed to create value for potential customers and how the company will capture value from innovation. Becton

Dickinson's (BD) strategy around medical device safety in the 1990s had a clear value proposition to focus its innovation efforts. BD makes a wide range of medical devices for either delivering therapeutic products into the body (e.g., syringes and infusion therapy systems) or removing fluids from the body (e.g., blood sample collection systems and catheters). What they all have in common is some kind of sharp cannula to pierce the patient's skin. "Sharps"—as they are called—expose health-care workers to risks of fluid-borne diseases like AIDS or hepatitis through accidental "needle sticks" or through inappropriate disposal. Recognizing that safety could create a lot of value for the health-care system, BD began to focus its innovation efforts around designing safer devices (e.g., syringes with auto-retractable needles). This was not a one-off effort. It required focused investment over years and over multiple projects, and a commitment to redesigning the entire product portfolio. There was no ambiguity inside the company: safety was not optional. BD's safety-focused innovation strategy is one of the key reasons the company maintained its dominance and attractive margins in a business that had been rapidly commoditizing.

The innovation strategies of many companies focus on a coherent value proposition. Over the decades, Apple has launched multiple different innovations (the Apple II, the iPod, iTunes, the iPhone, the iPad, the App Store), but they all share a common value proposition theme—make the user experience easy and delightful through intuitive interfaces, integrated hardware and software design, and (increasingly) seamless integration of different aspects of our digital lives (music, photos, communication, shopping, etc.). Amazon's focus on making the shopper's experience as convenient and secure as possible shows up in a constellation of innovations—from their one-click checkout and user product reviews to Amazon Prime and Amazon Echo.

Without an explicit innovation strategy, no one actually knows what kinds of innovation are really important to the organization. Anything is possible, and, when anything is possible, everything is potentially important. And when everything is potentially important, *nothing* is *particularly important.* If nothing is particularly important, nothing gets done. That's why good strategies lay the groundwork for good execution. Without clarity around the questions of how innovation is supposed to create value and lead to value capture, different parts of the organization can easily wind up pursuing conflicting priorities. Sales representatives hear daily about the pressing needs of the biggest customers. Marketing may see opportunities to leverage the brand through complementary products or to expand market share through new distribution channels. Business unit heads are focused on their target markets and their particular P&L pressures. R&D scientists and engineers tend to see opportunities in new technologies. A corporate venturing group is looking at riskier long-term bets on young firms with new business models. Every one of these perspectives may be legitimate, and diversity of perspective is critical to successful innovation. But, without a strategy to integrate and align those perspectives around common priorities, the power of diversity is blunted or, worse, becomes self-defeating.

An innovation strategy is also needed to focus the organization's resources and energy on building the right set of capabilities. Without an innovation strategy, innovation improvement efforts easily become a grab bag of much-touted best practices: dividing R&D into decentralized autonomous teams, spawning internal entrepreneurial ventures, setting up corporate venture-capital arms, pursuing external alliances, embracing open innovation and crowdsourcing, collaborating with customers, and implementing rapid prototyping, to name just a few. There is nothing wrong with any of those practices, per se. The problem is that an organization's capacity for innovation stems from an *innovation system*: a coherent set of interdependent processes and structures that dictates how the company searches for novel problems and solutions, synthesizes ideas into a business concept and product designs, and selects which projects get funded. Individual best practices involve trade-offs. And adopting a specific practice generally requires a host of complementary changes to the rest of the organization's innovation system. A company without an innovation strategy won't be able to make trade-off decisions and tailor its innovation capabilities to it specific needs (a topic to which we return in Part II). An innovation strategy should provide a framework that sets priorities and clarifies objectives across multiple innovation projects over time.

Mapping Innovation Opportunities

If you are trying to get good at something, it helps to define what that something is. The same with innovation. Many organizations set out on their journey to build innovation capacity by stating something to the effect of, "We want to become excellent at innovation." But what exactly does this mean? The problem is that "innovation" is a very broad term. It generally conveys something positive, but what specifically it implies is not clear. "Innovation" can mean anything—and, as a result, on its own it means nothing. We need to think about innovation in much finer-grained ways to make it useful.

Some things are obviously innovative. Think about breakthroughs like the telegraph, Edison's light bulb, Ford's assembly line, the first semiconductor, the first television, the first genetically engineered drug (human insulin), Intel's microprocessor, the Netscape browser, or the iPad. There is not a lot of debate about the magnitude of these innovations. They were entirely new concepts that revolutionized industries and even major swaths of the economy after their introductions. However, if you think only about these headline-grabbing breakthroughs as innovation, you are missing about 99 percent of the innovation landscape.

Most innovation is much less obvious. It does not make headlines, and it does not even seem all that new. In fact, when you look at some of these innovations, you are tempted to ask, "So what's really new here?" Consider ready-to-eat salad that comes already washed and cut in bags, first introduced in 1984 by a small California lettuce producer.[2] It did involve some process innovations around mechanized cutting of the lettuce leaves and washing processes to ensure product safety and integrity, but the core components—lettuce and plastic bags— were hardly new (lettuce was cultivated by the ancient Egyptians as far as 3500 BC, and plastic bags were introduced in the early part of twentieth century). While such packaging innovations may not have the "whizz bang" character of an iPad, they are nonetheless economically important. Ready-to-eat produce now represents about half the US leafy vegetable market.[3] Innovation pundits often dismiss improvements in packaging, manufacturing processes, and product features as "merely incremental," but that misses the point. The way to judge innovation is not by whether it gathers headlines, but by whether it generates value. Many "merely incremental" innovations create a huge amount of economic value!

A lot of innovation actually has nothing to do with technology at all. I am going to venture a guess that at some point you have shopped at IKEA, now a dominant global force in the home furnishings market. How did it come so far? By offering a relatively unique value proposition: attractively designed furniture at low prices. The shopping experience is totally different at IKEA than at a traditional furniture store. It is essentially all self-serve, including the picking and packing. The novel part of IKEA is the value proposition combined with the way it has organized the shopping experience and structured its operations. Sure, it uses technology systems to track inventory and sales, but this is pretty standard stuff in retail. The innovation at IKEA is the business model.

Even some new companies that start in Silicon Valley are not necessarily technology innovators. Think about the original Netflix business model of sending DVDs through the mail. Yes, Netflix had some new software to track customer preferences and to make recommendations, but the bulk of what it did was not new. It was taking DVDs, sticking them in envelopes (by hand), and mailing them (using the US Postal Service, which was established in 1775!) to customers' homes. Yet although there was not a lot of new technology, this was a completely new business model for the video rental business. It had a new value proposition (you did not have to go the store and the selection was huge) and new pricing structure (you paid a fixed membership charge, no late fees).

There are many examples of companies that have transformed industries through business model innovation. Think about Ryanair in the airline industry, Boston Beer Company in the craft beer business, Uber or Lyft in ride-sharing services. They may all use technology, but the novelty of these players lies in their business models. We return to the topic of business model innovation in Chapter 3.

You can see why statements like "We want to be a leading innovator" are not particularly helpful. If different people inside a company have a different definition in their minds about what *they* mean by innovation, the organization can easily get pulled in many different directions. And it is going to be impossible to build the required organizational capabilities to achieve any one priority if you are chasing after them all. A key part of an innovation strategy is deciding which types of innovation are most important to you. Which types of innovation can create the most value for customers and lead to the most value capture for your company? This enables the organization to focus resources and attention on those specific types of innovation that will matter most to it.

A Framework for Innovation Strategy

Whenever we are faced with choices, it helps to have a framework to categorize the different options and to provide nomenclature. Over the past thirty years, there has been quite a bit of careful scholarly research attempting to identify economically and strategically meaningful distinctions among different types of innovation.[4] There are many differences in these studies. They investigated a variety of different industries and at different times in history. And, not surprisingly, each developed somewhat different concepts and different nomenclature. But, as a whole, they highlight two critical dimensions of innovation that are relevant across a broad range of industries: first, the degree to which innovation involves a significant change in *technology;* and, second, the degree to which innovation involves a significant change in *business model.*

We can use these two dimensions to map a firm's innovation opportunities (Figure 1.1). For the technology dimension, we can think about whether a particular innovation will either leverage a firm's

FIGURE 1.1

The Innovation Landscape Map

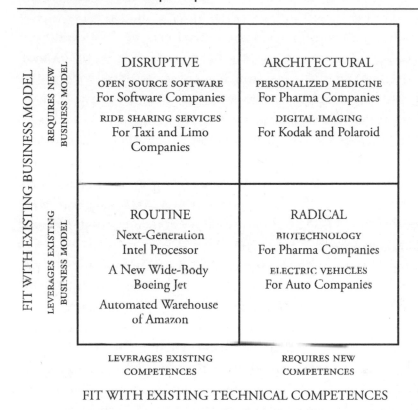

FIT WITH EXISTING BUSINESS MODEL

REQUIRES NEW BUSINESS MODEL

DISRUPTIVE

OPEN SOURCE SOFTWARE
For Software Companies

RIDE SHARING SERVICES
For Taxi and Limo
Companies

ARCHITECTURAL

PERSONALIZED MEDICINE
For Pharma Companies

DIGITAL IMAGING
For Kodak and Polaroid

LEVERAGES EXISTING BUSINESS MODEL

ROUTINE

Next-Generation
Intel Processor

A New Wide-Body
Boeing Jet

Automated Warehouse
of Amazon

RADICAL

BIOTECHNOLOGY
For Pharma Companies

ELECTRIC VEHICLES
For Auto Companies

LEVERAGES EXISTING
COMPETENCES

REQUIRES NEW
COMPETENCES

FIT WITH EXISTING TECHNICAL COMPETENCES

Source: Gary Pisano, "You Need an Innovation Strategy," *Harvard Business Review*, June 2015.

existing technological capabilities or require it to develop new ones. For instance, if you are a leader in a business whose traditional technological competences are in software development, an innovation embedding novel software is much closer to existing competences than, say, an innovation requiring new hardware. The same logic applies for the business model dimension. Does an innovation build upon our existing business model (say, selling products), or does it require us to master a new business model (say, selling services)? Although each dimension exists on a continuum, together they suggest four distinct categories of innovation.

- *Routine innovation* leverages a company's existing technological competences and fits with its existing business model. An example would be Intel launching ever-more-powerful microprocessors. This exploits Intel's deep technological expertise in the design and manufacture of microprocessors while fitting perfectly with the business model that has fueled its growth for decades. New wide-bodied aircraft from Boeing, next-generation iPhones from Apple, additional automated warehouses at Amazon, or new animated films from Pixar are all examples of routine innovation. I should note that "routine" does not imply easy or trivial. In each of these cases, the companies involved are investing significant resources and are working on and solving tough technical problems. It just means that they are working within the bounds of their existing repertoire of competences.

- *Disruptive innovation,* a category named by my Harvard Business School colleague Clay Christensen, requires a new business model but not necessarily a technical breakthrough. For that reason, it also challenges, or disrupts, the business models of other companies. For example, Google's Android operating system for mobile devices is a potentially disruptive innovation for companies like Apple and Microsoft not because of any large technical difference but because of its business model: Android is given away for free; the operating systems of Apple and Microsoft are not.

- *Radical innovation* is the polar opposite of disruptive innovation. The challenge here is purely technological. The emergence of genetic engineering and biotechnology in the 1970s and 1980s as an approach to drug discovery is an example. Established pharmaceutical companies with decades of experience in chemically synthesized drugs faced a major hurdle in building competences in molecular biology. But drugs derived from biotechnology are a good fit with the companies' business models, which call for heavy investment in R&D, funded by a few high-margin products.

- *Architectural innovation* combines significant technological and business model changes. An example is digital photography. For companies such as Kodak and Polaroid, entering the digital world meant mastering completely new competences in solid-state electronics, camera design, software, and display technology. It also meant finding a way to earn profits from cameras rather than from "disposables" (film, paper, processing chemicals, and services). Not surprisingly, architectural innovations are the most difficult for incumbents to pursue.

Like any framework, this one comes with some caveats and instructions for use. First, I want to emphasize that although we talk about these as types, there can be quite a bit of variance within any given category. Not all routine innovations are identical to one another. The same is true for the other categories.

Second, where a particular innovation falls into this matrix depends partly on the inherent nature of the innovation and partly on the choices made by firms. That is, innovation types are not "God given" but instead are endogenously determined by firm decisions and strategies. The Innovation Landscape Map can help you see the different strategies and possibilities for pursuing innovation. Consider autonomous driving vehicles, an innovation you've been reading a lot about these days. Google and several other companies, including major auto companies, are working on these types of vehicles. Where does the autonomous vehicle fit into the Innovation Landscape Map? Technologically, these are quite novel systems. No one, after all, has developed a fully operational, commercially feasible autonomous vehicle yet. It is a new configuration of various technologies (sensors, artificial intelligence, etc.) and creates completely new functionality. So, is this an example of a "radical" technological innovation (the lower right quadrant)? That depends on how it is commercialized. Let's assume that someday, when the technology is ready, a car company like Ford decides to offer an autonomous vehicle. The company decides to sell it through its existing dealers for $45,000. You can buy or lease it. You bring it to your dealer for service periodically. You use the car much like you use your car today, except you don't actually have to drive it. You just jump in, tell the car where you want to go, and then sit back like a passenger. Under such a scenario, the autonomous vehicle is a *radical* innovation. Although it embeds a very new configuration of technology, it is commercialized through a traditional automobile business model.

Now consider a scenario where Ford does not sell you the car at all. Instead, it maintains a huge fleet of these autonomous cars for use on a per hour basis. Whenever you want a car, you just use an app on your phone to call one, and, within three minutes, a vehicle arrives and takes you wherever you want to go (around the corner or across the country). If Ford were to pursue this approach, it would be attempting an *architectural* innovation. It would be developing a novel business model to commercialize a novel technology.

Or Ford might decide that it wants to be a ride-sharing company but not a technology innovator by buying autonomous vehicles from another company (say, Google). In this case, Ford would be pursuing a *disruptive* innovation strategy. Ford could also decide to enter the ride-sharing business through its existing internal combustion human-driven cars. (This is not far from reality: Audi has been piloting its own ride-sharing service in selected US locations, called Audi on Demand.[5] These are regular Audi cars that you can rent by the hour.) The Innovation Landscape Map framework allows you to consider and compare the possibilities and ask questions about how much value can be created and captured through different combinations of innovation.

The Challenge of Innovating Outside the Home Court

Sports teams tend to have a better winning record when they have the home court advantage. Playing at home is more comfortable. You do not have to travel. You know the arena or the field. And you have a friendly crowd rooting for you (and harassing the competition). Everyone would rather play at home. The same preference also applies to innovation. Routine innovation is the "home court" for most established organizations. It is where they are most comfortable. It is where they have developed and honed their capabilities. It is where they understand the technical and market risks best, and where their prior experience helps them avoid blunders. It is where they understand how to create and capture value from innovation. Innovation, even routine innovation, is never easy, so playing on the home court is a nice advantage.

The problem, of course, is that companies can also get trapped on their home courts. Unlike sport teams—who normally have to follow a schedule of home and away games set by their league—companies can choose their venue of play. And, unfortunately, the comforts of the home court can prove all too seductive. Proposals to explore outside-the-home-court opportunities for radical, disruptive, or architectural innovation can have a hard time gaining traction. Within an organization, many processes, structures, and management behaviors act to reinforce the home court bias. Existing project selection processes and criteria, management incentive systems tied to short-term performance metrics, pressures to utilize existing factories or distribution networks, demands from business units to address urgent competitive needs, and the technical biases of R&D personnel blow like prevailing winds toward the relative safety of home court innovation. Unfortunately, it is this very dynamic that makes established companies vulnerable to the gales of creative destruction described by Schumpeter.

And this why an innovation strategy matters. An explicit innovation strategy is required to counterbalance the automatic tendency to focus on the home court. Recall the example of the contact lens company at the outset of the chapter. They were victims of these prevailing winds. This is not to say that routine (inside the home court) innovation is bad. As I discuss in the next chapter, it is not. It can be quite valuable. The issue, though, is one of making explicit choices around the trade-offs that work best for the company *given its unique strategic circumstances*. Effort should never be allocated to innovation by default. Good innovation strategy is about finding the right mix of projects across routine, radical, disruptive, and architectural categories. Coming up with the right balance for *your* company requires an analysis of technological opportunity and market dynamics. This is the subject to which we turn in the next chapter.

2
NAVIGATING THE ROUTE
Creating Your Innovation Portfolio

Strategy is where you spend your money and time. Strategy is *not* about intent or vision or aspiration. It is about action. Skip the dense Power-Point presentation. Just tell me how resources are allocated and how you spend your time, and I can pretty much tell what your company's *real* strategy is. The same principle applies to innovation strategy.

An innovation strategy is ultimately a commitment to an allocation of resources across project types. Alphabet, for instance, has a policy of allocating 70 percent of its resources to its core search business (Google), 20 percent of its resources to ancillary businesses (such as cloud services), and 10 percent of its resources to "moonshots" (like autonomous vehicles) that could potentially bring the corporation into completely new technology and market spaces.[1] Corning's strategy and capital allocation framework specifies a target allocation of the company's R&D and capital investments across its core technologies (glass science, ceramic science, optical physics), its four engineering and manufacturing platforms (vapor deposition, fusion, etc.), and its five market areas (e.g., optical communications, mobile consumer electronics).[2] The purpose of this framework is to help the company make trade-offs between near-term routine innovation opportunities and longer-term opportunities outside its home court.

Executives often ask me, "What's the ideal proportion of resources to allocate to routine, radical, disruptive, and architectural innovation?" After all, if the 70:20:10 rule is good enough for Google, why shouldn't it be right for your company? There is, of course, no magic formula or golden rule that applies to all companies. What's best for Google or Apple or Amazon is not necessarily what is best for you.

Like any strategic question, optimal resource allocation is company specific and contingent on factors such as technology trends, market dynamics, competition, the company's capabilities, and environmental conditions. In this chapter, we examine how to take these factors into account in creating an innovation strategy that works best for *your* company.

Value Creation and Capture as Your Compass

If you go to innovation conferences or read the business press, it is easy to get the sense that "real innovators" do not do routine innovation. Radical, disruptive, and architectural innovations are viewed as the key drivers of growth. Routine innovation is denigrated as a sign that a company's leadership lacks vision and is trapped in the past. As noted in the previous chapter, companies can overcommit to routine innovation if they are not careful. But the notion that routine innovation is somehow inferior to outside-the-home-court innovation is simplistic and often just plain wrong. Innovation is not a beauty contest. The right way to judge the merits of any innovation (and an innovation strategy) is value created and captured.

Looking at innovation through a value lens, we can see that routine innovation can be extremely attractive. Let's take some examples. Since Intel launched its last major disruptive innovation (the x386 chip), in 1985, it has earned cumulatively more than $260 billion in operating income, most of which has come from next-generation microprocessors.[3] Microsoft has often been criticized for milking its existing technologies (like the Windows operating system) rather than introducing true disruptions. But this strategy has generated $395 billion in operating income since the introduction of Windows NT, in 1993 (and $353 billion since the introduction of Xbox, in 2001).[4] Apple's last major breakthrough (as of this writing), the iPad, was launched in 2010. Since then, Apple has produced a steady stream of upgrades to its core platforms (Mac, iPhone, and iPad), generating more than $400 billion in operating income.[5] Do not let anyone tell you that routine innovation does not generate economic value!

The point here is not that companies should focus solely on routine innovation. Routine innovation, as part of a balanced portfolio of innovation programs, can be quite profitable. Where companies get themselves into trouble is when they lose the appropriate balance. For instance, trying to "milk" a routine-innovation cash cow too long can leave a company vulnerable to major shifts in technologies or markets (a challenge that both Intel and Microsoft have experienced in recent years). In contrast, a company that introduces a transformational innovation but gets stuck on "generation 1" because it cannot follow up with a stream of routine performance-enhancing innovations will likely not develop the market or keep new entrants at bay. EMI pioneered the CAT scanner in the early 1970s but was unable to sustain its position when GE Medical Systems proved far better at making the routine innovation needed to enhance performance, increase manufacturing capacity, and reduce cost.[6] MySpace, a pioneer in social networking, failed to fend off Facebook because it could not make the stream of routine enhancements required to improve the user experience.

Architectural, radical, and disruptive innovation are analogous to financial options. They create future opportunities to invest. Routine innovations are akin to exercising those options. If a company cannot create options through architectural, radical, or disruptive innovation, it will eventually run out of opportunities to exploit routine innovation. But, likewise, a company that is great at architectural, disruptive, or radical innovation but cannot follow up with a stream of routine innovations is unlikely to thrive for long.

While there is no simple rule for deciding, there are some principles that can serve as guideposts. Specifically, there are four critical questions you need to ask to figure out how best to allocate your resources among different types of innovation opportunities: How fast is your core market capable of growing? What are the unmet customer needs? How much potential does your existing technological paradigm offer for improvement? Where can you create barriers to imitation?

How fast is your core market capable of growing? Just as some oil fields have more potential for exploitation because of higher in-the-ground reserves, some markets have more potential for demand growth. Consider Google. Between 2002 and 2017, Google's revenues (most of which came from advertising) grew at an eye-popping compound average annual rate of 53 percent. It now dominates the Internet search market with 63 percent share but still looks to have plenty of headroom to grow in its core market.[7] Its 2017 advertising revenues of $95 billion are indeed impressive but constitute only about 17 percent of the total global market for all advertising.[8] Google's core business looks to be the equivalent of a newly discovered, massive oil reserve. What do you do if you are sitting on top of the equivalent of a newly discovered, massive oil reserve? You exploit it—you keep drilling wells there. If you are a company like Google that has a strong position in a fast-growing market, routine innovation that builds and exploits the core advertising business makes a lot of sense. It is how you exploit your growth options.

Look, in contrast, at a company like Goodyear, one of the world's oldest and largest tire manufacturers. Between 2001 and 2017, Goodyear's compound average annual growth rate was about 0.5 percent.[9] This is not because Goodyear is a bad company or badly managed—it is not. The market for tires is relatively slow growing. Certainly, routine innovation in tires helps Goodyear keep and even grow its market share, but it is unlikely to spark significant growth—tire demand is constrained by the number of cars and trucks on the road. If you operate in a market like this, then you need to think about innovation in business models that can create more value or even potential radical innovation in technology that can lead to a massive share jump. Goodyear does a lot of routine innovation in areas such as improved and environmentally sustainable materials, self-inflating tires, better tread designs, and many manufacturing process technologies. But, to its credit, it has also innovated outside its home court by evolving its business model to include a range of services such as retail tire and auto service centers, roadside assistance, fleet maintenance solutions, retreading services for trucks, and direct-to-consumer online retailing.

The Goodyear versus Google example illustrates how the right mix of innovation projects will vary considerably across companies depending on the growth prospects of their respective markets. It is important to emphasize, though, that very rarely should a company's portfolio of innovation projects be limited to only one type. Despite the spectacular prospects for growth in Internet-based advertising, Google's parent company, Alphabet, is exploring radical and architectural innovation opportunities such as autonomous vehicles. Alphabet's leadership is smart enough to realize that someday Internet advertising could look a lot more like tires, and they want to build other options for long-term growth. Likewise, despite the fact that the tire business is tough, slow growing, and competitive, Goodyear still pursues routine innovation in that space. As in any portfolio decision, the issue is one of mix and balance, rather than all of one or the other.

It is also important to recognize that growth potential in any given market is not completely exogenous. Google's market is rapidly growing because of Google's innovation efforts—Google is not just along for the ride; it's been paving the road. Industries, unlike living creatures, are not doomed to follow a natural progression from vibrancy and growth to decline and mortality. An industry can, in fact, "demature" through innovation.[10] Back in the 1980s, cars were considered a classic mature industry. The basic technology and product concepts were fairly well established, innovation was incremental, and competition increasingly favored companies (like Toyota) that could manufacture efficiently. Today, the auto industry lies at the intersection of transformative innovations in powertrains (electrification and fuel cell), computer science and artificial intelligence (autonomous vehicles), and business models (ride sharing). The same story could be told of consumer electronics (think about RCA vs. Apple) or retail (e.g., Amazon). Ironically, companies are often told that if they are in a mature industry, they should either divest or just focus on incremental, cost-reducing innovation. This is horrible advice because it ignores the potential for reinvigorating an industry through transformative innovation. So-called mature, slow-growing industries may be exactly those most ripe for transformative innovation.

What are the unmet customer needs? Innovation—whether routine, radical, architectural, or disruptive—creates value when it solves a "problem" for someone. Routine innovation that solves an important (or expensive) problem is going to be much more valuable than a disruptive innovation that doesn't (and vice versa). Your decision about how to allocate your efforts to different types of innovation really depends on where you think there are valuable problems to be solved. Routine innovation will continue to create value as long as your existing technologies and your existing business model are capable of addressing customers' unmet needs. A better Internet search that reveals more about our potential purchasing plans is valuable to us as consumers and valuable to advertisers—so improving Internet search algorithms is a good (routine) innovation for Google to make. For the past few decades, we all craved faster, more capable personal computers, and we were willing to pay more for a machine with a faster microprocessor. So, introducing a new generation of microprocessor every eighteen months was good (routine) innovation strategy for Intel for a long time.

The challenge, of course, is that our needs are not unlimited. There are diminishing returns to how much we are willing to pay for any one dimension of improvement. It's something I think about many mornings. Since age fifteen, I have shaved with a Gillette razor. When I started shaving, I used a Gillette Trac II, which was the first twin-blade shaving system. Over the years, my Gillette razor has evolved—it got lubricating strips, a pivoting head, batteries to vibrate the head, and most of all more blades. The current Fusion ProGlide contains five blades. In men's shaving products, Gillette has had a clear and coherent innovation strategy: invest in technologies and designs that provide a closer, more comfortable, and safer shave. Judging by the price premium Gillette gets for its Fusion ProGlide (about $3.29 per unit on Amazon) versus an older design like the twin-blade Sensor (about $1.30 per unit on Amazon), the company has clearly created (and captured) significant value from this routine innovation strategy.

The question though is how much more I would be willing to pay for yet an *even closer,* more comfortable, safer shave. After all, at some point, a shave can only get so close before you require medical board certification. And, frankly, I am probably past the point of really knowing the difference. My shaves are already very comfortable, and I rarely nick myself. But, this morning, I noticed I was down to my last blade, and it was starting to feel dull. This means going to the store to endure a process—shopping—that is worse than nicking myself shaving. Apparently, because of theft, my local drug store no longer keeps the razor blades out on display. I will have to go to the counter, wait in line, and then ask a salesperson to get the one I want (which involves reaching across the counter and trying to direct them by pointing). When I get home, I am confronted with what appears to be bullet-proof plastic packaging, presumably again because of theft, that requires a very sharp scissor to open (I have not recently cut myself shaving but I have cut myself opening shaving cartridge packages!).

This example illustrates a common problem—an innovation strategy that may no longer be solving the most important problem for customers. The close, comfortable, and safe shave has become a "given" for me. I want it, but I will not pay more for it. My need for shaving performance is satiated. My need for convenience in acquiring and opening the product is not. I hate that part of the experience, and I would pay to avoid it. My guess is that other men have the same view, and this is why new, purely online players, who offer convenient subscription services like Harry's and Dollar Shave Club have become so popular. They are offering razor systems (they claim) that are equivalent to traditional brands like Gillette but are cheaper and more convenient to acquire. Last year, Unilever bought Dollar Shave Club for $1 billion.[11] We see similar business model innovations happening in other markets where basic product functionality needs have been met, but where customers' need for convenience has not. Long ago the performance of men's dress socks probably hit their peak in terms of comfort, appearance, and durability. My willingness to pay more for dress socks based on their physical attributes is limited. If you are in the sock business, it is hard to think of a technological solution to this problem. Socks are not like my iPhone—there are just not a lot of features I am going to pay for. But I will pay more for the convenience of not having to physically go to the store. And that's why Internet-only vendors like BlackSocks or

Tommy John can sell socks and underwear at a price premium. While my needs for "high-performing" socks have long ago been met, my needs for convenience are far from satiated.

As an innovator, you have to be aware where your customers are in terms of their degree of satisfaction along various product attributes. If customers' needs along particular attributes are not being met, those areas are ripe for continued innovation. If most men feel unsatisfied with their shave, then continued innovation in razor design (more blades, thinner blades, coatings, geometry, etc.) makes sense. This might be routine innovation if it builds off existing technologies or even radical if new technology is needed to create even higher levels of desired performance. But if customer needs are satiated along a particular dimension, continued innovation along this trajectory of performance is going to be less profitable over time because while it is costing you more and more to squeeze out improvements, customers are less and less willing to pay for them. Companies often get this wrong by sticking too long to improving product attributes that are no longer important differentiators for most customers. Clay Christensen has dubbed this "overshooting the market," and he argues it is exactly what makes companies vulnerable to disruption. His canonical example is the disk drive industry, where leading companies' obsessive focus on improving storage capacity blinded them to the threat posed by new entrants offering smaller (and cheaper) devices.[12] If you have seen signs that customers are less willing to pay for incremental improvements in the attributes that have always been focal points of your value proposition, then you need to think about different attributes. This might lead you to explore alternative technologies that drive improvement in other product attributes. Some needs (like product performance) can be addressed with improvements in technology, but others (like cost or convenience) might require a change in business model.

How much potential does your existing technological paradigm offer for improvement? In every industry at any point in time, there is a *technological paradigm:* a broadly shared consensus on the critical technical problems and the set of feasible designs, technology configurations, theories and concepts, know-how, materials, methods, and skills required to address those problems.[13] The internal combustion engine is an example of a long-established technological paradigm in the auto industry. The internal combustion engine is, of course, a physical artifact, but it also represents a specific body of knowledge and assumptions about focal technical problems (increasing fuel efficiency, reducing emissions, increasing horsepower, etc.) and critical design choices (combustion ratio; the size, number, and configuration of cylinders; piston geometry; fuel-oxygen ratios; ignition timing; etc.). Over time, companies within an industry develop deep expertise in the predominating paradigms.

A lot of technological innovation involves evolutionary refinements and improvements within existing paradigms. Occasionally, though, new paradigms emerge that displace established ones: semiconductors replaced vacuum tubes, and the jet engine replaced the propeller. A shift in paradigm is marked by a change in the fundamental parameters that describe the technology. So, for instance, parameters like compression ratio, cylinder configuration (V6, V8), displacement, and bore and stroke (all pretty basic ways of describing an internal combustion engine) have absolutely no meaning if describing an electric motor.

Routine and disruptive innovation involve evolutionary refinements in your existing technological paradigm, while radical and architectural innovation require exploration of new paradigms. How do you decide whether "sticking to your knitting" (technologically speaking) or exploring new terrain is worth it?

The first consideration is whether there even is a feasible alternative available. Much of the discussion about innovation today focuses on the major upheavals in technological regimes (shifts in paradigms) such as the impact of electrification on autos, the digitization of retail, the potential replacement of fossil fuels with renewable energy, and so on. When such transformations occur, they can have dramatic effects—destroying long-dominant enterprises and altering fundamental aspects of our daily lives. But, in reality, such upheavals happen relatively infrequently. Typically, most technological advances occur through more prosaic evolutionary innovation within a paradigm. This often happens for decades before being punctuated by a paradigm shift.[14] For almost a century, the internal combustion engine was essentially the only feasible technological paradigm for powering an automobile. In instances like this, the option of exploring alternative paradigms may not even exist.

In some contexts, fundamental advances in science create new paradigms rich with new opportunities. Think about pharmaceuticals. Until the early 1980s, pharmaceutical innovation was based largely on exploiting long-established technological competences in medicinal chemistry and random screening. Over the past several decades, a series of major scientific upheavals have created several new paradigms for drug discovery, including genetically engineered proteins and monoclonal antibodies, mechanism-based drug design, high throughput screening, combinatorial chemistry, system biology, cell therapy, RNA-interference, messenger RNA, and, most recently, gene editing. If you operate in a context where scientific progress can upend existing paradigms, your technology strategy has to put relatively more emphasis on exploring and absorbing capabilities related to new paradigms.

What about if you operate in a context (like say apparel, shoes, or restaurants) where the existing paradigm is quite mature and progress along existing trajectories has hit diminishing returns? In some cases, there are possible new paradigms that might rejuvenate the industry's innovation potential. Thirty years ago, it was beyond dispute that the auto industry was a technologically mature industry. Innovation focused on incremental refinements of existing concepts and on styling. Today, with alternatively powered vehicles and the potential for self-driving cars, I do not think anyone would say anymore that the auto industry is mature. Advances in bodies of know-how (largely outside the auto industry) have created the potential for paradigm shifts. So if you are in industry that feels a bit "sleepy" technologically, do not be lulled. You still need to keep your eyes open to explore new bodies of knowledge.

But what should you do if your core technologies are mature and you see no alternative technologies that can transform the business (e.g., you are in the apparel industry). In these contexts, it is hard to create a lot of value for customers through technological innovation, and so you need to focus your innovation strategy elsewhere. This is exactly the circumstance that should lead you to consider exploring new business models. Today, we see several technologically mature businesses being transformed by business model innovators, such Warby Parker in eyeglass frames, Uber and Lyft in taxis, Tommy John in men's underwear, and Airbnb in hotels.

If a potential alternative exists (or could at least be contemplated), a second consideration is the richness of future innovation opportunities in dominant and alternative paradigms. The oil field analogy is helpful once again. Some technological paradigms are like big, unexploited oil fields. They offer plenty of opportunities for productive exploitation. Here, the right innovation strategy is to exploit it through evolutionary innovation. Others are like old fields that have nearly exhausted their possibilities. Innovation is still possible, but R&D investments are hitting seriously diminishing returns. When you are operating in the equivalent of an old oil field, you need to explore potential alternative paradigms (if any exist).

The dominant paradigm for semiconductor design and production since the 1960s has been etching a greater density of ever-smaller transistors into a silicon-based substrate and increasing the rate at which electrons move through circuits (known as clock speed). This has proven to be a remarkably productive paradigm, with a doubling of transistor density occurring approximately every eighteen to twenty-four months. Thus, in the semiconductor business, exploiting Moore's Law, as it came to be known, has proven to be a very productive innovation strategy. However, like a giant oil field that has been pumped for decades, semiconductor improvements appear to be hitting their physical limits. As the electrons had to move faster through circuits that were ever closer together, heat became a serious problem. This has led to a flattening of microprocessor clock speeds since 2004.[15] The other problem is that there are physical limits to how tightly one can pack circuits on a chip—today's chips have "line widths" that can be measured in atoms, and by 2020 it is expected that quantum effects will make it impossible to scale further. Of course, chipmakers like Intel have proven remarkably creative at circumventing the limits (the demise of Moore's Law has been predicted since the mid-1980s), but there is no doubt that continued improvements are getting more and more difficult. It is not surprising then that many chip makers and computer companies are exploring alternative paradigms such as quantum computing. In Chapter 4, I will have more to say about timing these types of transitions.

We view shifts in technological paradigms as threatening to incumbents—and for good reason. Extensive academic research demonstrates what many practitioners have experienced firsthand: established companies have a hard time transitioning from their long-held technological paradigms to new ones.[16] Part of the problem is cognitive. A paradigm is a way of thinking, and it tends to filter how reality is perceived. Thus, it's easy for players operating within a paradigm to overestimate the potential of that paradigm relative to the alternatives or to dismiss the alternatives as not feasible. In the mid-1980s, when I was doing research on the then-fledgling biotechnology industry—which was creating an alternative to the century-old medicinal chemistry paradigm of drug discovery—I interviewed many medicinal chemists who expressed skepticism about the potential of molecular-biology-based approaches to revolutionize drug discovery. The large protein molecules and antibodies derived from biotech, they said, would be too hard to manufacture, too hard to administer (they need to be given by injections rather than as pills), and too likely to cause dangerous immune system reactions. To some extent, they were right *at the time.* Biotech came with much hype, but in the early years the industry witnessed its fair share of failures. What the skeptics missed, however, was that molecular biology had massive improvement potential.

Not all shifts in paradigms are bad for incumbents if they understand the implications and develop an appropriate innovation strategy. Consider the example of the high-end bicycle frame industry. Targeted to biking enthusiasts (you can spot them most Saturday mornings wearing bright, tight Lycra outfits, hanging out in front of coffee shops), high-end bikes typically sell for $2,000 (frame and components), but the prices can go as high as $30,000 for fully customized bikes made from esoteric materials. Most "bicycle" manufacturers are actually bike frame manufacturers: components like brakes, shifters, gears, seats, and wheels are typically made and marketed by specialists like Shimano. Until about thirty years ago, the frames used in high-end bikes were made from alloy steels. Bike frame manufacturers like Pinarello would buy tubes from one of the major suppliers (usually Reynolds or Columbus) and then fabricate frames based on their own designs. Value was created through frame performance (weight, stiffness, strength, etc.). Since scale economies of production were relatively low, many niche players like Pinarello (Italy), Scapin (Italy), Eddie Merckx (Belgium), and Serotta (United States) thrived in the high end of the market.

Starting in the late 1980s and continuing throughout the 1990s and 2000s, carbon fiber—which is both lighter and stronger than steel— emerged as the material of choice for high-end frames. Traditional steel frame producers were not able to make carbon frames for two reasons. First, the technology requires fundamentally different capabilities (e.g., steel frames are welded from individual tubes, whereas carbon-fiber frames are molded as single pieces). Expertise in carbon-fiber fabrication is geographically concentrated in Taiwan, far from the European and American bases of traditional frame builders. Second, because of the required investments in tooling and molds for carbon-fiber frame fabrication, higher volumes were needed for cost-efficient production.

Not surprisingly, carbon-fiber technology led to the demise of many traditional bike producers, as production moved to third-party specialists in Taiwan. Because a few major carbon-fiber producers dominated the value chain, they could charge relatively high prices for production contracts, leaving most bike frame manufacturers with little remaining value. But Pinarello, a leading producer of high-end steel frames near Treviso, Italy, adapted its innovation strategy to take advantage of carbon fiber. Pinarello recognized that, because of carbon fiber's malleability, it opened up new opportunities for innovative frame architectures and geometries (e.g., carbon-fiber frames can have curved tubes). A $7,000 bike frame can be considered a luxury good. People buy high-end Pinarellos for much the same reason (much richer) people buy Ferraris. They are buying a dream. Unless you race professionally, you really do not need the functional performance of a Pinarello frame, but that is not the point. You buy a bike like a Pinarello because you love the idea of having the same bike a professional rides. Selling that dream means having seductive designs and beautiful paint jobs. Pinarello decided to outsource production to high-quality Taiwanese producers and focus its resources on designing higher-performance and aesthetically attractive frames. The company invested heavily in design, engineering talent, sophisticated computer-aided design tools, and new prototyping methods. It focused production on painting since this has such a big impact on the aesthetic appeal (the company's highest-priced frames are hand-painted in its Treviso factory).

These new design capabilities not only allowed the company to create new value (more innovative and more beautiful frames increased customers' willingness to pay), they also provided a powerful means to capture value because they are hard to imitate. While competitors might be able to reverse engineer individual frame designs, the capabilities to *design* innovative and seductive bike frames is much harder to imitate because they are rooted in a complex set of interdependent elements—like talent, culture, design methods and processes, intellectual property, and experience. Pinarello also uses team sponsorships to bolster its brand and received a big boost in 2016 when its team won the Tour de France. Pinarello illustrates how a major upheaval in technology can create additional opportunities for innovation by an incumbent developing novel capabilities and adjusting its business model.

Where can we create barriers to imitation? Imitation is endemic to innovation-based competition. Every good (value-creating) innovation will quickly attract imitators, and imitation erodes the value you capture. If patents and other legal mechanisms were perfect, imitation would be a nonissue. You would patent (or copyright) your innovation and then sue anyone who dared to violate your intellectual property rights. And, in a perfect world, you would win these suits and get your legal costs back in addition to full damages. Reality is *very* different. First, the degree to which patents and other legal mechanisms can protect from imitation varies dramatically across technologies.[17] In many fields, prior art is so widely diffused that patents are almost impossible to get, or there are simply too many (legitimate) ways for rivals to engineer their way around your patents. Second, some technologies are inherently easier to copy than others because the key insights can be gleaned by making a detailed physical inspection of the product. With few exceptions, it is hard to rely solely on patents and copyrights to stave off imitation. You need to build or find other barriers. That is what companies like Amazon, Apple, Google, and Facebook do. Yes, these companies patent heavily, and they vigorously safeguard and enforce their intellectual property rights—but they also pursue innovation strategies that help protect their value streams from imitation.

There are three innovation strategy options for dealing with the threat of imitation.

Option 1: Build Complementary Technological Capabilities That Are Hard to Imitate

Most products or services are systems composed of multiple complementary technologies. Some may be easier to imitate than others. For instance, in many product categories today, functionality is determined by both hardware and software. Hardware tends to be easier to imitate than software because it can be physically inspected and reverse engineered. Software is much harder to imitate and much harder to reverse engineer. A good strategy for protecting value is to build capabilities in those parts of the technology ecosystem that are inherently harder to imitate. This explains why traditional hardware-oriented companies have focused more heavily on software (and many have even gone as far as to outsource design and production of their physical products). While you often hear people say that "the software is where the value is added," it's not really true. It would be more accurate to say, "Software is where the value is captured."

A variant of this strategy is to pursue complementary technologies that are not only harder to imitate but may also become bottlenecks in the overall ecosystem. Consider the electric vehicle market. It is impossible for anyone to patent the concept of electric vehicles (the first electric vehicles go back to the late nineteenth century, so the concept is hardly novel). And, today, just about every major auto company has a serious electric vehicle program, and many have electric vehicles on the market. So how will value be captured? Judging by its $5 billion investment in a "gigafactory" to produce batteries, it is clear that Tesla believes batteries will be the bottleneck in appropriating value.[18] Batteries are a potentially more effective way to capture value because they require complex process technologies that can be safely shielded behind factory walls. In addition, the potential for steep learning curves creates strong first mover advantages, which can be a difficult advantage for rivals to circumvent.

An extreme version of this strategy is to simply focus on the part of the technology system that is hardest to imitate and easiest to protect with intellectual property. This is essentially what Intel and Microsoft did in the personal computer industry. Neither firm became a personal computer maker or marketer in the first decades of the industry. Instead, they focused on two core elements of the personal computer—the microprocessor and the operating system—that heavily shaped overall performance and user experience. Each of these elements was well protected by both intellectual property (e.g., design patents) and inherently complex to imitate (e.g., Microsoft could keep its source code hidden inside the operating system).

Option 2: Focus on Business Model Innovation

In some cases, it is impossible to find any one technology that is hard to imitate. When imitation comes easily, the technology becomes a commodity and cannot be a source of advantage. In these circumstances, business model innovation can be used as a means of protecting value. Business models tend to be hard to imitate because they consist of many interdependent elements.[19] Dell was one of the few personal computer companies in the 1990s and early 2000s to earn profits. It was selling essentially the same "Wintel" machines as every other vendor. They performed the same, looked the same, and ran all the same software. How did Dell escape the commoditization that trapped other personal computer makers? It created a completely different business model based on online sales and customer configuration of machines. It focused on operational innovation and supply chain innovation to quickly and efficiently respond to changes in the market. Customers liked Dell because it offered the convenience of custom-configuring a machine online and then have it delivered within days. This protected Dell somewhat from the pricing pressures faced by other vendors. But it was also a much lower-cost model. Dell did very little design itself and outsourced all its manufacturing. Its supply chain capabilities and innovative operational configuration enabled very high inventory turns, which boosted Dell's return on invested capital.

Option 3: Crank Up the Treadmill
Through Rapid Routine Innovation

In cases where imitation is easy and business model innovation opportunities are limited, the only viable strategy to beat imitators is to outpace them through rapid and continuous routine innovation. You accept that imitation will happen and that prices will erode, but you try to keep just far enough ahead to earn premium prices. This is the strategy Apple now follows in the iPhone business. When the iPhone first came out, it was like nothing we had ever seen—it was a phone with no keypad that could seamlessly browse the web and run applications. But, within a year or so, we began to see the imitators arrive using alternative operating systems, like Google's Android. And, over time, the new phones began to look an awful lot like iPhones. They had the same basic design and same basic functionality. So how did Apple continue to make huge profits from the iPhone? From iPhone 2, iPhone 3, iPhone 4, iPhone 5, iPhone 6, iPhone 7, iPhone X, and so on. Apple engaged in rapid routine innovation. It kept upgrading functionality, features (better camera, sharper screen), performance, and aesthetics. It stays just enough ahead and just different enough to earn a good price premium. Intel also followed a similar rapid routine innovation strategy to stay ahead (and earn giant profits) in microprocessors, long after it became feasible for its chief rival, AMD, to offer its own compatible designs. If you pursue this strategy, you have committed yourself to being on a treadmill that keeps getting faster, which requires a significant allocation of resources to routine innovation. Of course, this strategy has limits. Eventually, you will hit diminishing returns to customers' willingness to pay for additional features and functionality. You can also hit fundamental limits of technology. Apple seems to be well aware of this, as we can see that it has already begun a heavier focus on integrating its devices with new service offerings, which represents a business model innovation.

Getting the Balance Right

Though much maligned, routine innovation can be extremely profitable for quite a long time and can be a winning strategy when

- your current market segments have excellent growth potential,
- the customer's most important needs are a long way from satiated,
- your current technological paradigm is still rich with opportunities to find innovations that will meet those important customer needs, or
- your current technological capabilities or your existing business model are powerful barriers to imitation.

The most-talked-about type of innovation—disruptive—is a widespread goal. But disruption is not a universal strategy. Like any strategy, it works under some circumstances but not others. It is an attractive strategy under the following circumstances.

- Growth in your current market segments is beginning to slow. This creates both opportunities (and threats) for new business models to address new segments of the market.
- The customer needs historically most important are becoming satiated (e.g., a closer shave), and customers are increasingly placing more value on new attributes (e.g., convenience).
- These new attributes are not easily addressed with technology solutions, but rather require different business models.
- There are strong first movers or scale advantages in the new business models needed to address these customer needs. These provide a barrier to imitation.

Like disruptive business model innovation, radical (technological) innovation has the capacity to transform industries and to destroy once-seemingly unassailable enterprises. Paradigm shifts in technology are relatively rare, but this does not mean you can ignore them. When they happen, they have a huge impact, and missing such a shift usually spells death for players in an industry. Radical innovation strategies involve exploring potential new technology paradigms. Such a strategy will be attractive when

- growth in your current market is robust enough to support investment in creating fundamentally new technological capabilities,
- customers' most important needs are a long way from satiated,
- the current technological paradigm is experiencing diminishing returns to making improvements that meet customers' most important needs, or
- the new technological paradigm is characterized by strong appropriability (i.e., it is difficult to imitate and easy to protect with legal mechanisms) *or* your current business model is difficult to imitate.

Architectural innovation involves a combination of radical technological innovation and disruptive business model innovation. In many ways, this is the most difficult innovation strategy to pull off because it involves mastering two entirely new capabilities: a new technological capability and a new business model capability. The risks of failure are high, and perhaps this is why architectural innovation by established firms is so rare. But it can also be a very attractive strategy, given its potential to transform entire industries. Architectural innovation will be attractive when

- growth in your current market segments is beginning to slow,
- the historically most important customer needs are becoming satiated and customers are increasingly placing more value on new attributes,

- these new attributes cannot be addressed with either your existing technology capabilities or your current business model independently, or
- your new technology capabilities or your new business model (or both) can be used as a barrier to imitation.

In practice, the leaders of most organizations will find themselves in circumstances that require them to pursue multiple types of innovation. That is, they will have a mixed portfolio of projects. The factors discussed in this chapter should influence your relative weighting of efforts toward each, rather than suggest any "pure play" strategy. You can utilize the questions in this chapter to evaluate your current portfolio of projects and to identify areas where you may be missing opportunities or where you may be exposing yourself to risks. In the next two chapters, I build on some of the concepts presented in this chapter to explore more deeply the problem of business model innovation (Chapter 3) and the challenge of dealing with uncertainty in assessing both your opportunities and your threats (Chapter 4).

3
WHATEVER HAPPENED TO BLOCKBUSTER?
Competing Through Business Model Innovation

We can usually touch, see, and feel technological innovations such as new electronic devices and self-driving cars, so it is easy to forget that a lot of *very important* innovation has little to do with technology. That is especially so with business model innovation, even though humans for millennia have innovated the way we organize and conduct business. When ancient merchants in Babylonia and Assyria decided to make loans to farmers and traders who transported grains from one city to another, they innovated their business model to create a primitive form of banking. Then, when someone came up with the idea that a merchant could pay an extra sum to have their loan forgiven in case a shipment was lost or stolen, they created a business model innovation for what we now call insurance. When moneylenders in ancient Greek and Roman temples decided to accept deposits, they were introducing a very durable business model innovation to the banking world. Medieval guilds were a business model innovation. The Dutch East India Trading Company was a business model innovation that introduced the world to the concept of publicly traded enterprises. Supermarket and retail chains were business model innovations. Business model innovations have been transforming societies and economies for thousands of years, and it would be hard to argue their effect has been any less powerful than that of technological innovation.

Not all technological innovations have the breakthrough impact of the microprocessor or the telephone; likewise, not all business model innovations are as transformative as the first bank or first insurer. Just as there are many incremental technological innovations (e.g., a better screen on your smart phone), there are also many incremental business model innovations (e.g., free shipping for Internet retail). But if you are not thinking about business model innovation as part of your portfolio of innovation activities, you could be missing big opportunities. Or, worse, you could be exposing yourself to great threats. Clay Christensen has written extensively about disruptive business model innovation, and he documents clearly its potential to transform industries, to propel some companies to stardom, and to doom others to the dustbin of Chapter 11.[1]

The power of business model innovation is clear to most senior executives I meet. Less clear is how you can design and implement effective and potentially transformative business models. A big part of the haziness lies with ambiguity about the concept itself. Most of the talk about "business model innovation" takes place without a precise understanding of what exactly it is. "Business model" is often used as a synonym for strategy or for describing the structure of a business or its revenue and profit streams. The literature on the subject is equally frustrating. A quick perusal of definitions reveals a plethora of abstract descriptors such as "a framework," "a structure," "mission," "a rationale," and so forth. It is hard to imagine becoming excellent at business model innovation if we cannot even agree on what a business model is! Thus, let's start by trying to get our arms around this concept, and make it as concrete as possible.

The fundamental task of a business enterprise—whether a global multinational like IBM or a kid selling lemonade on the corner—is to create, capture, and distribute value from some set of resources. *Every* business gathers resources, transforms those resources in some way to create value, utilizes mechanisms to capture some share of that value, and ultimately must distribute value back to those who provided resources. *Resources* include the tangible assets and inputs required by the business such as financial capital, human capital, intellectual property, raw materials, capital equipment, and information, as well as intangibles like reputation, customer relationships, and know-how. A business *creates value* by transforming those resources into products, services, intellectual property, or other tradable commodities (cars, financial

FIGURE 3.1
Business Model Framework

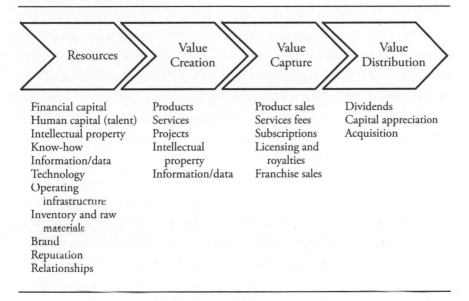

Resources	Value Creation	Value Capture	Value Distribution
Financial capital	Products	Product sales	Dividends
Human capital (talent)	Services	Services fees	Capital appreciation
Intellectual property	Projects	Subscriptions	Acquisition
Know-how	Intellectual	Licensing and	
Information/data	property	royalties	
Technology	Information/data	Franchise sales	
Operating infrastructure			
Inventory and raw materials			
Brand			
Reputation			
Relationships			

advice, patented or copyrighted property, lemonade, etc.). It *captures value* by finding ways to monetize the output of this process (e.g., it sells lemonade, charges for subscriptions, bills for the time of professionals, licenses intellectual property, etc.). Finally, the business has to *distribute value* to the people and organizations that provided resources (equity investors, employees, suppliers, etc.) in order to ensure continued or future access to those resources.

Business model design involves making choices about *resources, value creation, value capture, and value distribution* (Figure 3.1). For shorthand, we will call this the RV^3 business model framework.

Typical resource choices include capital structure issues (private equity vs. public equity, levels of debt relative to equity, etc.), human resource strategies (e.g., skill levels), investments in technologies and intangible assets (e.g., brand), and outsourcing strategies. Value creation has to do with both the form in which value is created and the specific value proposition of the firm. In the biotech industry, we find companies that are trying to create value by focusing on drug discovery, some are trying to take drugs all the way to market, others are offering contract development services, and still others are offering access to intellectual property or information on a subscription basis. Value capture choices involve decisions about what to charge for and the sources of profit. GE's aircraft engines business unit creates value by designing, making, selling and servicing aircraft engines; but, increasingly, it captures value in this business by charging fixed lease fees per hour of operation on the engines that bundle both the value of the engine and the value of the maintenance. Finally, companies can choose a wide range of approaches for value distribution. Some companies distribute value to investors through steady dividends or stock buybacks. Others offer the potential for significant capital appreciation. Some start-up companies are "built to be sold" (thus creating the potential for significant capital appreciation). Some companies pay employees relatively fixed salaries with small bonuses; others rely more heavily on stock options.

As you can see, decisions about each of these elements—resources, value creation, value capture, and value distribution—are not wholly independent. Attracting financial capital from dividend-hungry institutions will commit you to a specific value distribution model. Deciding to franchise your restaurant chain will have big implications for how you capture and distribute value. Business models are systems in the sense that each component is connected to the other. Good business model design is good system design. It takes into account and exploits the interdependencies among components.

Before examining the principles of business model design and innovation, let's illustrate the RV^3 by analyzing the salient differences between the business models of traditional taxi companies and Uber, one of the most widely discussed business model innovations of the past few years.

Uber Versus Traditional Taxis: An Illustration

A critical difference between Uber and most traditional taxi companies is that they operate with very different resources. Taxi companies own vehicles and employ people as dispatchers (the people you call to request a taxi). They also own government-granted licenses to operate in specific locales. Uber does not own cars, nor does it employ dispatchers. Instead, it uses a web-based app (a resource) in lieu of a human dispatch system. Its other critical resource is the network of independent drivers it can attract to be part of the Uber system. As discussed below, this network becomes fundamental to Uber's value proposition. Uber also invests heavily in its brand. Most of us have no idea which taxi company we might have used last Thursday in New York City or London. We just went out to the corner and stuck our hand up, went to a taxi stand, or found the number of a local taxi company to call.

Both Uber and traditional taxis ostensibly create value the same way. They offer the convenience of ride at a time (approximately) and place of your choosing. Because they leverage an expensive fixed asset (a car) across many users, they can offer this convenience at a relatively low cost. But Uber and taxis differ in the specifics of how they create this value. Traditional taxi companies have relied on licensing requirements, regulations, and government oversight to position themselves as a safer alternative to private rides (or worse, hitchhiking). Uber creates value by building a network of private individuals who are willing (for a fee, of course) to give you rides in their car. In essence, Uber is high-tech hitchhiking: instead of sticking out your thumb, you use it to open the Uber app. Because it does not own its own cars, Uber's economics are different than those of a traditional taxi company. Uber cultivates the biggest network possible because the more drivers in its network, the faster it can respond to your requests for rides (which is usually valuable for customers). Uber is less worried about having underutilized cars because its drivers own the cars. Uber cars do not look like taxis so, in most cases, Uber drivers are using their vehicles for both Uber work and personal use. Uber offers some extras that many find valuable, such as convenient payment (no cash, credit card on file, automatic e-mail receipt), information about the whereabouts of your driver and the ability to contact them easily, and driver ratings.

Uber and traditional taxi companies also capture value in very different ways. Traditional taxi companies have several revenue streams. First, they usually keep about 30 percent of the fare generated by drivers (the other 70 percent is for the drivers).[2] Second, they can also charge taxis in their network a dispatch fee for the privilege of being connected to their dispatchers. Third, they lease vehicles to drivers who do not have the capital to own a taxi. And, finally, in places where taxi licenses are tradable, they capture value by selling licenses to anyone who wants to operate a taxi. Uber largely makes money by collecting a 20 percent share of the fares generated by its drivers (although Uber will also lease vehicles to drivers who want to drive for Uber). Note, the value capture dimension of business models makes us differentiate between a company's business and how it makes money. From a customer's perspective, Uber and a traditional taxi company are essentially in the same business: they offer ways to get rides from one place to another. They are close substitutes. But each makes money (captures value) in very different ways.

Finally, because of the different choices they have made around resources, Uber and traditional taxi companies have different value distribution approaches. Uber has attracted considerable venture funding with the prospect of generating considerable capital appreciation (Uber is valued at approximately $70 billion at the time of this writing).[3] Taxi operators tend to be local. Even if owned by a larger group, they operate independently because they are regulated locally (usually by city or county jurisdiction). This means they cannot offer the massive potential capital appreciation of Uber. Instead, they seek to generate positive cash flow that can be distributed to owners (usually private entities) in the form of dividends or profit sharing.

What's the Relationship Between a Business Strategy and a Business Model?

We can illustrate the difference between the distinct concepts of business strategy and business model with groceries. Whole Foods clearly follows a different strategy than traditional grocery chains like Stop & Shop. Whole Foods focuses on organic and natural foods, appealing to health- and socially conscious consumers through its strict food standards, its strong emphasis on sustainability, its requirement that meat suppliers conform to stringent animal welfare standards, and its emphasis on "fair trade" and local farm sourcing. In addition, Whole Foods offer a broad selection of non-GMO, vegan, gluten-free, dairy-free, and other specialty foods. The company also tries to offer superior service through a human resource model that emphasizes teamwork and gainsharing. Whole Foods, though, also appeals to consumers with enough disposable income to afford its higher prices. It is a classic upscale provider—offering a differentiated product (and service) that customers are willing to pay a premium for. Traditional supermarkets like Stop & Shop position themselves differently in the market. While they recently have started to offer organic and natural foods, the bulk of their sales comes from mass-market (nonorganic, nonnatural) grocery products and brands. They do not utilize sourcing policies as restrictive as Whole Foods'. Traditional supermarkets appeal to more budget-conscious consumers who place less value on organic, natural, and sustainable foods.

Whole Foods and traditional supermarkets may follow divergent strategies, but their business models are similar (although not identical). Both utilize broadly analogous types of resources—they own or lease large retail establishments and have heavy investments in inventory. They both create and capture value by selling products (although despite differences in their specific value propositions). Their economics both depend on generating high revenue per square foot (although Whole Foods' higher cost base means it must generate greater revenue per square foot). Inventory turns are critical for both. And both Whole Foods and most traditional grocery retailers are publicly traded companies (or subsidiaries of public traded companies) that must ultimately distribute a portion of value captured to their shareholders through dividends or stock appreciation.

It is also entirely possible for companies to follow a similar strategy with different business models. Consider a new entrant into the grocery business that decides it will carry a product offering similar to Whole Foods' (with similarly restrictive sourcing practices). It too targets health- and environmentally conscious customers with high disposable income. But, instead of having retail stores, it sells its products strictly through the Internet with home delivery. In appealing to the same customers with the same type of product offerings, these two strategies are similar. Yet, the business models are completely different. One has stores as a key resource; the other does not: its critical resources are warehousing and distribution systems, and most likely data about all your past purchases. One creates value by having product available on the shelf; the other creates value by having products available for home delivery. The value distribution components of their business models could also be different if they had different ownership structures. Of course, the example of Whole Foods (which is now owned by Amazon) illustrates that a company can simultaneously pursue multiple business models (in this case, a physical retail store model and an online model).

We can find many real-life examples of similar strategy-different business models. For instance, in the quick service food industry (better known as fast food), chains often follow a similar strategy—consistent food served quickly and conveniently. Particular offerings may vary (pizza vs. hamburgers vs. chicken, e.g.), and they may also differ in some other aspects of their strategy (e.g., breadth of choice). Their broad strategies are similar, yet we see a variety of business models. Some chains like Pal's or Chick-fil-A have restaurants that are wholly owned by the company; others like McDonald's use a mix of franchising and company stores; still others like Penn Station rely almost exclusively on franchised operations. Franchising is a fundamentally different business model than a company-owned store. It completely changes the capital structure of the enterprise (resources) and generally changes the way value is captured: company-store models generate profits for the enterprise directly, whereas in the franchise model, value is captured largely through the sale of the franchise rights and ongoing licensing fees.

Obviously, some degree of coherence is required between a strategy and a business model. A company trying to differentiate itself, for instance, through extraordinarily high levels of personalized "high-touch" service might find it difficult to execute this strategy through a business model that did not utilize physical touch points between service providers and customers (such as stores or offices). Innovation in your business model should be consistent with your organization's long-term strategy.

Business Model Innovation as a Competitive Weapon: The Case of Netflix Versus Blockbuster

Many of us remember a time, not that long ago, when renting a home video required a trip to a local rental store.[4] You had to physically search for a video on the shelf, check it out, bring it home, and then bring it back to the store (hopefully in time, to avoid a late fee). You may also remember that, by a certain point in time, the "local" video store was very likely an outlet of a big chain like Blockbuster. All this began to change in 1997, when Reed Hastings came up with the idea of online video rental and founded Netflix. Instead of going to a store, you picked out a movie (or television show) online, and the DVDs were mailed to your home. You could keep the video as a long as you wanted. When you were done, you just mailed it back to Netflix. Today, of course, many of us are not even getting physical DVDs in the mail but instead are streaming or downloading content directly to our televisions, computers, and phones.

The history of this market provides an illuminating window into how rapid business model innovation—from the video rental store to the Netflix DVD-by-mail to video on demand—can shape competitive dynamics. Using the RV³ framework, we can pinpoint how different choices impacted the fortunes of different companies.

Blockbuster: A (Once-) Successful Retail Business Model

The ultimate failure of Blockbuster (it filed Chapter 11 in September 2010) makes us forget that Blockbuster once had a very successful business model. Blockbuster's critical resources were its huge network of stores (at one point, approximately 90 percent of the US population lived within a ten-minute drive of a Blockbuster store) and its library of new releases. We also tend to forget that, when Blockbuster started, it was a pioneer in using data to pinpoint neighborhood-level differences in movie tastes. So, for instance, if people in Charlestown, Massachusetts, tended to like films about bank robberies, the local Blockbuster stores there would carry a greater inventory of films like *The Town* (set in Charlestown), *Heat,* or *Inside Man,* whereas if people in Cambridge, Massachusetts, liked films featuring crusty professors, that local Blockbuster might stock up on films like *The Paper Chase.* These data were an important resource for the company. As the name of the company implied, Blockbuster focused on carrying movies that had a strong box office performance in the theaters. It *created value* by providing customers convenience and availability of new releases. With just a short drive, you could find a selection of movies for rental that perhaps just weeks before could be viewed only in theaters. At an average price of four dollars per one-day rental, this was a much less expensive way to enjoy a movie than seeing it in the theater (with average per-person ticket prices at twelve to eighteen dollars). It *captured value* through per-movie (fixed time period) rental fees and through late fees imposed if the video was returned after the due date. Late fees accounted for approximately 10 percent of Blockbuster revenues. The company also captured value on the sale of ancillary "movie night" items such as popcorn, ice cream, and candy. Finally, Blockbuster captured considerable value by selling previously rented videos. This not only generated additional value from its film library but was necessary to free up shelf space for each wave of newly available, more in-demand videos for rent.

The coherence between Blockbuster's choices of resource, value creation, and value capture methods helps to explain how the company rose to be the dominant rental video chain. The value distribution component of Blockbuster's business model is more complicated because the company went through a number of ownership structure changes. Blockbuster was initially a privately owned company but was acquired by Viacom in 1994 for $8.4 billion. Viacom then spun off Blockbuster in 2004. Prior to the spin-off, Blockbuster paid out a special dividend of $905 million (going largely to the shareholders of Viacom, which owned 81 percent of the company). This special dividend required Blockbuster to issue more than $1 billion in debt, which it ultimately had difficulty repaying as its business declined in the face of competition from Netflix.[5]

Netflix: A Business Model Innovator

Netflix entered the video rental market with a different mix of resources than Blockbuster. Most obviously, it eliminated stores. But its film library was also different. Rather than focusing on the latest films, Netflix initially carried older, less known films (sometimes referred to as "art house" or "independent" films). A big advantage of such films is that they tend to be cheaper to acquire from the studios because there appears to be less pent-up demand for rental. When Warner Brothers experienced record box office returns from the movie *Titanic,* it was pretty obvious to them that they had a hot commodity on their hands. Copies of *Titanic* to rent out would not come cheap. On the contrary, a film like *Hotel Rwanda* did relatively poorly at the box office despite winning many awards. For a studio, *Hotel Rwanda* was a commodity that offered seemingly poor prospects for rental. It was likely to gather dust in the studio's library. Which film would you rather negotiate for?

The good news is that if you are Netflix, you can likely acquire films like *Hotel Rwanda* relatively inexpensively. The bad news is that many people may not have heard of it, and thus might be unlikely to rent it. So Netflix created another resource that helped movie watchers find films they may not have heard of before. The Netflix software algorithm translated a viewer's ratings of films into recommendations of other films that seemed to match the viewer's tastes. The more films you watch and rate (and the more films other Netflix users watch and rate), the better the recommendation system becomes at understanding your tastes and matching them with potential films.

Netflix created and captured value in a completely different way than Blockbuster. Netflix was creating value by offering renters the convenience of renting from home. No need to drive to a store and browse a shelf. No need to return the video. You selected films on the computer, and delivery and return were provided through the US Postal Service. It was also convenient in the sense that you could keep a designated number of videos (depending on your plan) at the same time, which offered flexibility about which film to watch when. The recommendation engine also created value as it enabled viewers to discover films they liked that they might not have known about. Value was captured through a flat-fee monthly subscription (e.g., $9.99 per month for four films). There was no per-film rental and no late fees.

Netflix is a publicly traded company. The value distribution component of its business model appears oriented around capital appreciation rather than dividend payouts. This is not uncommon for companies that operate in businesses with strong "increasing returns" to scale economics.

What made Netflix's business model ultimately superior to Blockbuster's in the traditional video (DVD) market? In some industries, different business models can coexist to serve different segments of the market. In the beer industry, both craft brewers and big mass brewers carve out different niches of the beer market. Both have done pretty well. But that did not happen here as the Netflix subscriber base grew at the expense of Blockbuster. Clearly, Blockbuster failed to anticipate this. Shortly after Netflix went public, a spokesperson for Blockbuster was quoted as saying that online video rentals would never be more than a small niche.[6] The RV³ framework helps us understand why this turned out not to be the case.

Let's begin with value creation. Blockbuster created value by offering availability of the latest popular movies to rent and convenience of having a store close by. This value creation formula required a heavy investment in two expensive resources: an extensive store network and an ever-changing library of the newest available films. Investment in expensive resources is fine, as long as the they create enough value for customers in terms of willingness to pay and as long as Blockbuster can charge a high enough price to capture this value. Before Netflix existed, both of these were likely true. Having a Blockbuster within ten minutes of your house offered the best available convenience for video rental. Blockbuster's scale gave it enough bargaining power with studios to get reasonable prices on content. In addition, because it was a dominant player in the traditional market, Blockbuster had some degree of pricing power (and it likely had lower costs, given its scale) relative to smaller chains or independents. However, once Netflix entered the market with its business model, the dynamic changed. The relative convenience advantage of the store model began to erode—in fact, once Netflix could deliver DVDs to most locations within one to two business days, it may have gained an overall convenience advantage. Furthermore, because Netflix did not have to invest in an expensive store network, its cost structure was lower, and it could therefore charge a relatively low subscription rate (at $4 per movie rental, the breakeven for a $20 Netflix subscription was just five movies per month). This made it harder for Blockbuster to capture value through higher pricing. In essence, Blockbuster was saddled with an expensive resource (stores) that could no longer be supported by the value created or captured.

Even worse, a critical ingredient of Blockbuster's pricing strategy was late fees. These not only generated revenue, but they were critical for ensuring timely return. Why was timely return so important? For instance, why not just charge an extra day of rent? Why "punish" the renter with a late fee? Again, we have to go back to resources. Unlike Netflix's film library, Blockbuster's was composed largely of the perishable good of "new" films. After four weeks, a new film is no longer "new." If your business model centers on providing customers access to the latest new releases, you need to make sure these are available. Renters who hold onto films (even if they pay for them) create a cost for others. Thus, Blockbuster used late fees to induce timely return. There is only one problem with late fees. Everyone hated them. I have taught the Netflix versus Blockbuster case to more than a thousand students and executives over the past few years. Whenever I ask what people liked least about Blockbuster, almost universally the number one answer is "late fees"; and what they like most about Netflix—you guessed it, lack of late fees. For customers, late fees were value destroying. They made the experience worse (even the threat of late fees seemed to bother some people, even if they never paid them!). Blockbuster eventually responded by eliminating late fees, but this was costly to them in two respects. First, there was the direct revenue hit (recall that late fees accounted for 10 percent of Blockbuster's revenue). Second, as renters freed from the prospect of late fees held on to videos longer, they caused inventory turn to drop (and revenue per square foot to fall). This is a huge problem for an organization like Blockbuster with a high fixed cost base of stores. Now, add the heavy debt burden created by the value distribution component (remember the special dividend to shareholders), and you have a death spiral. Revenue falls, fixed costs largely stay the same, cash flow dwindles, and high interest payments on debt remain. Chapter 11 is all but inevitable.

Netflix's business model innovation was a success because it attacked Blockbuster's biggest vulnerability—the high fixed costs of stores and its video library (see Figure 3.2). Netflix not only substituted cheaper

FIGURE 3.2

Comparing the Business Models of Blockbuster and Netflix Using the RV³ Framework

	Resources	Value Creation	Value Capture	Value Distribution
Blockbuster	8,000+ retail outlets (at peak) Most recently available to rent, well-known movies (theatrical "blockbusters")	Availability of high-profile movies for rent immediately Convenient locations Tailoring inventory to local tastes	Per film rental fees Late fees Sales of videos Sales of "movie night" ancillaries (popcorn, candy, etc.)	Paid one-time special dividend to shareholders
Netflix	Warehouses and logistics system "Tail of distribution" film library Recommendation engine	Convenience of ordering from home Availability of previously unknown films Discovery of new movies	Flat monthly subscription fee	Capital appreciation

resources but was able to offer comparable (and eventually better) value in terms of convenience. It was also a coherent model. Its choice of resources was aligned with its chosen mode of value creation that, in turn, was supported by its approach to value capture.

Netflix: Innovating the Business Model for Video on Demand

The Netflix-Blockbuster saga increasingly feels like ancient history. Most of us are not sticking physical disks into DVD players but streaming content through the web using video on demand (VoD), a set of technologies that enables content in digital form to be stored and then delivered at a time and screen of a user's choosing. VoD, offered by Netflix since 2007, is a great example of new technology that also requires a new business model (it is, in the terminology of Chapter 1, an architectural innovation). What's different about VoD, and what are the implications for business model design?

First, obviously, no physical disk, meaning that two of Netflix's key resources—the film library and its distribution system—are no longer valuable. Because there is no more inventory, you do not have to worry about inventory management. Those independent art house films were never going to be attractive for the old Blockbuster because they were not an efficient way to use scarce shelf space. But, once content is completely digital, this no longer matters, creating competition for content. The other problem is that VoD technology is relatively ubiquitous. Many companies offer it: Amazon, Apple, Google, phone companies, and other Internet service providers. This means it is harder to create value for the user through the viewing experience. In the old world of DVDs, Netflix could create a different user experience in terms of ordering movies and having a super-convenient way of receiving and returning disks. That is no longer the case. Everyone can get VoD on their televisions (or phones or tablets).

How do you create value in a business like this? What makes you unique? Content clearly becomes critical. If Netflix has content that Amazon does not, then maybe I will pay more for a Netflix subscription. The problem is that this just triggers competition for content that leads to higher content prices. Expensive content is great for content producers (like studios) but not so great for content distributors like Netflix. VoD has shifted the source of value creation upstream from content distribution to content creation. This helps to explain, then, why Netflix shifted its business model to focus heavily on content creation. It has produced its own hit series like *House of Cards* and *Orange Is the New Black*. Such content now becomes the scarce resource that determines which business models will be profitable. Scale also helps. Netflix's large subscriber base (a critical resource) better enables it to capture value on both acquired and organically created content. Not surprisingly, Netflix spends more on content creation and acquisition (about $6 billion in 2017) than any other media company except ESPN (which must purchase expensive rights to sporting events).[7] Netflix now uses its proprietary content as a way to create and capture value.

The Netflix example shows that companies with successful business models can, contrary to popular wisdom, innovate new business models to thrive as technology and markets change. When Netflix innovated its business model to address VoD in 2007, it was not a small company. It was the dominant player in the traditional DVD rental market, with revenues of $1.2 billion. It is also a great example of business model innovation that leverages the advantages of scale. VoD meant a shift in the source of value creation from distribution to content. There are high fixed costs of acquiring or developing original content. This gives an advantage to larger players, and thus it should come as no surprise that the VoD market is dominated by larger, established companies: Netflix, Amazon, Google, Apple, Hulu (a joint venture of Disney, 21st Century Fox, and Comcast), and Internet service providers. Not only is business model innovation possible at scale, sometimes scale is actually required.

Principles of Business Model Design and Innovation

The Netflix business model innovation succeeded. That, however, is clearly not always the case,[8] as even very successful companies can fail at business model innovation. Consider Lego. In 2005, it introduced a business model in the form of a new service called Lego Design byME.

Today, you can buy a growing variety of Lego-designed kits. The idea behind Design byME was to allow consumers to design (using a simple CAD program) their own Lego kit, and then custom-order the required bricks. Sounds like a cool idea, right? The problem was that custom-configuring kits is extremely costly for an operation like Lego's, which is oriented around mass production (to give you some idea of just how "mass" Lego's production is, it manufactures more [mini] tires than any other company in the world). To profit from this concept, Lego had to charge much higher prices for custom kits than for stock kits. Not only did it charge for the bricks ordered, but it charged a separate service fee (for custom-picking bricks) along with the costs of shipping. Customer may have liked the idea of custom kits, but they were not willing to pay the higher price. In other words, Design byME did not create enough value relative to the cost of the resources required and was discontinued in 2011.

It should not be surprising that many business model innovations fail—after all, many technology innovations fail. Innovation—whether a business model or a physical technology—means pushing the limits on what's known. New combinations of resources, value creation, value capture, and value distribution can be just as uncertain as new combinations of technology. So how can you decide what business model innovations might be reasonable bets?

One popular approach, using reasoning by analogy, is imitating seemingly successful business models from other sectors:[9] "We want to be the Uber of business X" or "We want to be the Amazon of business Y." Nothing wrong here since analogies help simplify complex things and stimulate creativity.[10] Reed Hastings said he got his idea for Netflix's subscription pricing model on his way to the gym, where he paid a flat monthly membership fee.[11]

We will have more to say about analogies as a means of stimulating innovation in future chapters, but suffice to say flawed analogic reasoning can lead you astray. This can happen even to the most successful entrepreneurs. Consider the example of Stelios Haji-Ioannu, the founder of easyJet, one of Europe's leading discount airlines, carrying about 70 million passengers per year (second only to Ryanair).[12] Its business model revolves around maximizing utilization of its airplane fleet (an expensive resource) by maximizing the load per flight (the percentage of seats sold). Typically, easyJet's load factor is around 90 percent (compared to about 70 percent average for the European airline industry).[13] It gets such high loads by charging low fares, thus attracting more passengers. The company creates value for passengers by giving them a lower cost alternative to other airlines. It only captures this value through lower costs by flying out of secondary airports, providing no meals or frills, using Internet-only ticketing through its own site (fewer personnel and no travel agent commissions). And, of course, with higher loads, easyJet's capital cost per passenger flown is lower. This is a great example of a business model where each component reinforces the others. Expensive planes require high loads, which requires low prices, which, in turn, require a low cost structure. That is, easyJet's choices in its business model are complementary.

The idea of porting this successful business model over to other industries was not lost on Stelios. The parent company of easyJet is called easyGroup, and its subsidiaries include easyCar, easyBus, easyPizza, easyHotel, easyOffice, easyProperty, easyGym, and other "easy" brand concepts. But as the case of easyCar shows, business model concepts do not always translate across industries.

In April 2000, Stelios launched a car rental company based on the same principles as easyJet.[14] Stelios noted, "The car-hire industry is where the airline industry was five years ago, a cartel feeding off the corporate client."[15] Like easyJet (but unlike major rental operators like Hertz or Avis), easyCar targeted price-sensitive customers and aimed to be the lowest-cost provider in the market. It did not operate at airports or other expensive city center locations; booking was strictly through the Internet. And just as easyJet used only new Boeing 737s, easyCar offered only one type of car—the new Mercedes A-Class. And as was the case for easyJet, the economics of easyCar hinged heavily on the utilization of its fleet (depreciation of vehicles accounts for about 30 percent of the costs of a car rental company). The "easy" business model was very different from that of the traditional rental operator: it employed a different resource mix (e.g., one type of vehicle) and different value creation and capture models (low prices and low cost, high volume).

However, easyCar has not achieved anything like the success of easyJet. By 2013, the company reported profits of only £800,000 on revenues of just £15 million. The problem was that easyCar did not achieve the cost advantage needed to drive the model (unlike easyJet). In addition, it learned that part of the value creation equation for customers involves the convenience of rental locations: by avoiding airport rental locations, it made itself less convenient for customers. In 2014, the company switched models to focus on becoming a broker of private vehicles owners are willing to rent out. It calls this peer-to-peer model the easyCar Club. In essence, easyCar Club wants to be the Airbnb of the car rental business.

The case of easyCar is a cautionary tale about imitating business models. Analogies can be a helpful start, but additional analyses are required to help you identify what parts might need to be modified. Just as in technological innovation, it is impossible to *eliminate* completely the uncertainty of business model innovation. There are no sure-fire business models and none that universally work under all conditions. A business model needs to be tailored to the specific market, technological, and competitive conditions of the industry. Although there are no universal models, there are some design principles that can help you.

Business Model Design Principle 1: Search for Complementarities. By definition, the word "model" means a representation of a *system* using rules and concepts.[16] Like any system, a business model requires coherence among its components to be effective. Your choice about resources, value creation, value capture, and value distribution should complement one another. Netflix is a good example (Figure 3.3). Carrying the lesser-known art house films (a resource) was complemented by software algorithms to help users discover new films. And discovering new films became part of the appeal (value creation) of Netflix. The software algorithm also interacted with the company's inventory

FIGURE 3.3

Key Complementarities in Netflix DVD Rental Business Model

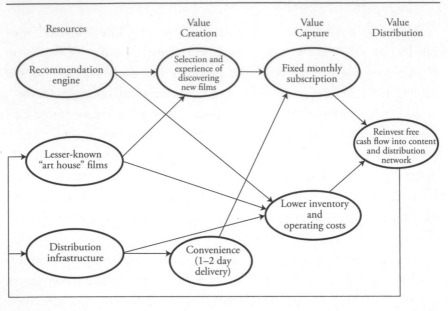

system to promote films it had in stock (the perfect Netflix film for you was a film that fit your tastes *and* that Netflix had in stock and was ready to ship to you). The connection to the inventory management system provided you better service (value creation) in terms of reducing your wait time for films. And the pricing model (fixed monthly fee to check out a specific number of films at any one time) made users more comfortable taking risks on a film they never heard of. In the mind of users, the fixed fee with no late charges was also a source of value creation since they hated late fees charged by video stores. A subscription model for value capture also generates somewhat predictable cash flows. When combined with a no-dividend value distribution policy, you get an enterprise with the financial resources to continue to invest in building out its distribution network—which enabled it to improve delivery times, which, in turn, created more value for users (which, in turn, increased the subscriber base). Later on, Netflix's strong cash position and big subscriber base enabled the company to invest in creating and developing proprietary content—a key resource in the world of video on demand.

Complementarities can clearly make your business model more effective, but the added benefit is that they make it harder to imitate.[17] Strong complementarities among the parts mean that would-be imitators have to replicate the whole system, rather than picking off one or two critical practices or policies.

Business Model Design Principle 2: Create Value for the Ecosystem. All too often, business model design is egocentric. Management teams design and propose models focused solely on the value captured by *their* organization without considering the value created for other critical members of the ecosystem—like suppliers, partners, investors, customers, and employees. The only way to secure the necessary cooperation of these players is to make sure your model also creates value for them. This requires a very different way to think about business model innovation. Instead of thinking strictly about the value you can capture, you have to think about the value you create for your partners in the ecosystem. Good business model innovators make the whole pie larger, not just their own slice.

Think about Uber's business model. It only works if there are independent drivers (with cars) willing to join their network. The more Uber drivers in the network, the better it is for customers looking for a ride. The more customers who routinely use Uber, the more business there is for drivers. Uber attracts drivers to join their network by making it economically advantageous and by making the arrangement flexible. If you drive for Uber, you have a high degree of latitude when and where you operate. You are not assigned shifts. Many Uber drivers have other jobs or other commitments and use Uber as a way to supplement their income. Uber also provides its drivers access to their technology platform. Uber drivers do not have to wait in lines at taxi stands. They can potentially be more productive driving for Uber than for a traditional taxi company or a limo service. Amazon creates value for third parties to sell on their platform by providing access to a massive customer base. Companies like Apple, Intel, and Microsoft provide independent software vendors the development tools they need to create applications that run on their systems. Toyota has long followed a strategy of supporting the long-term financial viability of their critical prime suppliers as a means of inducing them to make long-term investments in technology and operational capabilities. Investing in training, providing good working conditions, and paying well are means by which companies attract talent.

Business Model Principle 3: Exploit "Free" Resources. When it comes to resources, nothing beats free. A resource that costs you nothing but creates value is pure gravy. It sounds too good to be true, right? After all, economic theory has drummed into our heads that there is no such thing as a free lunch. But, it turns out, this is only true for commodities and resources for which there are well-functioning markets. Not all resources are tradable in markets. And this creates opportunities to find resources essentially for free *if you can figure out the right way to access them.*

Google's business model creates and captures value through advertising. The beauty of Google's advertising model (i.e., the reason it creates value) is that it based on information about our specific needs, tastes, and intentions. This means a dollar spent advertising with Google is likely to be more efficient than a dollar spent on ads in newspapers. But to make this business model work, Google needs *a lot* of information about us—what we like doing, what we might want to buy, where we are thinking of going on vacation, whether we have children, and so on. Information is a critical resource for Google's business model—it could not create value without it. And we are critical resource providers to Google. Our participation in Google's ecosystem is clearly worth a lot to Google's shareholders. As of this writing, Google's market capitalization is about $775.17 billion.[18] Google does not pay us one cent for all this valuable information. And here is the crazy thing—we do not seem to mind. We give away this massively valuable resource for free.

How does this happen? Why are we willing to subsidize Google by just giving away our information? Is it just pure generosity? Not really.

We give away our information to Google because we have no alternative means to monetize the value from it. There is no market in which we can sell information about what we ate for breakfast, what we might be planning to do this weekend, or what kind of car we like. Why not, you may ask? There seem to be markets for everything. Why is there no market for information? It goes back to what Nobel Prize winner and seminal economic theorist Ken Arrow called "the fundamental paradox of information." Now known as Arrow's paradox, it says that the only way to price a piece of information (say, what I ate for breakfast) is to reveal the information. But, once I reveal the information, no one really has to pay for it. Without a market for information through which we could monetize information about ourselves, that information has essentially zero value for us. Before Google, our personal information was like a massive oil reserve trapped underground that no one could access, and the value of anything that cannot be accessed is precisely zero.

The brilliance of Google's business model is that it figured out a way to access this information by giving us tools that simultaneously performed functions we valued (like Internet search, sending e-mail, keeping calendars, finding videos, etc.) and that automatically collected information about us. Every time we use a Google application, we give the company information. But it's a quid pro quo—we get to use the applications for free. So we get something we value in exchange for giving Google something that we as individuals are not able to extract value from in the first place.

Facebook follows a similar model, providing its members, for absolutely free, a means to interact virtually with a network of "friends." But, in return, it gets something really valuable. It gets information about what we are doing, what we like to do, what pieces of news we find interesting, and so on. This is extremely valuable information to advertisers and others interested in influencing our behavior.

Crowdsourced review sites like TripAdvisor, Yelp, and even Amazon also utilize undervalued resources. Reviews are a critical feature of sites selling products and services. These reviews provide a vital source supporting their business models. And yet how much are we paid to provide such a valuable resource? Absolutely zero. The motives for people to contribute to crowdsourced ventures (including open-source software projects) have been widely studied by economists and sociologists. The general conclusion from this research is that people gain a certain degree of psychological satisfaction from sharing their opinions.[19] The cost of contributing is the time required to actually write the review. But, remember, there is no additional opportunity cost because there never was a market into which you could sell your independent reviews.

You may have noticed a link between the principle of "exploit-free resources" and the earlier principle of "create value for the ecosystem." They tend to go hand-in-hand. One of the ways you get access to resources for "free" is to provide something else in return that is valued by those resource contributors. Google and Facebook provide services of tremendous value to their users that they do not even charge for. In essence, this is good old-fashioned bartering. I give you something for free (like my information), and you give me something in return for free (like access to e-mail or a social network). If there is no market for a particular resource, then bartering might just be a good way to access that resource for "free" or at least for a relatively low cost.

Business Model Design Principle 4: Build upon Hard-to-Imitate Resources. Good business model innovations are just as vulnerable to imitation as are good technological innovations. McDonald's may have pioneered the concept of the modern quick service restaurant chain, but there are now hundreds of rivals competing in the market. Uber and Lyft both offer ride-sharing services based on similar business models (albeit with different strategies). In the video on demand market, Netflix competes with literally dozens of other players who have adopted a similar subscription-based business model. Business model innovations can quickly commoditize if you cannot keep imitators at bay.

The question is how. For technological innovation, you can often (but not always) resort to patents or other legal devices. Patents get much trickier when it comes to business models. Technically, business *methods* can be patented (such as Amazon's 1-click shopping). Generally, these patents are issued on the software that underpins a particular business method (e.g., an online auction).[20] There was a surge in business method patenting after 1997, but subsequent court rulings have tightened the criteria.[21] And, while individual *methods* might be patented, the possibility of patenting an entire *model* seems remote. It is probably best to proceed under the assumption that your business model innovation cannot be protected by patents. If it works, you are likely to have imitators, and you need a strategy to defend against that imitation.

The best way to prevent your business model from being imitated is to base it on some set of hard-to-replicate resources—like brand, unique operating know-how, proprietary technological capabilities, and reputation. This explains why successful business model innovators often invest very heavily in building brand equity early on. *Increasing returns to scale*, if properly exploited, can be a powerful barrier to imitation since either the value created for customers increases with the number of customers you have or the costs of serving those customers decreases with the number of customers. Facebook is a good example of the former since people like joining and using Facebook because a lot of friends are already using it. The more friends they have on Facebook, the more fun it is to use and so the more they are likely to use it. And the more they use it, the more fun it is for *their* friends to join and use. We have a virtuous circle. Amazon is a good example of a company that has exploited increasing returns to scale. As it attracted users (initially just those interested in buying books), it became attractive for more and more vendors to sell through its platform. As more vendors joined the Amazon marketplace and the variety of products increased, Amazon became a more convenient place to shop for us. As more people shopped online at Amazon, more companies wanted to sell their products there. Amazon's size meant it had a great deal of bargaining power and so it could offer lower prices—which of course attracted more users. As volume increased, Amazon could afford to invest in more sophisticated and distributed warehousing and logistics infrastructure. This not only lowered costs, but it also shortened delivery lead times, which drove more demand to Amazon. Again, we have a virtuous circle.

Once that virtuous circle wheel is in motion, competitors can be hard pressed to imitate your model. They simply cannot imitate your volume or the cumulative size of your user base. But it is also important to "keep your foot on the gas." Just being first is not enough: you need sustained investments. Social network sites like Friendster and MySpace failed to exploit their potential first mover advantages. It is hard to believe today, but in 2006 MySpace surpassed Google as the number one site visited on the web.[22] MySpace should have been unbeatable, but in just a few years Facebook crushed it. In 2011, MySpace sold for just $35 million.[23] How did this happen? Part of the reason is that MySpace did not continue to evolve and improve its user experience (in other words, it started to create less user value). In addition, MySpace's user base—while impressive at its peak—was still a relatively tiny fraction of the total market potential. Whereas both MySpace and Facebook started with focused user segments (high school students for MySpace and college students for Facebook), Facebook quickly expanded beyond that demographic boundary.

Another way to protect your business model from imitation is to build a specialized ecosystem around it. Almost all business models require the support of providers of complementary resources, such as software developers who write apps for the iPhone in Apple's ecosystem. They make the iPhone platform more valuable for users. If your business model requires specialized complementary resources (like, say, software or accessories), then cultivating a network of complementary resources can not only enhance the value of your business model but can also become itself a powerful barrier to imitation. By the time Nokia realized that one of Apple's key advantages was its deep ecosystem of app developers, it was too late to catch up. It was simply impossible for Nokia to convince independent software developers to write software for its proprietary platform (based on the Symbian operating system). Eventually, Nokia was forced to abandon its proprietary operating system and sold itself to Microsoft. But at less than 1 percent of the total smartphone market, Microsoft's mobile operating system faces the same problem vis-à-vis the Apple and Android platform.[24]

Conclusion: Evolving Your Business Model

Technology can become obsolete, and so can your business model. Most companies are well aware of the risk of technological obsolescence and take steps like continued investment in R&D to defend themselves against it. Ironically, though, the forces making their business models obsolete are often missed. New competitors may introduce new business models to the market. New technologies may change which kind of resources can be monetized. Customer preferences may change in ways that cause your basis of value creation to decline. Competitive conditions may alter the economics of the way you capture value. An obsolete business model can be just as deadly to corporate health as obsolete technology. Just ask Blockbuster.

How do you keep your business model fresh? Part of the answer lies in the principles discussed in Chapter 2: an overall strategy that identifies business model innovation as a priority, allocating resources to business model innovation (just as you need to allocate resources to technological innovation). Second, business model innovation also requires the focused efforts of people within the company. That is often missing. For instance, at most companies when I ask who is in charge of technological innovation, I can generally get a pretty clear answer. People will point to the R&D organization or even name the chief scientific officer or senior vice president of R&D by name. If I ask the same question, though, about business model innovation, I usually get one of two responses: "it's no one's job" or "it's everyone's job" (which is the same as the former). Someone and some organization within the enterprise needs to be responsible for exploring, testing, and selecting ideas for business model innovation.

Finally, business model innovation like technological innovation requires experimentation and learning. No company would ever think about launching a significant innovation without building and testing prototypes. Experimentation is a natural and inherent part of every

R&D organization's repertoire. But, too often, companies do not apply the same logic to business model innovation. They either refuse to tamper with their model, or they try to introduce business model innovation without experimentation. The former dooms you to business model obsolescence, and the latter is highly risky. It is simply impossible to figure out all the details of business model innovation in advance, no matter how smart you are or how much analysis you do. Netflix's business model evolved. Initially, the company's pricing strategy was similar to Blockbuster's: you paid per video. But, when that didn't work, Netflix tried a subscription model. Amazon is a master at business model experimentation. Amazon Web Services—today the most successful cloud computing provider—grew out of an experiment to make the company's application interfaces available to third-party developers.[25] Business model innovation does not require having all the answers. It requires a capacity to experiment and to learn and a tolerance for risk. In essence, the organizational capabilities and culture required for business model innovation are no different from those required for technological innovation.

4

IS THE PARTY REALLY OVER?
Why You Should Not Always
Eat Your Own Lunch

It is hard to think of a business today that does not face some kind of potential threat from transformative innovation. If you run an automobile company, you have to think about how radical technological innovations in electric engines and autonomous vehicles and business model innovations like ride sharing could upend your business. A leader of a grocery chain has to be concerned about the threat of Internet-based home-delivery business models—especially now that Amazon owns a major grocery chain. If you run Marriott, peer-to-peer networks like Airbnb have certainly attracted your attention by now. One of the perennial questions of innovation strategy is how you should deal with these threats.

You have heard the advice on this question many times. Perhaps you were at a conference on innovation. Perhaps it was in a conference room at your company. Perhaps a consultant told you. The topic turned to future innovation trends and the potential threat to your business, and then someone said it: *eat your own lunch before someone else does.* It is one of the most ubiquitous pieces of advice in the management of innovation. According to this logic, you should make your existing technology or business model obsolete before someone else does. Embrace the future—let go of the past. Like all clichés, it's tiresome for its lack of originality. But "eat your own lunch" offends for a more important reason: it can be downright misleading. While the logic might seem impeccably obvious (better to be alive than dead), it is founded upon assumptions that do not always hold up. Dealing with the potential threats of disruptive innovation is a game requiring deep consideration of the nuanced interplay of technological and economic forces. It requires a strategy, not a slogan. In this chapter, we will explore how to develop such a strategy.

When Old Does Not Mean Obsolete: The Case of the Mainframe Computer

The mainframe computer has been commercially available since the late 1950s, and IBM's dominance of this business over several decades propelled it to become one of the largest, most profitable, and most admired corporations in history. As we all know by now, the picture changed dramatically in the late 1970s with the emergence of the personal computer. Computer power was now on our desktop (and a bit later, on our laps), and we were unshackled from the tyranny of time-share computing. As personal computers became more and more powerful with each generation of microprocessors (Moore's Law in action), businesses had less and less use for bulky mainframes. This was not good news for IBM, of course, which not only enjoyed a dominant market share in mainframes but also garnered juicy profit margins on them.

The PC looked exactly like the type of disruptive innovation that could sweep away a giant like IBM. But to its credit, IBM was not asleep at the wheel. By 1981, still relatively early in the PC revolution, IBM entered the market. And, in fact, one might argue that IBM's entry into PCs played a key role in propelling the revolution forward into the corporate computing market. IBM leadership understood that PCs would eat into the company's mainframe business—it was exactly for this reason it set up its PC organization in a separate stand-alone unit (in Florida, safely away from corporate headquarters in Armonk, New York). IBM was eating its own lunch.

For a while, this strategy seemed to be working. IBM's PC sales skyrocketed and quickly grabbed a significant share of the market. IBM was widely heralded for its bold move into PCs—it looked like the perfect business school case study to demonstrate how a large, highly successful organization could in fact be nimble enough to duck the forces of creative destruction. As mainframe sales declined, the strategy looked quite prescient. Predictions that the mainframe's days were numbered were not hard to find.

There was only one problem with this strategy—the PC market was never that profitable and was never going to be. Partly thanks to decisions made by IBM to outsource the operating system (to a then little-known software company called Microsoft) and the microprocessor to Intel, the structure of the personal computer industry made it very hard for personal computer manufacturers and marketers to be profitable. Because Microsoft and Intel controlled key components of the system architecture, they were in a position to extract all the economic rents from the industry. Sure, IBM and others could sell a lot of personal computers, but the profits flowed back to Microsoft and Intel. Personal computers became a brutally competitive business because it was hard for IBM to really differentiate itself from others like Dell, Compaq, and Hewlett Packard based on the performance of its machines because everyone (except Apple) was using the same basic "Wintel" architecture. Facing declining margins and eroding market share, IBM decided enough was enough and sold its PC division to Lenovo in December 2004.[1]

In the meantime, the old dinosaur known as the mainframe has been resurrected by the emergence of cloud computing and more recently big data. What few anticipated in the early days of the PC revolution was that the Internet would usher in a whole new era of networked computing. Applications and data would gravitate back to remote locations, eventually giving rise to what we now call "cloud computing." Some applications of cloud computing, like transaction processing, require massive amount of data storage and computational capacity, not to mention security and reliability—exactly the kind of thing mainframes are good at. Fortunately for IBM, it never listened to all of those who told the company to get out of mainframes. IBM's System Z mainframe utterly dominates the mainframe market. In 2017, almost 90 percent of all credit card transactions globally were processed by an IBM mainframe.[2] For IBM, mainframes are still a multibillion-dollar business with healthy margins. Mainframes will probably never be the gourmet lunch they were back in the 1960s and 1970s, but they turned out to be commercially far more durable than anyone predicted. Old? Yes. Obsolete? Not really.

The Assumptions Behind the Eat Your Own Lunch Logic

If you are going to follow (or discard) advice, you should understand the logic behind it. The logic of "eat your own lunch" rests on two fundamental assumptions. The first, which is often not true, is that you can perfectly predict the future. You think you know for sure that a particular transformative innovation will make your current technology or business model obsolete. But, as we saw with IBM, technology trends in reality are very hard to predict. The second assumption behind the eat your own lunch argument is that the potential disruption in question offers profit opportunities that are at least as good as your alternatives. That is, it presumes you are better off abandoning your current market position to embrace the new regime because if you do not, you will go bankrupt. But, as IBM discovered, PCs were never as profitable as mainframes. Deciding how to respond to a potential disruption threat requires you explore whether these assumptions hold. Let's explore them in more detail.

Assumption 1: You Can Predict the Timing of Disruptive Threats

Those who preach the eat your own lunch gospel have plenty of examples to illustrate the dire consequences of failing to follow the advice. They can point to all those traditional bricks-and-mortar retailers who failed to embrace the Internet and were wiped away by the likes of Amazon. They can describe the downfall of traditional media companies who were slow to realize how Google and other online platforms would ultimately disrupt the advertising business model of the industry. They can evoke the ghosts of once-dominant companies like Nokia, RIM, Blockbuster, DEC, Wang, Kodak, Polaroid, and many others who were swept away by the Schumpeterian gales of creative destruction. In each of these cases, so it seems, leaders could not bring themselves or their organizations to swallow the bitter reality facing their industry.

They could not jettison their past in order to have a better future. They could not, in short, bring themselves to eat their own lunch. What else could explain such suicidal behavior?

These cases can be persuasive and frightening. When I read them, I am reminded of watching a horror movie—the type where creepy villains hide in the basement. As you see the story unfold, you want to shout the business equivalent of "don't go in the basement" or "get out of the house now"! But, just as they do in the movie, the leaders in these cases ignore your pleas, and bad things happen. It all seems so predictable.

And yet, at least in the case of innovation, it is not. *It only tends to look that way after the fact.* In reality, technological and business model evolution is a messy and uncertain process—full of dead-ends, wrong turns, and random effects. What might look obvious in retrospect was by no means obvious at the time leaders of these enterprises peered into the future. Predicting technological trends is brutally difficult. Even the most visionary business leaders can get it wrong.

The Future of Electric Cars

A visionary technologist sits across from the journalist and calmly proclaims that the electric vehicle will be the car of the future. There is good reason to believe the speaker—he has been a successful entrepreneur, with deep technical knowledge of the trends transforming the contemporary economy. Surely, I must be talking about Elon Musk, founder of electric car producer Tesla, Solar City, and PayPal. But I am not. The technology visionary in this case is Thomas Edison, who in 1914 told an interviewer, "I believe that ultimately the electric motor will be universally used for trucking in all large cities, and that the electric automobile will be the family carriage of the future."[3] And Edison was not the only visionary who believed in the future of electric cars. Henry Ford was also enthusiastic about their future. Ford collaborated with Edison to develop an electric car, buying more than 100,000 of Edison's batteries and committing more than $30 million (in today's dollars) into the car's development—over a fifth the size of the $135 million investment that a much larger Ford Motor Company made in electric vehicles in 2010.[4] As late as 1917, the *Wall Street Journal* published an article about a new electric automobile company with the title, "Another Wonder of the Age on the Threshold: Dey Electric Automobile, Noted Engineers Say, Promises to Revolutionize the Auto World," in which a world authority on alternating current argued the electric car would lead the automotive field with low prices.[5] Noting increases in electric cabs, another 1917 article from the same newspaper pondered whether, "should the electric vehicle assume sufficiently great proportions, it is possible that many cities may compel drivers of cars to use electric power within city limits rather than the smoky and noisy gas motor."[6]

Of course, as we now know, by the early 1920s, the gasoline internal combustion engine became the entrenched dominant design for automobiles. This happened because of a confluence of forces, not all of which would have been predicted at the time. Technical improvements in internal combustion technology made the engines quieter, cleaner, and smoother. The invention of the electric starter by Charles Kettering in 1912 eliminated the inconvenience (and danger!) of having to start the engine with a hand crank.[7] That same year, perhaps not coincidentally, Ford introduced the Model T for $850.[8] The internal combustion engine was also boosted by the dramatically expanding availability of gasoline, thanks to a combination of greater domestic crude oil production and refining capacity.[9] The expanding supply of crude drastically reduced the price per mile of gasoline vehicles. One advantage gasoline cars had over electric vehicles at the time (and even today) was greater range. This range advantage, however, was of little use to consumers until there were enough roads to take them longer distances. Thanks to federal support of road building and maintenance (in no small part influenced by the growing popularity of the Model T), the US road system (particularly in rural areas) expanded dramatically between 1916 and 1921.[10] The expansion of the road system made the gasoline-powered car an alternative to the railroads' monopoly on long-distance and interstate travel. While charging stations for electric cars existed in the 1910s, much of the country did not have electricity, let alone standardized electricity (AC vs. DC).

Why You Should Take Innovation Predictions with a Grain of Salt

The world is awash in predictions about future technologies and business model innovation. You hear them at industry conferences and in TED Talks. You read them in blogs, books, newspaper articles, tweets, and consulting reports. In fact, there is a whole cottage industry of people dedicated to making these kinds of predictions. They are called "futurists." Futurists are usually the ones cautioning you about the next big disruptive wave that will kill your business. Sometimes they are right—sometimes they are wrong. And that's the problem. It turns out to be *really* hard to predict technology and business model trends.

There is a tendency to emphasize how quickly things are changing and how different the future will be from the present (a predictable bias of people who, after all, call themselves futurists). But as with mainframe computers, supposedly obsolete technologies can be surprisingly tenacious. There are other examples. The transition from sail power to steam power for ocean going vessels took more than sixty years.[11] The first electronic fuel injection for the car was introduced in the 1950s, but it was not until the 1980s that it overtook carburetors, thanks largely to tighter government standards on emissions.[12] The first commercial airplane to use a jet engine (instead of a propeller) was introduced in 1952, yet propeller aircraft engines are still being designed, manufactured, and used for smaller, shorter-haul aircraft today.[13] When Steve Jobs introduced the iPad, he predicted tablets would replace notebooks. In 2013, tablet sales surpassed notebooks, partially validating his vision.[14] But, with unit sales of more than 160 million in 2017, notebooks have by no means gone away.[15] Internet-based banking has surged in the past twenty years, leading many to expect the end of the branch. Yet, the number of branches in the United States continued to grow steadily until 2009 (when it peaked at 35.72 per 100,000 adults). The number of bank branches in 2014 (32.40) in the United States was essentially the same as it was in 2004 (32.5 per 100,000 adults).[16] We all know about the decline of print newspapers as digital channels have ascended. While it is true that print circulation has been declining for years, print still made up 78 percent of daily circulation and 86 percent of Sunday circulation in 2016.[17]

But it is also just as easy to underestimate how quickly things do change. Consider what happened in the smartphone market. In 2008, a year *after* Apple introduced the iPhone, Nokia's proprietary operating system for smartphones, Symbian, still commanded a 48.8 percent share of the market (a slight *increase* from the prior year).[18] So if you were running Nokia at the time, you must have been feeling pretty good—Apple's much-vaunted iPhone had no negative effect on your share. But then came Google's Android operating system, introduced in 2008. Within just four years of its introduction, Android's share soared to 74.4 percent, Apple's iOS held most of the remaining with 18.2 percent, and Nokia's Symbian vanished to a 0.6 percent market share.[19]

There are other examples of rapid disruption. Video on demand displaced the market for rental DVDs within about three years of introduction. Within eight years of its founding, Amazon was selling more books online than Barnes and Noble was selling through its stores. In 2004, about 90 percent of US households had a wired landline for telephone service. By 2014, only slightly more than half did—households relying on cell phone telephone service only jumped to about 45 percent.[20]

Prediction is always inherently difficult, but predictions about technology and business model trends are particularly vexing for three reasons. The first is what I call the "systems problem." Few technologies exist in isolation. They are part of more complex systems. This means that the economic viability of any given technology depends on the interaction of multiple complementary technologies and economic forces, each subject to its own uncertainty. The performance of complex systems tends to progress in a nonlinear fashion. Inflection points are extremely hard to anticipate because their timing is influenced by the interaction of multiple factors. For instance, if you want to predict the market penetration of electric vehicles in the next ten years, you have to get your arms around trends in battery technology (in itself a highly complex space), advances in electric motors, materials that affect vehicle weight, potential advances in internal combustion technology, advances in fuel technology, the cost of gasoline, the cost of electricity, future government policies, and future customer preferences, to name just a few factors.

Such system interdependencies are also at work in business model innovation. Netflix initially became viable because the video storage technology shifted from bulky VHS cassettes to cheap-to-mail DVDs. But television screens were also getting larger and sharper, thanks to advances in display technology and graphic circuitry, and this made watching movies at home a more pleasurable experience. This increased demand for at-home viewing fit perfectly with Netflix's fixed price ("all you can eat") subscription pricing model. This all looks so predictable now, but at the time it was not. In fact, Netflix's original business model did not include a fixed subscription price—it was a per-film rental like Blockbuster. It was not until later—after disappointing market penetration—that Netflix shifted to the subscription model.

The second impediment to technology and business model predictions is what I call "endogenous customer preferences." The textbook description of entrepreneurial innovation is one where a visionary leader "sees" an unmet need and then develops a breakthrough innovation to serve that need. Reality is a bit messier. Customer needs and preferences are neither static nor given. We discover what we want by seeing things that we never imagined. This means that it is hard, ex ante, to determine market demand for needs that do not currently seem to exist. Intel did not invent the microprocessor because its leaders saw the potential to transform the world's economy and turn itself into a colossus of the digital age. The story has more prosaic origins. In 1969, Bussicom, a Japanese calculator company, asked Intel to design a set of twelve integrated circuits to handle the logic (mathematical functions) for a new line of calculators. Intel engineer Ted Hoff got the idea of combining the functionality of all twelve chips into a single chip—a device we now call a "microprocessor."[21] But it is not as if Intel immediately understood the potential applications of its new invention. In fact, originally, the rights to the microprocessor were assigned to Bussicom. It was only later that Intel bought back the non-calculator rights to the technology, in what must be considered the greatest business development deal of all time. But, even then, Intel did not fully understand the potential markets for microprocessors.[22]

Initially, the uses for microprocessors appeared limited. They were underpowered relative to traditional multichip modules used in existing mainframe and minicomputers. The market for personal computers had not yet been created. When the first PCs did hit the market, Intel's visionary leader, Gordon Moore (after whom Moore's Law is named) did not see its potential. He dismissed home computers as devices that might find limited use as a way for "housewives to store recipes." The point is not that Intel was incompetent. It clearly was not. The ultimate big market for Intel microprocessors was one that did not exist, and forecasting a market that does not exist, or is in its infancy, is nearly impossible. None of us knew we *needed* a personal computer until we had one. Customers do not always know their own preferences, and they reserve the right to change them any time they please without notice!

Finally, whether and how fast a new technology triumphs depends not just on its own (uncertain) rate of progress, but also on the (uncertain) rate of progress of the technologies it seeks to replace. There is often a presumption that technologies that have existed for a long time are somehow "out of gas." When confronted with "new" technologies, they will quickly collapse. But, as documented by the work Dan Snow of Brigham Young University, old technologies often continue to progress and improve quite dramatically in the face of potentially disruptive innovations, a phenomenon he called "last gasps." For instance, carburetors continued to improve after the mass introduction of electronic fuel injection in the early 1980s, a task partly accomplished by integrating some elements of electronic fuel injection into their carburetor design.[23] Snow's work shows that such last gasps can be quite prolonged.

The point is not to urge you to ignore technological or business model threats, nor is it to dismiss ominous forecasts. That would be myopic, and myopia is never useful. Companies do get destroyed by radical changes in technology and by disruptive business model innovations. Instead, I hope to have sensitized you to the delicate balance you have to strike in responding to potential threats. On the one hand, something may not look like much of a threat today that could quickly become so due to unexpected changes in complementary technologies, regulations, or markets. On the other hand, you don't want to prematurely abandon existing technologies and business models that may actually have long economically productive lives in front of them. Abandoning an existing strong position too early can be just as costly as abandoning too late. We need to accept that our radar screens are much foggier than we realize. Uncertainty has important practical implications for how we conduct innovation strategy. Later in this chapter, we will examine these. Before we do that, however, we must examine another critical assumption of the "eat your own lunch" logic.

Assumption 2: All That Glitters Is Gold

Let's start with a thought experiment. Like many such experiments it stretches reality a bit by endowing you with unparalleled powers of prediction. I am going to assume that all the challenges of technology and business model prediction we examined above do not apply to *you*. You can predict the future perfectly. Now let's assume you are CEO of Kodak in 1983, and, because you are such an omniscient visionary, you can see the future of digital imaging perfectly. You know how fast it will improve; you know the rate that all the required complementary technologies will improve; you know the rates of investment of all your competitors. You have exact dates when images of different quality will be available, and you even know the prices. You are pretty much a wizard. And, obviously, you can see the dire implications for your core film business.

If there was ever a time to eat your own lunch, this would appear to be it. Abandon film and go headfirst into the digital future. Right? Not so fast. There is another assumption made the by "eat your own lunch" logic that also needs to hold up before you leap. You have to assume that the new technology (say, digital imaging) is as profitable as your existing technology (say, film) or all the alternative things you could do with the shareholders' money (like give it back to them). That may or may not be true, depending on the circumstances. There is no economic law that says new technologies offer the same profit potential as old technologies.

Digital imaging is actually one case where technological change dramatically reduced the profit potential of the business. The usual story about the fall of Kodak is that it was too slow to respond to digital technology because it was so wedded to its traditional business—film. That is, in theory, Kodak failed because it did not eat its own lunch. But this story has been convincingly challenged by the recent work of my Harvard colleague Willy Shih.[24] Willy should know the Kodak story well, because he joined Kodak as an executive in 1997, just as digital photography was ascending. As Willy describes it, Kodak was not slow at all in responding to digital. It was tracking trends carefully and investing heavily in critical digital technologies (like sensors).[25] The problem was that digital technology transformed the structure of the photography market in a way that completely eroded its profit potential. Digital photography was based on general-purpose semiconductor technology available from multiple suppliers. As Shih notes, "Suppliers selling components offered the technology to anyone who would pay, and there were few entry barriers. What's more, digital technology is modular. A good engineer could buy all the building blocks and put together a camera."[26] With such low entry barriers, it is not surprising that hundreds of companies (many small start-ups like GoPro) were able to enter the market. Moreover, broad availability of the core technologies made it difficult for companies offering digital cameras to differentiate their products from others. Low barriers to entry plus low opportunities for product differentiation equals very low opportunities for profit for *everyone*. Eating your own (very profitable) lunch is not necessarily a good strategy when the alternative is table scraps.

There is no guarantee that new technologies and new business models offer you, or others in the market, attractive profit opportunities. Profit potential in a market is determined by a set of structural factors, like barriers to entry, intellectual property, opportunities for differentiation, supplier and buyer bargaining power, and the availability of substitutes.[27] In some contexts, technological and business model innovation might alter these forces in a way that leads to higher overall profit potential for some players. Strong increasing returns to scale has enabled Google to sustain a highly profitable position in Internet search/advertising. Facebook exploits inherent positive network economies in social media to sustain a dominant position in its market.

But, as in the case of digital photography, innovation can also level the playing field, which can make profitability very hard to achieve. The personal computer market is an example, as I discussed earlier. Personal computers were a transformative technology that created lots of value for society and lots of profits for Microsoft and Intel but not much for companies who sold them (with the exception of Dell for a short period of time and Apple, which used a proprietary operating system). Newspapers are another example. Over the past two decades, newspapers have jumped headfirst into digital channels. This is a classic "eat your own lunch" strategy. The presumption is that print is dying and that the only way for newspapers to survive is to embrace digital. As noted above, print may be declining, but there is still a large print market in the United States. And, according to new research on the topic, digital channels have not been very profitable for traditional newspapers.[28]

In determining how aggressively you should embrace a new technology or business model, you need to focus not just on revenue but on profitability. Revenue opportunities might be enormous, but this does not necessarily translate into profit (again, think about the case of PCs or digital photography). Let's consider Walmart. The long-successful retail giant is certainly under threat from online retail, and Amazon in particular. Walmart's profit growth in recent years has stagnated after decades of predictable growth, and today Amazon's market capitalization is almost twice as large as Walmart's. Yet let's put Walmart's situation in perspective. In 2016, Walmart generated operating income of $19.5 billion on $482 billion in revenue, for a return on sales of 4 percent.[29] In comparison, in the same year, Amazon's *retail* business generated approximately $1 billion in operating income on $123 billion in revenue, for a return of 0.8 percent.[30] For all its dominance in retail, Amazon has not been particularly profitable in that segment. This creates a serious dilemma for a traditional (and still-profitable) retailer like Walmart. It cannot ignore online channels. Those channels seriously threaten its existing business. And yet those channels are not all that profitable—and may never be. Or consider the situation faced by auto companies today, which hear they will be disrupted by ride-sharing platforms that will make owning a vehicle an obsolete concept. Some are taking this threat seriously, as they should. Audi and GM, for instance, are experimenting with offering their own ride-sharing services. But will ride sharing ever be profitable for them? To date, ride sharing has not been profitable despite its hype. Industry leader Uber, even with strong revenue growth, reportedly lost more than $5 billion over the years 2015 and 2016.[31] Uber's leading competitor, Lyft, has promised its investors that it will not *lose* more than $600 million per year.[32] This does not mean these companies will not be profitable in the future. Investors seem to be betting they will. But there are no guarantees for either of these companies or auto companies who enter the space.

We can see the dilemma some companies confront in dealing with fundamental transformations: if they stick with their current technology or business model, they run a potential risk of extinction. If Kodak had just stayed with film, eventually that market would have dried up. But if they move aggressively, they might be exchanging dollars for dimes. Neither of these are particularly palatable options. How you might navigate this dilemma is the subject to which we turn below.

Strategies for Navigating Threats to Your Business

I've highlighted two main forces you need to take into account when deciding how to respond to a potential threat of technology or business model disruption. The first is the nature of the threat: How certain are you that the threat will destroy your current business, and over what time horizon might this happen? The second is the impact on your profitability: If you do adopt the new technology or business model, can you still achieve reasonable profits? Each of these requires its own in-depth analysis. And, in reality, each requires a mix of cold analytics and artful judgment.

That technology predictions are often difficult does not mean you cannot engage in deep exploration and evaluation of trends to develop insights about what *might* happen. Uncertainty is time dependent. By this I mean that the level of uncertainty depends on the time horizon over which you are evaluating the potential threat. Will there be fully autonomous vehicles capable of transporting people over highways while they sleep in the *next year*? Not very likely. Will there be such vehicles in the next *fifty years*? Much more likely. Start by picking a time horizon for your analysis that matches your window of response. That is, figure out how long it will take you to respond to the threat, and then use that as your window to analyze what might happen. If you have long product development cycles (like, say, Boeing or a pharmaceutical company), you need to be looking far out on the time horizon to assess technologies because you have to act now to be capable of responding to a threat in ten years. If you are an app developer, whose product development cycles might be only a few months, then your threat window is shorter. You do not have to assess threats to your business or core technology in ten years.

Once you have a reasonable time horizon, you can then conduct all the usual types of technological and economic analyses to assess various scenarios. These typically involve talking to experts, analyzing patent data, probing the scientific literature, conducting your own research and competitive intelligence, and getting detailed windows into a technology through partnerships. To assess your level of confidence in the likelihood of an impact, go back to the three factors that can make it hard to predict technology or business model trends.

1. Are there complementary technologies that need to be developed for the threat to be realized? What is the status of those? What are the critical technology bottlenecks that need to be overcome?
2. What can we really glean about customer behavior and tastes? What are the signs they are changing in ways that might make a particular threat economically viable?
3. How much improvement potential is left in existing technologies? How long is the runway for the "last gasp"?

The goal of these analyses is not to make precise predictions but to get a qualitative feel for the threat level from specific technologies. Is the threat imminent and highly likely? Or is it distant and, at this point, relatively unlikely to impact the business? The process of getting senior management teams to even discuss these issues can be quite valuable.

The second piece of analysis concerns assessing whether you can earn reasonable profits by adopting the disruption in question. So, for instance, if you are an auto company and thinking about ride sharing, you need to analyze your future profit potential in the ride-sharing business. To find this answer, you will need to examine how the technology or business model change will influence fundamental industry drivers of profit potential: What impact will it have on structural market factors like barriers to entry, intellectual property protection, ability to differentiate, supplier and buyer bargaining power, availability of substitutes, scale economies, network externalities, fundamental cost drivers, and the like? Importantly, how might a particular technological upheaval affect where in the value chain profits will be earned? How well positioned is your company to earn profits under a new technology scenario? You need to assess realistically your capabilities to compete effectively in the new technology. In some cases, the technological change in question is so distant from the company's base of expertise and experience that it is virtually infeasible to develop the requisite competences. A good example would be the situation faced by Smith Corona, once a dominant player in traditional typewriters. The PC, as we all know, completely replaced the market for traditional electromechanical typewriters, but becoming a PC maker was simply not a feasible option for Smith Corona.

Thinking through these questions will help you assess your alternatives. Figure 4.1 provides a simple framework combining the two dimensions we have discussed: the nature of the threat (how likely is the disruption in question to occur in the relevant time horizon?) and your profit potential *should you switch*. From it, we identify a set of potential responses to technological or business model threats. This is designed

FIGURE 4.1

Mapping Responses to Potential Disruptions

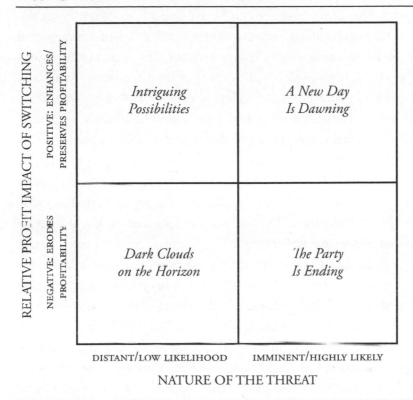

RELATIVE PROFIT IMPACT OF SWITCHING

POSITIVE: ENHANCES/ PRESERVES PROFITABILITY

NEGATIVE: ERODES PROFITABILITY

| *Intriguing Possibilities* | *A New Day Is Dawning* |
| *Dark Clouds on the Horizon* | *The Party Is Ending* |

DISTANT/LOW LIKELIHOOD   IMMINENT/HIGHLY LIKELY

NATURE OF THE THREAT

to help you figure out when you should, in fact, move aggressively (eat your own lunch) and when obstinate defense of your existing position may be a better, if less glamorous, response.

A New Day Is Dawning: The Case for Eating Your Own Lunch. Let's begin with the case for eating your own lunch. If the threat in question appears relatively likely to impact your business *and* the profits from it are at least as good as your current business, then aggressively moving into the new technology or business model makes sense. Here, your logic is, the change *is* coming, but we can still be profitable if we adapt.

Let's look at an example of how IBM dealt with this dilemma when confronted with the threat of open-source Linux software in the early

2000s. When graduate student Linus Torvalds first created the open-source operating system, Linux, from his dorm room, no one paid much attention. Linux appeared to be a hobbyist operating system—certainly no match for a proprietary enterprise-grade operating system like Unix. Being open source, Linux was not only free, but its source code was available to anyone who wanted to modify, fix, or improve it. Pretty quickly, a community of independent developers began writing new code for Linux, and its capabilities improved quickly. When its scalability, reliability, and security hit a certain level, companies began to install Linux on their servers to run business applications. If you were IBM in the late 1990s, this was not necessarily good news; after all, IBM had its own proprietary Unix operating system that came with its servers and garnered handsome licensing fees. It could fight by trying to improve its proprietary Unix, cut prices, improve service, and so on. Or it could switch: it could embrace Linux. This would almost certainly accelerate the demise of its own Unix system—a classic case of eating your lunch before someone else does. In this case, the threat was real and imminent. By 2000, there was little doubt in the minds of IBM leadership that Linux would penetrate the market. But how about profitability? How could Linux—given away for free—ever be a profitable business model for IBM? IBM realized if it embraced Linux, it would also need to adapt its business model. Rather than making money off licensing fees for its Unix operating system, it would instead make profits by selling "middleware" (the software that runs on the operating system), applications, and other services. Because these are highly profitable, the switch to Linux was actually quite attractive economically for IBM. It did lose revenue from Unix licenses, but it more than made up for them by additional sales of servers, middleware and applications software, and services.

Eating your own lunch is almost a no-brainer when you are moving to an equally attractive profit position. Netflix's move from traditional DVD rental to video on demand is another example where it seems to have paid off to eat your own lunch. VoD—the capacity to stream or download media content to your computer, television, or phone—was an emerging technology in 2005. Then, it took about an hour to download a film, and, in fact, you could only watch content on your computer (televisions were not Internet compatible). But, even then, it was apparent that these bottlenecks would be overcome. Apple was introducing a device to connect televisions to the Internet (Apple TV) and making a few films available online. Broadband speeds were accelerating. Storage was becoming cheaper and cheaper. Netflix realized that video on demand was inevitable and that it could displace its traditional DVD rental by mail business. But could VoD be profitable? After all, many companies entered the VoD space (Amazon, Apple, Google, Hulu, to name just a few). The key in VoD is proprietary content. Customers will pay for a subscription if they can get content not available elsewhere. Because there are high fixed costs of acquiring or creating proprietary content, Netflix's scale and its large subscriber base are a huge competitive advantage in the world of VoD. Netflix may have eaten its own DVD by mail lunch, but it continues to enjoy tasty profits in the world of VoD.

The Party Is Ending. In the worst-case scenario, your core business or core technology not only looks likely to become obsolete, but you do not even have a viable path to profit under the new regime. This was the scenario facing Kodak. This kind of dire situation reminds me of the line from the movie *Annie Hall* about a commencement speaker's admonition: "More than any other time in history, mankind faces a crossroads. One path leads to despair and utter hopelessness. The other, to total extinction. Let us pray we have the wisdom to choose correctly." What should you do if you are faced with such terrible alternatives?

There are two basic strategic plays. One is to pivot around your capabilities. Rather than trying to compete in a market where you have little chance of profiting, find new markets where you can deploy your existing capabilities. Kodak might have pivoted to markets where its existing and unique specialty chemical and materials capabilities could be deployed, a strategy successfully used by Fuji.[33] Smith Corona repositioned itself as a producer of thermal ribbon used in thermal transfer printers.[34] Such repositioning strategies are often more easily implemented in a diversified company that has organizational mechanisms to redeploy resources from one business to another or to start (or acquire) new business units.

The second possible strategy is *defend and extend*. In this strategy, you try to prolong the decline as much as possible by improving your technology, finding attractive sub-segments of the market where your technology still has an advantage, and reducing costs. Under this strategy, you are betting you can create a long and potentially profitable last gasp. This is by no means a cure. It may be purely a life extension. This strategy is not glamorous, nor is it a prescription for growth. But it may be the only possible alternative and can set the stage for an exit that is the least costly solution for shareholders.

Intriguing Possibilities and Clouds on the Horizon. How should you respond if you really do not know whether the threat in question will materialize (let alone whether it will create or destroy profit opportunities)? Almost all disruptions that do materialize once started out in this category—at one time, things that seemed inevitable were murmurs at conferences and wild speculations. Many companies do nothing at this stage, but that is probably a valuable opportunity lost. By the time something is inevitable, it may be too late to respond to either seize the profit opportunity in the new wave or to reposition the company for a transition.

This was a mistake made by Baldwin Locomotive, once the largest manufacturer of steam locomotives in the United States. The diesel engine was invented in the late nineteenth century and began to be used in locomotives as early as 1912, but they were not commercially successful because of poor power-to-weight ratio. Only a few prototype diesel locomotives were produced by the 1920s. At this stage, the diesel locomotive should have looked like the classic ambiguous threat to Baldwin. There was something there, but it did not appear anywhere close to commercially threatening. Could it advance enough to challenge the steam engine? Could it be made at attractive costs? Would rail operators adopt them? Could the steam engine be improved enough to maintain its superiority? This would have been an ideal time to begin exploring the technology as a means for Baldwin to hedge its bets and develop options to participate in the new technology should it advance rapidly. Baldwin chose not to do so. In fact, in 1930, the chairman of Baldwin, Samuel Vauclain, stated publicly that advances in steam technology would ensure the dominance of the steam loco- motive until at least 1980.[35] Baldwin bet on steam and on another emerging technology, all-electric locomotives.

If one recognizes the difficulty of predicting future advances in technology, then such "all-in" commitments are really quite dangerous. They make the precarious assumption that your technological forecast is correct (in this case, steam can improve and all-electric will beat die- sel). A better strategy under such conditions of uncertainty is to hedge and create options (e.g., make smaller R&D investments in diesel). In fact, Baldwin's largest competitors in steam locomotives, ALCO, did exactly that. It was investing in diesel technology as early as the 1920s. While GE eventually went on to dominate the diesel locomotive in- dustry, ALCO survived until being acquired in 1964. Baldwin filed for bankruptcy in 1935.

The best strategy when facing high degrees of uncertainty is to hedge and build options for the future. This might involve, for in- stance, making some small investments in companies developing potentially threatening new technologies. Or it could mean experi- menting with a novel business model to understand its challenges and its economics. If the disruption could come to fruition and put you in the "party's over" category, then it's particularly important to start, early on, exploring alternative strategic options, such as entering new markets where your existing capabilities provide an advantage. Again, given uncertainty, I am not advising you to abandon your core mar- ket. But it is prudent to experiment with alternatives well in advance as insurance against a potential disruption you may not be able to respond to.

Conclusion

One of the great puzzles scholars of innovation have grappled with is why companies often fail to respond to disruptive threats. Why are there so many cases like Baldwin Locomotive where senior leaders just do not seem to "see" the future? Scholars and consultants generally ascribe such behavior to inertia. The senior leaders are too wedded to their existing technology or business model, or simply too narrow minded to accept change. Certainly, such leadership failures happen. One reason why I think thoughtful leaders have trouble with these transitions is that they are framing the alternatives too narrowly. They can either stand pat in their market (and hope for the best) or they can eat their own lunch by embracing the new. I think many senior leaders have legitimate concerns with eating their own lunch. Intuitively, they recognize that a commitment to a new technology or new business model is very risky, given uncertainty. They also often realize that eating their own lunch may not be very palatable financially for the firm. But they feel stuck. Because they also know that standing pat on their home turf may ultimately lead to the extinction of the company.

What I hope is that this chapter has helped you see that you have more choices than to stand pat and pray versus eat your own lunch. The chapter has highlighted the conditions when eating your own lunch really is your best strategy. But it has also focused on conditions when standing pat and fighting (extend and defend) may be best. Hopefully, though, it has broadened your strategic palette to recognize that, even in dire disruptions, if you act early enough, you may be able to reposition your enterprise in a way that ensures its continued prosperity. Finally, hedging and exploration are essential features of a robust innovation strategy under many circumstances. Too often, innovation leadership is posed as a test of "guts"—are you willing to make the big bets? Such "all-in" bets make for great business headlines, but they are actually pretty foolish if you face high levels of uncertainty. Making smaller bets, experimenting, learning, and adapting are survival-enhancing behaviors in highly uncertain environments.

As I have pointed out, there are going to be circumstances where you have to transform your organization and innovate outside your home court. You will have to seek disruptive business model innovations, radical technological innovation, or architectural innovations. Having a clear strategy to undertake these kinds of innovations is indeed helpful. But they require different kinds of capabilities than your organization may have been using. To execute your innovation strategy, you need to develop a matching set of innovation capabilities. You need to develop an innovation system. This is the topic of Part II.

PART II
DESIGNING THE INNOVATION SYSTEM

In Part I, we learned about the different types of innovation (routine, radical, disruptive, and architectural) and that a good innovation strategy specifies the balance and mix of resource allocated to each type. To execute your innovation strategy, though, requires more than allocating resources—it requires that your organization have appropriate organizational capabilities. The capabilities deployed for routine innovation, for instance, are different from those required for outside-the-home-court innovation. Tight alignment between an innovation strategy and the organization's capabilities is essential for effective execution.

How can you build the capabilities you require to execute your innovation strategy? Many companies look to emulate so-called best practices. Today, for instance, they might hear about the power of such practices as crowdsourcing and open innovation, decentralization of R&D, co-development with customers, big data analytics, and so forth. Innovation writers and consultants will urge companies to imitate the practices of companies like Apple or Google. The problem with this approach is that every innovation practice involves trade-offs. There are no universal "best practices." What is best for Apple or Google is not necessarily going to be best for *your* company given its strategy and its circumstances. Creating capabilities for innovation is more like bespoke tailoring than buying off the rack. The leadership challenge is to *design* the particular approach to innovation that will work for your company and support its particular innovation strategy. This is the focus of Part II.

An organization's capacity for innovation is rooted in a system of choices and practices about people, processes, structures, and behaviors. Building appropriate capabilities for innovation is a systems design problem. As a leader, you are taking on the role of an organizational engineer. Good system engineers make it their business to understand the components of the system, the way components interact, and the desired performance trade-offs. The same principles apply to designing innovation systems. Innovation systems need to perform three basic tasks: (1) *search* for novel and valuable problems and solutions, (2) *synthesis* of diverse streams of ideas into coherent business concept, and (3) *selection* among opportunities. The three following chapters of Part II focus on each of these tasks.

5

VENTURING OUTSIDE YOUR HOME COURT
Search: Discovering Novel Problems and Solutions

On December 28, 2015, Michimasa Fujino stood before a gleaming white private jet at the Greensboro, North Carolina, airport. He was ready to deliver a new plane to a business owner from Cedar City, Utah, who had placed his order more than ten years before. This delivery was remarkable in two respects. First, this was the initial jet delivery of *Honda* Aircraft Company—a subsidiary of a corporation best known for automobiles and motorcycles. The HondaJet was the culmination of nearly three decades of work by Honda to innovate outside its home court. Second, with its two engines mounted *above* the wings, the HondaJet looked like no other airplane on the market. But this design was not about aesthetics at all—it was critical to solving a big problem for small jets—space. Normally, small jets mount engines on the rear of the plane body (the fuselage). But because this design requires putting structural supports through the fuselage, it devours interior space, leading to cramped cabins. And, with the engines right next to the passengers' heads, the noise can be uncomfortable. By putting the engines over the wings, Honda was able to create a light jet with a much roomier and quieter interior.

The HondaJet is creative construction in action—a very large and successful corporation not only venturing outside the safety of its home court but also creating a transformative product concept in the process.[1] The over-the-wing-engine design was so revolutionary that, prior to the HondaJet, most aeronautical engineers thought it violated basic principles of aerodynamics. When Fujino first proposed this design in

111

1997, his supervisor called it "the worst piece of engineering" he had ever seen. Boeing engineers were so skeptical of the design that they almost refused to let Honda test a prototype in their wind tunnel, fearing a catastrophic failure would damage their multimillion-dollar facility. Few could see then that, by the first half of 2017, the HondaJet would become the top-selling airplane in the light business jet market.[2] The biggest challenge for Michimasa Fujino, now Honda Aircraft's CEO, is ramping up production to meet growing demand.

How Honda accomplished this feat illustrates a central theme of this chapter: innovating outside the home court requires an organization to be willing and capable of *searching* in novel and unknown terrain. Search, the process by which people identify salient problems and explore plausible solutions, shapes the kinds of innovations an organization is capable of creating. Search generates hypotheses about problems that may be valuable to solve and solutions that might be worth exploring. Search shapes which problems and which potential solutions get on the organization's radar screen. Being willing to at least entertain the controversial hypothesis that an over-the-wing configuration might work is an example of how broad search is a prerequisite to transformative innovation.

When organizations search narrowly, really interesting problems and novel solutions usually don't get a chance to enter the discussion. Blinders, however, are not put on a search process by design. No senior leader says, "Let's close our eyes to really interesting ideas. Let's just focus on the same old things we have always done." I have never come across an organization with an explicit policy that stopped employees from using their imaginations. The problem is that many senior leaders are not really aware of how their organizations search for new innovation ideas. They do not *design* their search processes to purposely expose the organization to ideas that might be transformative. Exploratory search outside a company's home court does not happen automatically. Like most processes, search tends to become routinized over time, focused on the same familiar terrain. That is fine for routine innovation, but if your organization wants to innovate outside its home court, it may need to challenge its search process to venture into new and less certain places. How to design your organization's search processes to explore new terrain is the topic of this chapter.

Innovation as a Hunt for Problems and Solutions

Solving some "problem" of value is at the heart of every successful innovation. Some innovations tackle technical or functional problems. Statin drugs reduced serum cholesterol, a major contributor to heart disease; semiconductors enabled us to create a whole new array of computing and communications devices. Some innovations solve problems of convenience. Google's search engine, for instance, made it much easier to find information on the web. Some innovations address purely economic problems. New aircraft engine designs reduce airlines' operating costs per available seat mile. Some innovations address aesthetic issues. The iPhone is more than just a functional device—enabling mobile web browsing, communications, and a host of applications—it is also aesthetically pleasing to use and look at. Some innovations tackle social problems. Innovations leading to clean drinking water and better sanitation did more to improve health than most new pharmaceuticals over the past century.

Taking a problem-solving perspective on innovation highlights two key challenges: finding valuable problems to solve and then coming up with solutions to address them. In some instances, finding the right problem is not the hard part. Terrible diseases like cancer or Alzheimer's or big social challenges like clean water or the environment are well-defined problems. We know that solving such problems would reap large financial or societal dividends. The challenge is that good solutions to these problems have been *really* hard to find. In other instances, though, innovations address what economists call "latent demand"—they create demand for things we never knew we really needed or wanted until we saw or used them. That is, the innovation itself changes our perceived needs. We are surrounded by many of these. While experiencing the existential panic that comes from misplacing my mobile phone, I usually forget that I survived just fine without one for the first thirty-five years of my life.

There is a temptation to think about innovation as a one-way process flowing from problem identification to solution identification. After all, it is hard to imagine finding a solution for a problem without knowing the problem. However, despite its apparent infallible logic, innovation processes often do not follow this path. That is, they sometimes generate solutions in search of problems. Let's take a look at one classic example.

Beware the Hidden Customer: The Case of DuPont Kevlar

Kevlar, a lighter-than-steel, super-strong, heat-resistant material with a wide range of uses, from bulletproof vests to surfboards to wind turbines was invented more than fifty years ago by DuPont scientist Stephanie Kwoleck.[3] It now seems everywhere. Everywhere, that is, except the one application for which DuPont originally targeted Kevlar. Kwoleck's group in DuPont's research laboratories was searching for strong, lightweight fibers that could be used to make more fuel-efficient automotive tires. At the time, DuPont was the largest supplier of polyester used in bias-ply tires. The problem, DuPont foresaw correctly, was that this market was under threat as more tire makers converted to more fuel-efficient steel-belted radials (which were already dominating the European market). DuPont was highly prescient in anticipating the potential of serious gasoline shortages, increases in demand for fuel-efficient cars, and the conversion of the tire market to steel-belted radials. Kevlar itself was invented somewhat by accident. Polymers are typically synthesized in clear, highly viscous solutions that can be spun into fibers. While working with a particular polymer, Kwoleck got a cloudy, thin solution, which would normally be thrown out (under the assumption that such a solution could not be spun into a fiber). Initially, a technician refused to try Kwoleck's solution on the spinneret (a device that spins liquid polymer solutions into fibers) because he was worried it would damage the machine. But, ultimately, he went along. The result was a surprise. The solution yielded not only a fiber but one much stronger than any they had tested previously. This fiber was a precursor to Kevlar.

At first, it appeared that Kevlar had solved DuPont's strategic problem in the tire market. DuPont manufactured small samples for tire companies to test. Initially, feedback was promising. Tire companies liked its strength and performance, but there was a caveat: because tires are a low-margin business, costs of Kevlar tire cord had to be competitive with those made of steel (which was very cheap). DuPont invested heavily for several years in improving the processes and scaling the manufacturing facilities to drive costs lower. In 1980, based on forecasts for Kevlar use in automobile tires, the company committed $500 million (approximately $1.5 billion in today's dollars) to building a plant capable of producing 45 million pounds per year. It was right about this time, however, that auto tire producers decided to bet on steel, rather than Kevlar. Steel continued to be significantly cheaper, and, unless you drove a race car 200 mph, the performance difference was unlikely to be noticeable. Had the story ended there, Kevlar would be one of the greatest failures in innovation history.

But it did not end. Right about the time the tire industry was turning away from Kevlar, DuPont sent a proposal and samples to the US Army just as it was evaluating new materials for reinforcing soldiers' flak jackets. During the army's evaluation, DuPont reweaved Kevlar a number of times in search of a lighter and cooler material. In laboratory tests, Kevlar demonstrated that it could essentially stop a 38-caliber bullet. It was also about this time that Lester Shuman from the National Institute of Justice heard about Kevlar and began a campaign to sell Kevlar vests to police forces around the country. The vests became widely adopted, and eventually federal police agencies, including the Secret Service began using Kevlar-reinforced vests.

The success of Kevlar as protective clothing—never really considered one of the core markets for the product—sparked an idea at DuPont. Perhaps there were other applications where Kevlar might be attractive? DuPont decided to establish a dedicated applications development and market research group to systematically explore and test potential new applications and markets for Kevlar. This group's charter was wide ranging. It had no specific industry focus. Its sole job was to find markets for Kevlar. Nothing was ruled out (even some ideas that sounded crazy, like Kevlar-reinforced socks that resist wear in the toes). It is out of this effort that, over thirty years, Kevlar began to diffuse into the broad range of applications we are most familiar with today. By 2011, demand for Kevlar was increasing so rapidly that DuPont invested an additional $500 million to expand production capacity.[4] Today, Kevlar is everywhere. Everywhere, that is, except automobile tires.

The two acts—the first a failure and the second a success—of the Kevlar story offer insights into how search behavior impacts innovation. Act 1 was the story of Kevlar as a replacement tire cord. At some level, DuPont did many things right during this project. Its R&D effort was guided by a *clear strategic objective:* find a material to replace polyester in one of DuPont's most important markets. DuPont demonstrated great foresight in predicting that auto fuel efficiency would become critical in the face of fuel shortages. It foresaw disruptive competition from steel-belted radials and proactively launched a research program to find alternatives. This was no blue-sky research program. And DuPont did not just imagine what it thought was important. It talked to its big tire customers and even got early prototypes into their hands for testing. DuPont learned early on that while its customers liked the properties of Kevlar, they needed a lower-cost solution. And, in response, DuPont put extensive efforts behind cost reduction. So far, the initial DuPont Kevlar program looks like a textbook example of how you are taught to pursue innovation. Its failure, in some ways, seems baffling.

Yet, let us examine more closely DuPont's search behavior: The search effort was tightly focused on a very specific problem (i.e., find a new material to replace polyester as a tire cord). This effort generated a *potential* solution (Kevlar). Kevlar, it turns out, is a great solution to many problems, just not the particular problem DuPont was focused on solving. Kevlar was the wrong solution for the tire cord replacement problem, and tire cord replacement was the wrong problem for the Kevlar solution. But notice how DuPont searched. Its problem space was predetermined (tire cord). And this meant that it was never hearing from a whole bunch of other potential customers—like companies interested in making bullet-proof vests or protective industrial equipment or consumer electronics—who did have problems that Kevlar could solve. Notice, though, that someone at DuPont must have been aware of at least some other potential uses of Kevlar outside of tires, because DuPont submitted it to the army for testing for use in bulletproof flak jackets.

It was not until Kevlar failed as a tire cord product and interest began to percolate from other types of users that DuPont began to turn the innovation problem on its head. In Act 2 of Kevlar, DuPont shifted its pattern of search from trying to find a solution to the tire cord problem to exploring potential problems for which Kevlar might be useful. Innovation in Kevlar was about discovering new markets and finding the silent customers.

The DuPont Kevlar case reveals the complex interaction between problem discovery and solution discovery. It is rarely linear. In Act 1, DuPont had a well-defined problem but never really found a solution. In Act 2, DuPont had a well-defined solution but had to search for a problem. You may be wondering which approach is best. The answer depends on the innovation strategy you are pursuing. Routine innovation is generally best anchored with well-defined problems associated with specific customer segments and needs. If you are trying to penetrate your existing market with your existing business model utilizing your existing technological competences, you have essentially already defined the key problems to be solved.

Even in relatively new technologies, the critical problem may be quite well defined. Consider electric vehicles. While still a relatively new technology, the critical problem to be solved for market penetration is clear: extend driving range and reduce operating costs per mile to be competitive with internal combustion engine technology. In contrast, disruptive, radical, and architectural innovation often evolve through an iterative process of problem and solution search and refinement. In practice, it is usually very difficult to predict how radically new technologies will perform in particular uses or markets.[5] As the case of Kevlar shows, new technologies first targeted for one market may ultimately find most of their applications elsewhere. Moreover, customers themselves often need to learn how to best utilize new technologies.[6]

Complicating matters further is the potential for new technologies themselves to spawn new markets. The biggest market for Intel's microprocessor turned out to be personal computers, but at the time Intel invented the microprocessor (in response to a calculator company's problem), personal computers did not exist. The microprocessor helped to create the market for personal computers. Lithium-ion batteries were invented for powering small medical devices and later consumer electronics; their largest market today is electric vehicles. Discovering markets can be just as hard as discovering technologies, and just as important for innovation.

Expanding Your Search Arc

Expanding your company's capacity to search is both a personal and organizational challenge. It is a personal challenge because for you to lead your organization outside its home court, *you* need the capacity to explore novel terrain. If you are trapped in your own personal home court, don't expect your organization to venture too broadly beyond that. At the same time, you can't do it all alone. You need to create an environment and set of processes that enable the rest of the organization to explore a broader set of sources of potentially transformative ideas.

Many organizations I encounter in my research and consulting believe they already have in place a robust set of processes for finding new ideas. But often these processes are implicitly designed to reinforce the home court, rather than to explore new terrain. While there is no single process or set of practices that lead to broader search, there are some principles that can help you and your organization foster this capability.

Looking for the Missing Bullet Holes

During World War II, the US military asked a high-powered think tank a few blocks from Columbia University called the Statistical Research Group to help them figure out where to place reinforcing armor on combat aircraft. The military provided data on the distribution of bullet holes over the surface of the plane. The military initially thought it should place the most armor on the parts of the plane that got hit the most (which turned out to be the fuselage). But one statistician in the group, Abraham Wald, concluded that the extra armor should go where the bullet holes were *not*. His reasoning: since the military is examining only the planes that successfully return from battle, the part of the planes with the most bullet holes must be the least harmful places a plane can be hit. The fact that not many *returning* planes had holes in the engines meant that planes shot in the engines tended to crash. By reinforcing the surface around the engines, more planes should return from battle.[7]

This story always reminds me of the problem of where to look for new ideas for innovation. The problem for most companies is not where they look for ideas; rather, it is where they do *not* look for them. The customers, suppliers, partners, and experts you do *not* talk to are the ones whose problems you are not hearing. Those are your blind spots. Those are the problems you do not know about and therefore are not trying to solve. Those are your missed opportunities for innovating outside the home court.

How can you find the missing bullet holes in your innovation search? With all the advances in digital technologies, big data analytics, artificial intelligence, and machine learning, it is easy to forget that innovation in general, and the search for innovative ideas in particular, is an *intensely human activity*. What we see, what we experience, whom we listen to, whom we speak to, and whom we observe all shape our perceptions about problems worth solving and solutions worth pursuing.

As individuals, we often hear the advice that if we want to be more creative, we need to meet new types of people, travel to different places, try activities we have never tried, and so forth. If you are a chemist, you are supposed to be having lunch with musicians on Tuesdays and physicists on Thursdays and learning Mandarin on Fridays. In essence, we should be getting outside our personal home court. I could not agree more with this advice. The problem, of course, is that stepping outside one's personal home court is far easier said than done. Even with the best of intentions, the vast majority of us tend to graze in those familiar pastures that define our professional identities. Part of this is habit. My guess is that most of us attend many of the same professional or industry conferences year after year. Partly it's due to time constraints. We are so busy trying to keep up with our own field or industry that excursions to new territories feel like a waste of precious time. Part of it, though, is psychological. Our own field of expertise is where we feel most competent. It is where we know the language, where we know the problems, where we likely have built our reputation. When we interact with other experts in our own field, we can feel pretty confident we are not asking any embarrassingly dumb questions. And, at the end of the conversation, we can also feel pretty confident that we grasped critical messages and gained new insights into familiar problems. Expertise is very comforting.

Venturing outside our personal home court creates a sense of vulnerability. There is a real possibility of looking stupid, and few of us want that. Let me recount a recent experience of mine. A couple of years ago, the Harvard Business School and the Harvard School of Engineering and Applied Sciences ran a joint research symposium. Sessions were co-organized by a faculty member from each school. My job was to co-organize a session with Stuart Shieber, one of the leading experts in artificial intelligence and computational linguistics—two subjects about which I know *nothing*. We started our conversation with the usual "so, what do you work on?" type questions that are classic icebreakers for academics. In the sixty minutes Stuart and I chatted, not only did I learn an incredible amount about artificial intelligence, machine learning, and natural language processing, but I also discovered unexpected connections to the kinds of problems I studied in management. To this day, that conversation has influenced my work. The experience was intellectually exhilarating and quite productive. And yet, to be perfectly honest, it was also intimidating. Despite the fact that Stuart is one of the most approachable and humble people I have met, I felt embarrassed to be asking *really dumb* questions about things that the majority of his eighteen-year-old freshman computer science majors knew *before* they entered Harvard. Not far from the back of my mind was the thought *this guy must think I am a total bonehead.* And, no matter where you are in your career or what you have previously accomplished, these are not comforting thoughts! I was most definitely outside *my* home court. I am happy to report that we have continued to have conversations and I continue to learn immensely from them (and I no longer feel embarrassed, even if my questions continue to be just as naïve as they were in our first meeting). And, for his part, Stuart also took a big step outside his home court when he attended the vast majority of the sessions of my Commercializing Science course at Harvard Business School to get a better understanding of our case-centered method of teaching and how he might use elements of that approach in his computer science classes.

The point of my story is not to brag about how good I am at getting outside my home court. In fact, I am no better at it than anyone else. Yes, I can attest to the benefits, but I also know that in reality it is *really* hard. So, let me turn the problem on its head. Let's start with the fairly realistic assumption that most of us are reticent to venture outside our home courts. What then might we do as leaders of an organization to facilitate the broader search by our people (including, of course, ourselves)?

1. Create Forcing Mechanisms: When the deans of the Harvard Business School and School of Engineering and Applied Science decided to hold a joint symposium, they knew that one of the chief benefits of the exercise would be to force their respective faculties to talk to the other. Stuart and I had ample opportunities to interact in the thirty years we had both been Harvard faculty before the symposium. No one ever stopped either of us from contacting the other during those years. It is just that we never had a reason—or, at least, so it seemed. The symposium was a forcing function. Look for ways to force yourself and your people to have conversations with people they do not normally talk to. Sometimes this might be as simple as having meetings in new places or visiting companies outside your industry. Hospital managers, for instance, now spend plenty of time visiting companies like Toyota to gain exposure to world-class quality methods.

2. Move People Physically Outside Their (Geographic) Home Courts: Even in this supposedly flat world of instant communication and ubiquitous data, where people work and live matters. Where you are shapes with whom you tend to talk and thus the kinds of problems you hear about. Fujino decided to move his small team of Japanese aeronautical engineers to the United States so they could interact directly with American customers. He recounted, "You can read market reports, but you really only learn by talking to the customers." Living in two smaller US cities (Mississippi State, Mississippi, and later Greensboro, North Carolina) gave Fujino firsthand experience with the frustrations and time delays of hub-and-spoke travel through regional carriers. He noted that this would have been hard to understand sitting in Japan where a 320 km/hour bullet train can take one from Tokyo to Aomori in just three and half hours. This opened his eyes to the potential of a relatively inexpensive but comfortable jet that could serve smaller businesses that normally would not be able to afford their own planes. One of the chief advantages of scale is the ability to open a geographically diverse set of "listening posts" around the world. But it does not take a huge investment to spread your geographic wings. Fujino's team in the States for more than a decade consisted of only about twenty engineers working out of a simple hangar at the Greensboro airport.

3. Mix the "Gene Pool" of Your Workforce: If it's hard to get people in your organization to go outside their home courts, then bring people from outside their home courts to them. Hire a diverse array of people who can bring a broader variety of technical, functional, and industry perspectives. Too often, organizations become monocultures, dominated by a particular scientific function, educational background, or industry experience. I have been in R&D organizations, for instance, where just about everyone graduated from the same relatively narrow set of graduate programs in the same technical fields. Such an approach provides great depth in specific fields, but such depth also serves to reinforce the home court bias. And such homogeneity is not limited to R&D organizations. Think about how many companies recruit MBAs from only a select group of schools, often as a matter of formal policy.

There is ample evidence suggesting that a more diverse talent base stimulates innovation.[8] There are also some striking case examples. Think about Bell Labs, arguably one of the most prolific creators of transformative innovation of all time. Bell Labs spawned, among other things, statistical process control, shortwave communication, photo-voltaic cells, the transistor, satellite communication, wireless communication, fiber optics, the laser, packet switching, and the computer operating system Unix. By design, the company hired scientists and engineers from a vast array of technical and scientific backgrounds, including physicists, electrical engineers, chemists, materials scientists, metallurgists, mathematicians, systems engineers, manufacturing engineers, and so on.[9] As I discuss in the next chapter, many breakthrough innovations require the integration of diverse knowledge domains. This was clearly true for the inventions spawned at Bell. Without its high diversity of talent, it is hard to imagine Bell being able to identify, let alone develop, transformative innovations that drew from multiple disciplinary bases.

4. *Learn Through Analogies:*[10] Recall from Chapter 3 that learning from analogies across industries can stimulate business model innovation. Analogic reasoning can also help us broaden our search for product innovations. Early in the life of the HondaJet program, the idea of creating a "Civic" of light jets (efficient, inexpensive, and compact, yet as roomy and comfortable as possible) provided a powerful metaphor for both the design team and senior management. A real Honda Civic and a real business jet, of course, are completely different artifacts with completely different economic and technical properties (the HondaJet costs around $4 million and can fly more than 500 mph, whereas the original Civic cost less than $2,000 in the 1970s and topped out around 90 mph). Yet there were parallels that helped the jet design team envision a new product concept. Civic, introduced to the US market in 1973, altered Americans' perception of subcompact cars, which at the time were generally cramped, noisy, utilitarian affairs. As *Road and Track* reviewers commented at the time about its design, "While the Civic is clearly a small car in every sense of the word it is not, happily enough, cheap."[11] Like the car, the Civic of jets would offer more space, a quieter interior, and interior design normally found on more expensive models. The success of the Civic was also a source of inspiration for both the team and Honda. When funding for the jet

program became tight, Fujino didn't hesitate to remind Honda senior leadership of the impact the Civic had on Honda's fortunes.

The Civic analogy was more than symbolic or inspirational. It played a key role in defining the crucial design problems that needed to be solved. Fujino's breakthrough over-the-wing engine design was a direct result of the priority given to interior space.

5. *Challenge Sacred Assumptions:* Every field and industry has its "sacred" assumptions—things that everyone believes are true. And, because of our certainty, we never question these assumptions. In jet aircraft design, no one had questioned the assumptions about engine configuration. Over-the-wing configurations were a nonstarter. You learned this on day one of aeronautical graduate school. Assumptions are a two-edged sword. They can be helpful because, by constraining options, they focus our efforts. But this very benefit also means they can blind us to completely different approaches. Challenging assumptions, as Fujino did about over-the-wing engine configuration, is a simple way to expand the scope of search. It allows you to surface new hypotheses.

It is hard to challenge sacred assumptions. No one likes being wrong, so it is no surprise that search processes are biased toward ideas, concepts, and theories considered "sound." Anything that seems ridiculous (like, say, putting a jet engine over the wing) is typically dismissed out of the blocks. To find transformative innovations requires unshackling search from the bounds of existing assumptions. One company that has systematically addressed this challenge is Flagship Pioneering, a venture creation company in Cambridge, Massachusetts. Unlike a traditional venture capital firm, Flagship does not entertain business plan proposals from independent entrepreneurs. Instead, its business model is to create new ventures based on its own breakthroughs in science.[12] The company has designed a formal "exploration" process for identifying potential breakthroughs. One of the key principles of this process is to suspend belief early on about what is possible. Flagship founder and CEO, Noubar Afeyan, explains:

> Early on in our explorations, we don't ask "is this true" or is there data to support this idea. We do not look for academic papers that provide

proof that something is true. Instead, we ask, *"what if this were true, or if only this were true* would it be really valuable?"...In a nutshell, during an exploration we are trying to come up with hypotheses or hypothetical ventures. Hypothetical ventures comprise some scientific or technological advance, not one that has been produced or written about in the literature. You just have to assert one....As crazy as it may sound, when we start, we don't really care about how believable or concrete these things are.[13]

By suspending belief—just temporarily—Flagship employees allow themselves to imagine possibilities without constraints. Suspending belief was a behavioral trait of many scientists at Bell Labs, where inventions such as undersea cable, the transistor, and satellite communication were born of ideas raised years before they were considered technologically or scientifically feasible.[14] A century before the Honda-Jet was designed, and about 208 miles east of the company's Greensboro, North Carolina, development center, two brothers were busy testing their own assumption-busting airplane.

And the breakthrough potential of suspending belief is not limited to technological innovations. Think about all the business model innovations we see today that might have seemed downright crazy at one point. How many times, for instance, did you hear that people will never buy *product category X* over the Internet? My guess is that you never heard anyone at Amazon say it.

6. Experiment and Iterate: Suspending belief is a first step, but then you quickly need to test your hypotheses and really understand what is true (and not). Fujino first began to question the assumption about over-the-wing engine configurations after digging into some equations of aerodynamic theory contained in long-forgotten textbooks. But this was just his first step. He then tested his hypotheses through analytical calculations, computer simulations, and ultimately physical wind-tunnel tests. Likewise at Flagship: venture hypotheses are quickly tested with rigorous experiments. The point of the experiment is partly to assess validity (is this true?) but partly to point the way to different ideas. Afeyan describes the process at Flagship as converting a "what if" to "something that sounds more like 'it turns out that you can do this.'" Ideas serve as stepping-stones to other ideas, rather than as candidates to be sorted into "winners" and "losers."

Early experimentation is critical when questioning sacred assumptions for two reasons. The first is that some of these assumptions turn out to be true. The faster you test your logic, the faster you can discover whether you are on the right or wrong track. Going down blind alleys is part of the discovery process—but the best blind alleys are short ones! Second, as the case of Honda indicates, when you question sacred assumptions, you could face biting skepticism. Sure, you can argue your logic all you want, but, at the end of the day, rigorous experimental data is the best way to start winning converts.

7. Open Things Up: Bill Joy, the cofounder of Sun MicroSystems, once remarked, "No matter who you are, you have to remember that most of the smartest people work somewhere else." Known as Joy's Law, this statement reminds us that good ideas for innovation often come from outside your own organization. Sometimes the idea—in the form of a problem definition—comes from a customer, as was the case for Intel and the microprocessor. In some cases, innovative ideas come from partners. One of the most successful food innovations of all time—McDonald's Egg McMuffin—came from a McDonald's franchisee who was looking for a way to drive more breakfast traffic to his restaurant.[15] Many innovations have their origins in the tinkering of users, a phenomenon documented extensively by Eric von Hippel of MIT.[16] Mountain bikes, windsurfers, and surgical instruments are other examples where users—trying to solve their problem (or just looking for a way to have fun)—are the first to come up with innovative concepts. Some ideas come from academic laboratories, suppliers, or even competitors.

Over the past decade, companies have started to open their innovation processes at much larger scale through various types of crowdsourcing platforms. Think about the app stores where you acquire most of the applications for your smartphone. Independent software developers—not the major phone manufacturers like Apple or Samsung or operating systems providers like Microsoft or Google—create more than 99 percent of those apps. In essence, Apple, Samsung, Google, and Microsoft crowdsourced a vital part of the functionality of their products. Why did they do this? After all, these are huge enterprises with ample technical and financial resources to develop relatively simple apps. The answer is that the potential universe of apps is so massive and varied that it would be virtually impossible for any single organization—no matter how large—to figure out all the possible things one might want to do with their smartphone.

My colleague Karim Lakhani has done extensive research on these platforms and has found that they not only dramatically increase the number of people trying to solve a problem (which increases the odds of the problem being solved), but, more importantly, they increase the diversity of problem solvers.[17] Contest platforms give companies access to people with skills and from geographies they may never have known or thought about asking. In the wake of the *Exxon Valdez* oil spill off the coast of Alaska, the company responsible for the cleanup faced a novel problem.[18] Because this spill occurred in such cold waters, there was a problem with the "sludge" freezing as the company attempted to pump it from the ocean and onto barges. As you might imagine, solids do not pump well. But how could the crew keep the sludge from freezing in temperatures well below zero? It was a vexing problem that environmental engineers had never encountered before. So the company posted the problem on InnoCentive, an innovation contest platform, where an engineer from the concrete industry immediately saw the solution. In the concrete industry, they use vibrating probes to keep concrete from hardening when it is being poured. He reasoned the same approach would work for ice— if water keeps moving, it has a harder time freezing. The company tried it and it worked. In retrospect, the solution was obvious, but the company never would have thought to ask an engineer from the concrete industry for advice.

Conclusion

There is nothing predictable about transformative innovation. Exploring new technological or market landscapes is fraught with uncertainty.

This does not mean, though, that transformative innovation is the outcome of random luck. Transformative innovators do not just stumble onto interesting ideas by pure chance. Instead, their senior leaders design and manage their organizations to increase exposure to a broader palette of problems, perspectives, concepts, technologies, and user experiences. Fundamentally, they value diversity of ideas over sheer quantity. They value the learning that comes from exposure to novel ideas more than the predictability that comes from working in familiar spaces.

Broadening your organization's capacity to search widely cannot be reduced to a few magic practices. Search capacity is rooted in *organizational systems* composed of interdependent choices of people, processes, and structures. The capacity to search broadly requires a thoughtful combination of people who bring diverse perspective with processes and structures that facilitate exploration and learning.

Almost everything I discussed to enable broader search is facilitated by scale. Large organizations have the resources to hire a broader portfolio of talent. Larger organizations can invest in multidisciplinary capabilities in a way that is simply outside the reach of smaller companies. Larger organizations have the resources to mitigate risks through parallel efforts. They can attract and work with a broader cross-section of external parties.

Finally, while building a capacity for broader search is a necessary step in becoming a transformative innovator, it is, alas, not sufficient. Novel ideas are the raw material for innovation; having a diverse mixture of ideas sets the stage for transformative innovation. But to take that potential and create truly transformative innovations requires a capability to synthesize diverse ideas into coherent concepts. It is to this capability that we turn to in our next chapter.

6
SYNTHESIS
Bringing the Pieces Together

My six-year-old son *loves* Legos. This is good because I like to play with Legos too (and now I have a great excuse!). After we finish building a kit (which contains the set of parts and instructions to make a specific design), my son prefers to play with it, rather than to display it on the shelf. The play usually involves some version of good guys fighting with bad guys, and inevitably our creation gets destroyed during the battle. The kid inside me always finds this a bit heartbreaking, but my son does not seem to mind. He just takes the pieces and throws them in a big red box containing all his other random Lego bricks. Most of our building adventures come from the Legos in the red box. By combining and recombining the dozens of types of blocks in the red box, my son and I can create a seemingly infinite variety of cars, trucks, airplanes, buildings, and of course good guys and bad guys. Whenever we do this, I am reminded of one of the enduring principles of innovation: innovation is not necessarily about creating something new from the ground up. Quite often, innovation involves combining existing ideas and existing components in new ways.

Innovation through combination is all around us. Think about music. With just twelve notes, we can compose every genre of music at every level of sophistication, from Mozart's symphonies to "Chopsticks" and from opera to rap. Or, to take an even more extreme example from nature: using just four chemical components of the genetic "alphabet" (adenine, thymine, guanine, and cytosine), evolution has created an almost infinite variety of living species, from the tiniest viruses and bacteria cells to humans and sequoia trees.

Innovation through combination is also all around us in products and business models. If you have done a good job with search (discussed in Chapter 5), you have assembled a rich palette of potential ideas for innovation. But none of these ideas on their own are likely to be innovations. It is the rare innovation that germinates from a single idea. To spawn transformative innovations requires an organization to blend multiple strands of seemingly disparate ideas into coherent concepts. I call this process "synthesis." Like other aspects of innovation, synthesis does not necessarily come naturally to organizations. It is a capability that must nurtured and managed. How to build an organizational capability for synthesis is the subject of this chapter.

Innovation as Synthesis

We often think about transformative innovations as sharp breaks with the past. The transistor looked and worked nothing like the vacuum tube. Personal computers looked and functioned very differently than did the minicomputer and mainframe computers that preceded them. The first iPhone bore no resemblance to the mobile phones available at the time. Even business model innovations can strike us as sharp points of departure. Ordering books (and, later, just about everything else) on the Internet with a few clicks was an experience no one enjoyed before the arrival of online retailing. But if we peer deeper, even the seemingly most radically "new" innovations have roots deeply embedded in the past. The first commercially viable personal computers of the late 1970s, like the Apple II, embodied decades of ideas about computer architectures, microprocessors, memory, software operating systems, computer graphics, input-output devices, and user interfaces. The basic concept of the personal computer—one machine per user—had been around since at least the 1940s. The personal computer synthesized these elements into a new design form. Likewise, many of the basic concepts behind the original iPhone—mobile telecommunication, Internet connectivity of mobile devices, portable music, graphical user interface, solid state storage, and so on—predated the iPhone. But the iPhone brought these together in both a novel and appealing way.

The first genetically engineered drugs of the 1980s were born out of advances in genetics, molecular and cell biology, protein chemistry, analytical chemistry, immunology, and other fields of physiology. The transistor emerged from the confluence of research in solid-state physics, metallurgy and materials science, chemistry, electrochemistry, and electrical engineering. Transformative business model innovations likewise often result from combinations of old and new concepts. In some ways, Uber is like an old-fashioned taxi service. You can request a ride on demand from point A to point B. But it is also a bit like hitchhiking in the sense that the drivers are private individuals willing to offer rides to complete strangers. But it also organizes and monetizes this process through an online platform that makes a market between ride providers and ride seekers. In this sense, it shares a striking resemblance to other online market-making platforms like eBay or Amazon. There is nothing new about taxis, hitchhiking, or market makers. But the combination is new.

Synthesis is an act of creating something new out of the integration or combination of existing components. The idea that innovation is inherently synthetic has deep roots. Joseph Schumpeter, arguably the grandfather of the field of innovation economics, wrote back in 1911:

> To produce means to combine materials and forces within our reach. To produce other things, or the same things by a different method, means to *combine* these materials and forces differently....Development [or entrepreneurship] in our sense is then defined by the *carrying out of new combinations.*[1]

There is quite a bit of empirical evidence from both statistical and detailed case studies highlighting the importance of synthesis in innovation. For instance, drawing from more than two hundred years of patent data, Lee Fleming and Olaf Sorenson found that the most impactful innovations arose from broader combinations of interdependent technological components.[2] That is, inventors were more likely to generate breakthroughs when they worked with and integrated a greater variety of ingredients.

Synthesis often involves applying knowledge gleaned in one field (or for one specific problem) to another. Historically, cancer and heart disease were considered different fields because each was considered, biologically, a different problem. Cancer was viewed as a disease of uncontrolled cell growth originating from damaged or abnormal genes. Cardiovascular disease was viewed as a problem of blood vessel blockage caused by lipid deposits. Cancer researchers focused on finding ways to stop cell growth either by outright destruction of cancer cells or intervening in the metabolic processes causing uncontrolled cell growth. Cardiovascular researchers looked for ways to reduce blood lipids. It is not surprising that cancer researchers and cardiovascular researchers rarely, if ever, talked to one another. Today, we know inflammation plays a key role in both. This means that a cancer researcher may be interested in the studies on inflammation conducted by scientists interested in cardiovascular disease and rheumatology (and vice versa). Rebecca Henderson and Ian Cockburn's detailed analysis of R&D performance in the pharmaceutical industry showed that exploiting such spillovers *across* disease areas (cancer, cardiovascular, neuroscience, etc.) significantly contributed to research productivity among larger companies.[3]

Even within academic science, there is evidence that the highest-impact research stems from synthesis across fields. For instance, there is evidence that larger, cross-disciplinary teams are more likely to produce higher-impact research.[4] Think about the mapping of the human genome, one of the greatest scientific achievements of the past century. This effort required integrating insights from molecular biology, genetics, biochemistry, protein chemistry, mathematics, computer science and software engineering, and instrumentation engineering. It required not only a lot of people from many different fields but also bringing their insights together in new ways. It is no accident that the discovery of the structure of DNA—about fifty years prior to the mapping of the human genome—was the collaborative effort of a biologist (James Watson), a physicist (Francis Crick), and a biologist and physicist (Maurice Wilkins), with crucial contributions made by a chemist and x-ray crystallographer (Rosalind Franklin).

Exploiting opportunities for synthesis may be critical for creative innovation, but how does synthesis actually happen inside an organization? The laws of chemistry, physics, or biology do not of course govern synthesis within organizations. An artist who mixes red and blue paint will get some shade of purple, the result determined by the chemical reactions between the pigments and the physics of how light is reflected off the molecules. If you control the inputs precisely enough, you can pretty much control the synthesis of the color. Synthesis of ideas into innovations does not happen automatically. In fact, organizations are often designed and managed in ways that actually impede the process.

Having All the Pieces Is Not Enough

I have always been struck by companies that seemed to be ideally positioned to innovate through synthesis but yet were unable to exploit these opportunities. Usually, these were organizations whose business or geographic footprints had exposed them to a diverse set of ideas, technologies, markets, customer problems, or insights that could have formed building blocks for transformative innovation *if combined in the right way*. And yet they were not able to bring these ideas together.

Early in my career, I consulted for a diversified financial services company. The company was a major provider of transaction services such as record keeping, safekeeping of portfolio assets, trade settlement, and income collection on sales of assets to large institutional investors like pension funds and mutual funds. As this business matured and faced intensifying price competition, the company developed a strategy to differentiate its services to institutional investors. The company reasoned, correctly, that fund managers whose own compensation was based heavily on their risk-adjusted returns would be willing to pay for information that gave them even the slightest edge. And they also understood that the institutions that paid these fund managers would be very interested in better ways to measure risk-adjusted performance. The company was ideally positioned to develop these value-added services. Its custody business gave it access to massive amount of data on transactions, portfolio positions, and performance (in essence, this company had a big data strategy long before anyone knew what big data was). In addition to its trove of data, the company had all the required expertise in-house. Its custody business unit had the deep IT systems development expertise needed to build the requisite software platforms. The company's investment banking unit had world-class experts in designing sophisticated trading and hedging strategies, creating complex derivatives, and applying the esoteric mathematics of financial valuation and risk. The company's money management division was on the leading edge of using new trading strategies and financial investments for enhanced portfolio performance. In short, it had all the pieces of the puzzle.

The bad news was that all this expertise was scattered in different business units, each with its own strategic objectives, its own profit and loss incentives, and its own culture. These divisions operated independently. The corporate operating philosophy was one of extreme decentralization. Business unit heads were like CEOs of their own independent companies. Whatever interactions the divisions had in the past were done at arm's length (e.g., the custody division provided custodial services to the money management business unit on the exact same terms as all its other customers). Some of this was done for good legal and regulatory reasons, but some of it was a choice of business philosophy. While all the groups worked in reasonably close proximity to one another (all within the same major metropolitan city), they had never had reasons to interact before. And they had no incentives to do so. Bonuses were based strictly on how your business performed.

Even more challenging were the deep cultural divides between the groups. The investment banking unit and the money management unit were classic Wall Street cultures, dominated by MBAs and PhDs from top programs whose compensation depended heavily on performance-based bonuses. In both groups, speed was everything. They had to be able to pounce on market trends and move quickly in and out of positions. The custody group was composed of IT systems specialists and accountants. Pay scales differed between the two groups by an order of magnitude. For the custody group, reliability was everything. Systems had to be secure and 100 percent reliable. In describing the differences among the various groups, one senior executive told me, "The systems people think in terms of years and big projects. The money management folks are obsessed with quarters because that's how they are measured. And the traders—their attention spans can be measured in seconds." The custody people viewed the traders and money managers as arrogant; the trader and money management people viewed their counterparts in custody as dull. The traders and money management units made the bulk of the company's profit; custody generated most of the revenue.

It is not surprising that, for several years, talk about creating new ancillary services remained just that—talk. There were no mechanisms to mesh the capabilities and expertise of these different parts of the company. The strong decentralization philosophy inhibited cross-divisional collaboration. A new group was created to coordinate cross-divisional innovation efforts, but this group lacked a budget and any direct authority over innovation projects (those all remained in the divisions). Its impact was predictably limited. The different sets of skills and know-how needed to execute its strategy remained trapped in their own silos.

The company had a great strategy for exploiting information. It was in many ways decades ahead of its time. It had done a great job searching for and seeing an incredible opportunity that was well within its reach. But it lacked the capability for synthesis. It could not bring the pieces together.

Over the course of my career, I came to realize that what I observed at this financial services company was not unique. It is an inherent feature of many multidivisional corporations. Each division is focused on its own business and its own innovation agenda. I've seen it in other financial services companies, in health-care companies whose own pharmaceutical and diagnostic divisions struggled to collaborate on the potential of genomics to transform both businesses, in medical device companies whose different market-focused business units could not collaborate on developing common technology platforms, in hospitals whose attempts to create novel services were crushed by their inability to overcome walls between different medical and surgical departments. I've seen it stifle innovation in food and beverage companies as different divisions battled over "ownership" of the program and in the inability of hardware and software groups within the same company to synchronize their efforts. And, coming closer to home, frankly, I see it all the time in universities.

The consequences of failures to integrate existing knowledge and capabilities from within a corporation can be severe. An ominous example is Sony. For a couple of decades, Sony was a star of the consumer electronics industry. It launched a string of hit products like the Walkman and was a pioneer in digital photography. Academics fawned over its design prowess in case studies and articles in the *Harvard Business Review*. Yet, as we all know today, Apple clobbered Sony in portable electronic devices (a segment invented by Sony) with the iPod and then the iPhone. Walter Isaacson's biography of Steve Jobs has a terrific chapter on the development of the iPod that provided a vivid picture of how Sony missed the opportunity despite having had all the pieces in place. It already had a portable music player; it had expertise in critical component technologies like disk drives, displays, and batteries. Sony had its own music division with a strong ensemble of recording artists. But each of these was housed in a different division, each with its own profit and loss accountability and each with its own strategic interests. Sony had no capacity for bringing these pieces together. The head of a music company that had tried to work with Sony commented to Isaacson, "How Sony missed this is completely mind-boggling to me.... Steve [Jobs] would fire people if the divisions didn't work together, but Sony's divisions were at war with one another."[5]

Building a Capability for Synthesis

There is a magical quality to creative synthesis. Ideas of distant ancestry find their way to a common place and then give birth to something completely new and compelling. But there is nothing magical about this process. An organization's capacity for synthesis stems from the choices made by managers about how the organization works. We discussed examples above of how organizations are often designed to stifle synthesis. They create boundaries that block the flow of ideas across divisions or functions. They balkanize knowledge. Those examples help us understand what *not* to do, but how might we design organizations that are actually good at connecting ideas across markets, technical domains, and functions? Like any organizational capability, synthesis involves choices about people, processes, and structures.

People: Find, Develop, and Retain the Synthesizers

Earlier I made the point that being a business polymath is not possible for most of us. We tend to focus our attention on our well-ploughed fields of expertise. This specialization is, in general, helpful to both our own careers and to our organization. Having access to a broad portfolio of experts from different disciplines or backgrounds is probably one of the best ways to ensure your organization gets exposed to a rich diversity of innovation ideas. But, ultimately, capitalizing on this diversity—finding the novel combinations of seemingly disparate ideas that form the basis of transformative innovations—requires individuals who can span boundaries, who have the capacity to sort and filter ideas from different fields and see how they connect. These are people good at what I call "intellectual arbitrage." They leverage ideas across fields. They can see how a theory in physics might apply to biology, how the configuration of our brain's neurons might provide an apt analogy for computer architectures, how a business model designed for the consumer products industry might work for Internet-based advertising, or how a product concept for subcompact cars might revolutionize light jets. Posed simply, for an organization to be good at synthesis, it needs good *synthesizers*.

Some of the greatest inventors, scientists, and entrepreneurs of all time were spectacular synthesizers. Leonardo da Vinci, Isaac Newton, Thomas Edison, Nikola Tesla, Guglielmo Marconi, Albert Einstein, Henry Ford, James Watson and Francis Crick, Bell Labs' John Bardeen, and Steve Jobs were all incredible at seeing connections across fields. These are, of course, extreme examples of individuals with extraordinary intellects. The good news is that you do not have to be or have access to the likes of these geniuses to be a successful innovator. They are out there among us in "mere mortal" form, and innovating companies find them and cultivate them. In the drug industry, scientists who are particularly good at discovering drugs are called "drug hunters." Successful drug hunters are examples of good synthesizers. They integrate insights from chemistry, biology, physiology, and clinical practice to "see" molecular structures that might treat a particular disease. Drug hunters not only need to understand quite a bit about these different disciplines, but they need to be able to connect insights across them. In the entertainment industry, the animation studio Pixar fuses the highly technical world of computer graphics with the highly creative world of motion picture animation because it has people throughout its organizations—software engineers, technical artists, editors, or directors—who themselves bridge those worlds. Pixar has software engineers with interests (and even training) in art, and it has artists who understand technical aspects of computer graphics. The company's cofounder and CEO, Ed Catmull, is perhaps the epitome of this fusion. A PhD in computer science, Catmull had dreamed of becoming a film animator since childhood.

Paolo Fazioli, the founder of Fazioli Pianoforte S.p.A, an Italian company making ultra-high-end pianos played by some of the world's leading concert pianists, is an example of a person who spawned innovation by bridging different worlds. After graduating from the University of Rome with a degree in mechanical engineering, Fazioli, a gifted pianist from an early age, went on to study both piano and music composition. He dreamed of becoming a concert pianist. He earned a degree in piano (from the Conservatorio Gioachino Rossini) and a master's degree in music composition (Academy of St. Cecilia).[6] Despite his considerable musical talents, Paolo realized that a career as a professional concert pianist was beyond his reach. At that point, he joined the family furniture business, which specialized in office furniture made from exotic woods. Within a few years, though, Paolo left the company to start his own piano company with the mission to engineer and produce the best-sounding pianos in the world. This mission required Fazioli to integrate three different streams of know-how. The first was music and the piano in particular. How should a piano feel when it was played? How should it sound? He started by study-ing contemporary grand pianos to understand how their structure and design influenced their performance. The second was engineering. A piano is a highly complex piece of mechanical and acoustical equip-ment, consisting of thousands of parts. The design of each part, the mechanical connections between them, and choices of materials shape the performance and sound of the piano. Fazioli conducted extensive experiments on different types of wood to better understand their acoustical properties (Fazioli was fortunate that his first piano factory, located in Sacile, Italy, is only about a hundred miles from the forests of Fiemme Valley, where Antonio Stradivari sourced wood for his vi-olins). Fazioli was helped by the fact that his brother was an expert in wood technology. The final piece of the puzzle was manufacturing. The best-designed piano will be ruined by a poorly designed manufacturing process. Choices about myriad processes (such as joining techniques, wood forming processes, and finishing) impact a piano's performance. Here, Fazioli was able to draw on his own and his family's expertise in precision-crafted wood furniture (Fazioli's first piano factory was actu-ally located inside the family's furniture factory). Today, Paolo Fazioli plays *every* piano before it leaves the company's factory.

How can you identify, attract, and cultivate synthesizers? Identify-ing them is actually not that hard. There is usually something revealing in their educational background, career path, or even personal inter-ests that has caused them to cross fields. Maybe they are like Catmull, who studied and became proficient in one field and yet had dreams of another. Or maybe they are like Fazioli, who studied music and engi-neering (or other pairs of seemingly distant fields). Or maybe they are like the Israeli scientist I recently interviewed who was trained in phys-ics and computer science but became interested in how principles from these fields could be used to study the evolution of bacteria. He would now describe himself as a "systems biologist" (a description well sup-ported by his publication record) even though he has no formal train-ing in biology. Career-path movements and personal history can also hint at people's potential to be a synthesizer. Have they always worked in the same industry or in the same function for most of their career? That provides great depth but probably doesn't help them understand insights from other industries or functions, let alone leverage those creatively.

One problem that many organizations have in recruiting potential synthesizers is that they tend to undervalue people from "nonconforming" backgrounds. The "standards" established by many human resource departments are exactly that—standards. They create uniformity. They filter out the people whose backgrounds just don't quite fit the mold. And, in so doing, they screen out your future potential synthesizers.

Career paths within organizations can also be used to cultivate synthesizers. Whenever I am working in an organization doing research or consulting, I always ask the most senior people I meet about their previous positions inside the company: "How did you get to this position?" I am less interested in how they "climbed the ladder" than in how they moved across it. I am always surprised by how many companies' career ladders are etched within functional or divisional silos. Sales and marketing people enter and rise through the commercial ranks. R&D people stay in R&D—and often within their own technical or scientific disciplines. Movements away from your specialty are viewed as signs of failure (i.e., you weren't good enough to "cut it" in, say, R&D so you got "repurposed" to operations or marketing). From an innovation point of view, this model of human resource management is a disaster. It completely destroys your ability to promote and develop synthesizers. In fact, if the most capable people stay within their silos, it means that the only people moving across boundaries are your weakest players. And this means that the people potentially most important for your innovation efforts are not your strongest.

There is nothing easy about synthesis or being a synthesizer. Synthesizers have to be incredibly capable people. They need intellectual firepower across multiple domains and a habit of mind that can entertain complexity, contradictions, and ambiguity. They need the capacity to both learn from and communicate to specialists from diverse fields. This type of work requires people with the right backgrounds and temperament. It also requires recognition. The synthesizers in your organization should be among the most-coveted (and best-rewarded) positions.

Processes: Design for Exploration and Experimentation

The act of combining diverse streams of knowledge and experience is inherently unpredictable. And the more diverse the contributing streams get, the more unpredictable the outcome of the process becomes. Consider a cooking analogy. Let's say you have a lot of experience preparing Italian cuisine. You not only have a long repertoire of recipes, but you also have a good sense of which ingredients pair well with others (fresh egg pasta with butter and cream-based sauces; dry pasta with olive oil–based sauces, etc.). This familiarity helps you improvise and come up with new dishes that dazzle your friends. In fact, you are planning to dazzle a group tonight, and so you head to your favorite Italian food specialty market to see what looks good. To your horror, you discover the store is closed in celebration of the feast of Saint Anthony, and it is now too late to find another Italian market. Next door, though, is an Indian food market. In a fit of culinary desperation, you decide to prepare an Indian meal despite your utter lack of familiarity with this cuisine and the fact that you lack an Indian cookbook. You realize you will have to innovate, and since you have so far read up through Chapter 5 of this book, you know a good strategy is to search broadly in the market for a variety of ingredients and spices. When you get home, you will have just enough time to try a few experiments with different combinations of ingredients to see which ones come out best. As you can well imagine, this is a risky strategy. Unlike when you prepare Italian food, you have no prior experience about what combinations of ingredients yield sumptuous sauces and which produce acrid ones. You will have to learn through trial and error, and you do not even know where to start. The large list of ingredients you brought home provides a lot of potential combinations to explore. This is, of course, both the good news and bad news. The good: some random combinations of these ingredients may produce extraordinary results. The bad news: you have a lot of possible combinations to test, and many are likely to turn out horribly! To use the terminology, you are facing a high-variance out-come. You might win big, but the odds are stacked against you.

Lee Fleming's research (mentioned earlier) suggests that a similar dynamic is at work when it comes to combining different "ingredi-ents" (component technologies, etc.) for innovation. He found that the blockbuster innovations tend to result from exploring more novel combinations of component technologies that are also highly interde-pendent (that is, each one influences the performance of the other). But this approach is also the riskiest in that it usually results in failure. If you get the combination "just right," you may just have the big winner, but getting it just right is very difficult if the ingredients are unfamiliar to you.

Because the right combination of "ingredients"—whether they are component technologies, capabilities, engineering methods and prin-ciples, or business concepts—cannot be predicted in advance, cre-ative synthesis demands a fluid innovation process rather than the more structured processes that have become popular over the past decade. Let's contrast these two approaches. Structured approaches like phase-gate models (and the waterfall variant used in software engineering) typically prescribe a detailed sequence of steps and ac-tivities for every innovation project. These are generally grouped into well-defined "phases" (e.g., concept development, detailed engineer-ing) delineated by criteria for a project to move from one phase to the next. These structured models draw their inspiration from manufac-turing processes. Indeed, they aim to make innovation as predictable as manufacturing.

The problem with such approaches is that they cannot convert an inherently uncertain process into a predictable one. The analogy with manufacturing breaks down because, with manufacturing processes, the list of components and the specific steps are known in advance. For routine innovations, utilizing familiar technical and business concepts, that may be true. The job of the phase-gate or similarly scripted process is to make sure the organization executes what it already knows how to do. But, once we enter the realm of transformative innovation, where the underlying "ingredients" may be unfamiliar, then no amount of scripting the process removes the underlying uncertainty. In fact, imposing a structured process on an inherently uncertain one will only make matters worse by providing a false sense of control.

Because integrating diverse streams of knowledge is *inherently* uncertain, it requires a fluid process designed around rapid experimentation, iteration, and learning. Experimentation, iteration, and learning (from failure) are prominent themes in cases of both transformative technological innovation and business model innovation. You may recall from Chapter 5 the "suspend belief" principle at Flagship Pioneering. But, at Flagship, initial venture hypotheses are tested relatively quickly with rigorous experiments. The point of the experiment is partly to assess validity but partly to point the way to different ideas, what Afeyan described as converting a "what if" to "something that sounds more like 'it turns out that you can do this.'" This theme of iteration appears in other highly innovative organizations. Ed Catmull highlighted the central role of iteration at Pixar in his book *Creativity, Inc.*: "Creativity has to start somewhere, and we [at Pixar] are true believers in the power of bracing, candid feedback and the iterative process—reworking, reworking, and reworking again until a flawed story finds its through-line or a hollow character finds its soul."[7]

Fleming's case study of Hewlett Packard's creation of the first commercially viable ink-jet printer, a very significant innovation, highlights how the fluidity of HP's labs' process enabled rapid exploration of diverse technical concepts. Early prototyping was critical to testing which combinations of materials and concepts were technically viable. One participant he interviewed explained how a lead engineer on the program was "able to very quickly explore a multitude of prototypes by working informally with his friends in the integrated circuit laboratory."[8] By being able to test prototypes rapidly, the team was able to iterate through more potential design solutions to critical technical problems.

Business models also evolve through iteration. There is always a temptation to think that great entrepreneurs see the future perfectly and "nail it" with their first business plan. Nothing could be further from the truth. Amazon's business model has evolved immensely since the company's humble founding in 1994. Amazon's first attempt to create a market for third-party sellers failed. As Jeff Bezos recalled about that site, "I think seven people came, if you count my parents and siblings."[9] Its second attempt, an auction site called zShops, also failed ("again, no customers," in Bezos's words). It was not until the company began to let third-party retailers compete on the Amazon site that volume began to accelerate. Likewise, at Google's founding, the initial business model was not entirely clear to Larry Page and Sergey Brin (or their investors). The model evolved through experiments, experience, and, yes, some mistakes too.

Companies often squash iteration through processes that essentially require you to "meet your plan." In one pharmaceutical company I consulted for, each therapeutic area for drug R&D (cancer, cardiovascular disease, etc.) had to create a five-year plan detailing the kind of programs it wanted to pursue, the critical science it wanted to explore, the talent it required, and the external partnerships that were necessary for success. There is nothing wrong with asking questions about these issues or requiring a rigorous degree of planning for the future. Every two years, the heads of these groups were required to report to executive leadership on their progress. Again, there is nothing wrong with interim reviews, check-ins, and progress reports. The problem was that the groups were evaluated on how well they were tracking their plan. To not pursue the projects, technology, or partnership detailed in the original plan was considered a problem. This process assumes that you can plan everything up front—correctly—and that course corrections are a sign of failure, rather than the natural result of tackling highly complex and uncertain challenges. In essence, the process left no room for learning. It is hard to come up with transformative innovations this way.

Organizational Structure: Create Permeable Boundaries

There is a theory in the innovation literature that *the design of a product mirrors the design of the organization that created it*.[10] Physically inspect the product (or deconstruct the service), and you can pretty much figure out the structure of the organization that created it. You have probably endured products where the components just do not fit together either aesthetically or functionally. If you ever found yourself asking about a product, "Did the person who designed part A (say, your car's steering wheel) ever talk to the designer of part B (say, the instrumentation panel)?" the answer is probably no. Companies that create barriers between people from diverse technical specialties, functional expertise, experience, and knowledge—like Sony or the financial services company mentioned above—snuff out opportunities for the kinds of creative synthesis that lead to transformative innovations.

Restructuring an organization is one approach to overcoming these barriers. Bell Labs is a great example of how structuring to intentionally drive cross-disciplinary integration can produce big benefits. Starting with the design of its new campus in Murray Hill, New Jersey (which opened in 1942), everything about Bell Labs was organized to drive communication across scientists and engineers from different disciplines and functions.[11] The physical layout of the facilities was designed in a way that made it almost impossible for people from different departments to avoid one another.[12]

After World War II, the newly appointed head of Bell Labs, Mervin Kelly, replaced the lab's discipline-oriented department structure with cross-disciplinary groups focused on specific technologies or problems.[13] The solid-state electronics programs that ultimately gave birth to the transistor was one of the new programs created from this restructuring. The solid-state group contained theoretical physicists like William Shockley and John Bardeen, experimental physicists like Walter Brattain and Gerald Pearson, chemists, materials scientists, metallurgists, electrical engineers, and technicians.[14] Constant exchange of ideas and spontaneous meetings to discuss problems and hypotheses were the norm. The transistor group was clearly endowed with some of the best minds in twentieth-century science—Shockley, Bardeen, and Brattain would win Nobel Prizes for their work; Bardeen would go on to win a second Nobel Prize in physics for superconductivity (he is so far the only person in history to win two Nobel Prizes in physics); and Pearson would later invent the photovoltaic cell. It is hard to imagine the transistor being invented under an organizational structure that divided the work across separate discipline-based groups. Having the right talent on board is important, of course, but meshing that talent together is what is often needed for transformative innovation.

Of course, organizational design involves trade-offs.[15] No group can include every possible capability, technical discipline, or domain of expertise that might prove useful at some point. Attempting to do so would simply produce a bloated, unwieldy organization that can't get anything done. As in building architecture, choices must be made about where to put up "walls." And those choices will shape what the organization can do particularly well. They will shape the specific combinations of capabilities and technologies that are likely to be tried. As a result, they will influence the kinds of innovations that get created.

The problem is that, in dynamic technological or market contexts, the most attractive combinations that potentially yield transformative innovations change frequently. Putting some combination of disciplines together at one point in time (say, physicists, chemists, material scientists, and metallurgists, as they did at Bell Labs) might be a good idea, but what if new combinations become relevant to future innovations (say, electrical circuit engineering and process engineering, which were critical to the invention of the integrated circuit ten years after the transistor)? An organization can find itself laden with an obsolete structure. How can you prevent this at your organization?

One approach is to use "soft structures" like project teams or temporary organizations focused around specific innovation opportunities. These are like those temporary office walls or partitions than can be moved around to reconfigure space as needed. Temporary structures like project teams can be a more fluid way to respond to changes in the technological or market landscape.

The birth of Amazon Web Services is a great example of this approach.[16] Today it is a $12 billion business and the leading provider of cloud computing services.[17] This was a significant business model innovation for both Amazon (which, until that time, had been purely a retailer) and for the IT world. The concept, though, started innocuously enough in 2002 as a small experiment inside the company's retail operation (Amazon.com). The initial idea was to give companies that sold products on the Amazon.com website greater control over how they presented their goods (the kinds of display photos they used, the information they provided, etc.). The thesis was that, because sellers understood their own products best, giving them control over their presentation should drive greater sales. But the only way to achieve this goal was to give third-party developers access to Amazon's web infrastructure and the application interfaces used to display products. So Amazon decided to run a small experiment and temporarily open up part of its web infrastructure to see what third-party developers could achieve.

The results of this experiment were both surprising and dramatic. Amazon learned that developers were very interested in leveraging Amazon's platform. As Andy Jassy, who went on to run Amazon Web Services, recounted:

> It caused us to step back and wonder if something broader was going on. If developers would build applications from scratch using web services, and if a broad array of Web services existed (which we believed would be the case), then the Internet would become the operating system. We asked ourselves if the Internet became the operating system, what would the key elements be. Which had already been built, and which would Amazon be best-equipped to provide for the community? At the time we were looking at it in 2003, none of the key elements of the Internet operating system had been built. When we thought about Amazon's strength as a technology company that had simply applied its technology to the retail space first, and what Amazon had done well over the last decade, we realized we could provide a lot of the key building blocks.[18]

In many organizations, this idea would have died right here. After all, what did "the Internet as operating system" or "web services" have to do with the "core" business of retailing? And, structurally, Amazon was not well positioned to exploit this opportunity. Amazon had no services division or any other divisional home for it. But this is where the soft-structure approach came into play. Early in the process, the idea was escalated to the company's most senior management, who discussed it at a strategic planning meeting later in 2003. Amazon senior management decided to explore the concept and appointed Jassy (who had joined Amazon in 1997) to run a newly formed web services team (which was separate from retail). The team formed by Jassy was a vehicle for synthesis. It integrated sources of information and know-how from multiple sources. It tapped Amazon's technical community to understand the kinds of problems it faced when building applications. It also gathered twenty business and technical leaders from throughout Amazon to understand which Internet applications existed and which ones should exist. It spoke to outside developers who had been actively involved in the original experiment. For each candidate service (e.g., storage), Jassy formed an autonomous subteam that combined both technical and management talent pulled from various parts of Amazon and from external sources.

Notice the contrast to my earlier description of the financial services company (or perhaps what you have seen in your own organization). Amazon used small, nimble teams that were given a high degree of autonomy (and resources) to explore and integrate ideas from different sources and to develop and test concepts. Input and talent came from various parts of Amazon. Boundaries were fluid.

I want to stress that the kind of teams we saw at Amazon are infinitely different from the kind of limp "matrixed" teams that are so common in many larger companies. Matrix teams are cross-divisional or cross-functional teams built on the underlying divisional (or functional) structure of the company. The idea behind matrix organizations is to alleviate the trade-offs inherent in the company's structural design. So, for instance, if the company is organized around market-facing business units, it might create matrix teams for different kinds of cross-divisional integration efforts. In theory, this is not a bad idea. In practice, though, these teams usually have no real teeth. They lack budgets and authority—those usually rest firmly within the iron grasp of the existing business units. They lack dedicated people: everyone has two jobs in a matrix—the divisional or functional job and the team job, so in theory everyone has two bosses. (In reality, of course, everyone knows that the person who sets your pay is your boss.) Instead, the matrix team's job is pretty much limited to making sure information is shared across business units. Jassy's team was not a classic matrix team. It had authority, budget, and full accountability. It had its own dedicated personnel (picked by Jassy). Fluid does not have to mean weak.

An extreme example of using soft (but powerful) structures to drive transformative innovation through synthesis is how the Defense Applied Research Projects Agency (DARPA) organizes research.[19] DARPA is a government agency (part of the Department of Defense) responsible for developing technologies with potential military applications. It is well known for seeding such transformative technologies as the Internet, very large-scale integrated circuits (VLSI), global positioning systems (GPS) for navigation, carbon composites, and others. In many ways, DARPA has become a modern-day Bell Labs, but its structure is completely different. DARPA's current annual budget is about $3 billion. If DARPA were a company, it would rank in the top fifty of global R&D spenders. But DARPA lacks something that every major corporate R&D spender has. DARPA has no R&D lab of its own, and it employs a relatively small number of people directly. It organizes all its programs around temporary project teams composed of networks of external collaborators from both industry and academia. Each team is headed up by a DARPA program leader, a highly talented scientist responsible for assembling the right mix of collaborators and orchestrating their efforts. The program leaders own the program—they control the budget, manage relationships, deal with problems, and make all the critical decisions.

Every project has a fixed timeframe (usually two to five years), and the tenure of a DARPA program leader lasts only as long as the project. The network is fluid—external collaborators are brought in and out of the project as needs change. According to two former heads of DARPA, Regina Dugan and Kaigham Gabriel, the temporary nature of DARPA employment contracts and contracts with external collaborators enables a high degree of flexibility in pursuing innovation opportunities as both needs and technologies change:

The DARPA model allows a company to alter its portfolio of projects faster and at a much lower cost than a conventional internal research organization can. During our recent tenure at the agency, we were able to shift significant investment from programs in space and large air and ground systems to programs in cybersecurity, synthetic biology, and advanced manufacturing in less than a year.[20]

Again, with DARPA, as with Amazon, there was nothing weak about the soft structure. Program leaders are leaders; they are not co-ordinators or facilitators. They own the critical decisions, and they control budgets. Creative synthesis—pulling ideas and capabilities from different sources—is not easy and requires strong leadership and decision-making authority. Weak teams are not capable of the kinds of creative synthesis that leads to transformative innovation.

Which approach is right for your company? Structure your organization to integrate the right mix of skills, capabilities, and experience like Bell Labs? Or opt for more fluid soft structures like project teams like Amazon and DARPA? The answer is that both can be complementary tools in the pursuit of transformative innovation. An organizational structure is like the foundation of a house. The choices you make about its design will shape and constrain what you can do with what rests on top of it. If transformative innovation is part of your strategy, then you should think about creating structures that actively catalyze important connections among people with different technical and functional expertise, experience, and commercial perspectives. About your current organizational structure, you should ask, Does it impede the kinds of cross-disciplinary or cross-market collaborations that are critical to our future success? If so, then consider restructuring. But also recognize that you will never have the perfect structure. A shifting technological and market landscape will produce opportunities and threats that require you to quickly integrate new combinations of capabilities and skills both from inside and outside your organization. Amazon and DARPA show that soft structures—when properly resourced and led and endowed with the same authority as hard structures—can be very powerful.

Conclusion

Synthesis—the melding of ideas from distant sources into coherent innovation concepts—is crucial for transformative innovation. Unfortunately, synthesis does not come naturally to most organizations and is particularly challenging for large enterprises. To manage scale, companies typically divide themselves into ever more isolated compartments. They create market-facing business units or divide their R&D function into specialized subunits. They hire ever more specialized people in particular technologies or in particular markets. They reward people according to goals defined by narrow organizational boundaries (e.g., How many patents did your department file? How much market share did your business unit gain? How much cost did you take out of purchased components?). None of these are, by themselves, inherently bad things to do. But, unfortunately, they impede the kinds of cross-flow of ideas, talent, expertise, and experience that might lead to transformational innovations. What is ironic, of course, is that larger organizations may have more of the pieces for transformational innovation available to them, either within their broad portfolio of businesses or through their external networks. Unfortunately, having the pieces is not enough. They need to be melded.

Transformative innovation through synthesis doesn't happen through pure luck. It happens where organizations build that capability through a set of interrelated choices about people, processes, and structures. The capability for synthesis is rooted in people who can bridge diverse fields of knowledge and domains of expertise; it is rooted in processes that enable experimentation and learning; and it is rooted in structures that drive, rather than impede, the flow of ideas from diverse sources. All of these are, of course, completely in the hands of management. A company's ability to do synthesis well is a function not of size but of management.

7

WHEN TO HOLD 'EM
AND WHEN TO FOLD 'EM
Uncertainty, Ambiguity, and the Art and Science of Selecting Projects

In October 2003, Joshua Boger, CEO of Vertex Pharmaceuticals, and his team of senior management confronted a problem.[1] The company Boger founded twenty years before was at a critical juncture. It had four molecules that could potentially become drugs for treating several different diseases. Each "candidate" (to use the parlance of the pharmaceutical industry) had thus far been tested only in animals or in small groups of human patients, but the preliminary data for all were promising. To turn any of these molecules into a drug would next require much larger and more expensive clinical trials. The company had enough resources to invest in only two of the programs for further development. Boger and his team had to pick which to pursue. It was a high-stakes decision given that these would be the first programs the company would take forward on its own (its previous projects had all been conducted through partnerships with larger pharmaceutical companies). Picking the wrong projects could lead to financial ruin—picking the right ones could be worth billions of dollars. There were many possible criteria along which to evaluate the projects (e.g., potential market size, return on investment, likelihood of technical success, fit with the company's mission), and each project excelled along different criteria. In addition, pharmaceutical R&D is notoriously risky—most potential products do not prove to be safe or effective enough to reach the market. And even if approved, it is extremely hard to predict demand given that the benefits of the drug and thus its appeal can't be determined until years of clinical trials have been conducted. Further complicating matters was the fact that people in the different parts of the organization had different judgments and opinions about the prospects of each project for both clinical and commercial success. The commercial people liked two very different candidates from those the scientists backed.

The challenge for Boger and his team was not only deciding *which* two projects to pick. Equally important was *how* to choose. On quantitative analytical methods of project value and financial returns? On the judgments of its scientists about the likely clinical performance of each drug? On the judgments of its commercial people about the future market potential? What kind of information should be considered? How could Boger and his team get the best available information to make the decision? His dilemma, while somewhat extreme in terms of the stakes and the level of uncertainty inherent in his business, is fairly typical of struggles I have seen in many different organizations across a variety of industries. Picking projects is hard. You rarely have enough information to identify with precision the "best" alternative. Different metrics point in different directions, and, not surprisingly, people with different expertise have different judgments about what programs should be pursued.

An organization bad at project selection, no matter how extraordinary at search and synthesis, will not be very innovative. Prospective innovations that do not get funding for development remain just that: prospects. Companies profit only from innovations, not prospective innovation. Business history is riddled with examples of those quite good at generating innovative concepts but quite poor at figuring out which projects to fund. Xerox of the 1970s is a classic and well-documented example. Xerox's Palo Alto Research Center was clearly great at search and synthesis, inventing many of the key technologies of the digital age: laser printing using bitmapping (1971); object-oriented programming (1972); ethernet (1973); the personal computer (1973); graphical user interface windows (1975); and the page-description language used for desktop publishing (1978).[2] But, with the exception of laser printing, all languished inside Xerox for lack of commitment to full commercial development. Other companies commercialized them. Graphical user interface technology became the basis for Apple's first Macintosh. Ethernet and page-description language were commercialized by start-ups 3Com and Adobe, respectively, both founded by frustrated Xerox employees. Xerox is not an isolated example. AT&T lagged in com-mercializing the mobile phone technology it invented because a market forecast it commissioned in 1980 pegged the total phone market at only 900,000 units by 2000.[3] The real market in 2000 turned out to be 109 million units.[4] By the time AT&T realized its forecast was badly off, the only way for it to enter the market was to make a $12.6 billion acquisition of McCaw Cellular.[5] Contrary to popular belief, Polaroid was actually an early mover in digital imaging technology but lagged in committing resources to full commercial development.[6]

Xerox, AT&T, and Polaroid didn't fail from lack of ability to dis-cover a problem (search) or bring together diverse ideas into a novel solution (synthesis). They failed from an inability to make good project-selection decisions. Of course, bad selection decisions do not always manifest themselves as errors of omission—great opportunities squan-dered by lack of funding. Errors of commission—funding or keeping alive bad projects—is also a common problem. Not every prospective project is a winner. There will be many losers in the bunch, and the ca-pability for project selection means being able to cull them. Bad selec-tion cuts both ways. It can lead to killing winning projects or wasting money on losers.

The Challenge of Selection: On the Knife's Edge of Two Types of Errors

In principle, picking innovation projects is no different from any other resource allocation decision (like, say, deciding whether to build a fac-tory, buy a piece of equipment, or advertise a product). Every innova-tion project requires resources, like money and people's time. Because resources are scarce, you want to put them to the best use. This leads to a simple heuristic: pursue only those projects that are likely to generate more value than the alternative uses, adjusting, of course, for time hori-zons and risks. A set of well-known analytical tools such as discounted cash flow and internal rate of return for assessing whether the potential value generated from a project is worth the resources expended will be discussed in more detail later.

Selection sounds simple. Innovation projects, though, have characteristics that make choosing among them anything but a simple exercise. The first problem, as highlighted with Vertex, is uncertainty: you do not know in advance what you will find. Which project is a winner? Which one is a loser? Nor can you be certain about how many resources or how much time will be required to complete a project. Along the way, you may discover new problems that you never thought of, and these will require more time and more resources. If you are working with newer technology or less-familiar science, you may simply not know how long it will take to solve a particular problem (or, indeed, whether you can solve that problem at all). Finally, because by definition innovation means something new, estimating basic value parameters like revenues and profits can be very difficult. The more novel the innovation—from either a technology or market perspective—the greater the uncertainties associated with both the resources required and the potential returns.

Ambiguity is the second challenge for selecting innovation projects. Ambiguity differs from the uncertainty surrounding lack of information about known parameters of the future. Uncertainty can usually be measured in terms of probability: Will it rain tomorrow (the forecast says 40 percent chance of showers)? What is the probability that the FDA will approve the drug? What is the likelihood we can complete the project by the third quarter of next year? Ambiguity is lack of knowledge about the parameters themselves. It means you do not know what you do not know, or so-called unknown unknowns.[7] If I cannot tell you precisely the demand for a potential innovation next year, then that is uncertainty; if I don't even know for which market it may be suitable, that is ambiguity. With uncertainty, you at least know the options, but you may not have all the information you need to estimate which options are most attractive; with ambiguity, you have not yet discovered the options.

Both the levels of uncertainty and ambiguity vary, of course, with the type of innovation in question. A routine innovation like Apple launching a next-generation iPhone may involve relatively low levels of uncertainty and ambiguity. Apple has sufficient experience in the smartphone market to understand reasonably well what customers want and how they react to certain features. They have likely collected massive amounts of data on customer usage and buying patterns. The basic design is reasonably mature. This does not mean there is no uncertainty. There are new components and new software, which often involve surprises, and customers' tastes can be fickle. They do not know for sure what products Samsung and other competitors will offer or how they will price them. Some features may be a big hit, and some may flop. So there is some uncertainty, but it is bounded. Sales forecasts may disappoint or positively surprise.

As we move into the realm of disruptive, radical, and architectural innovations, an organization's lack of experience and understanding of either the technology or the business model creates ambiguity. When an organization first begins to explore a technology completely outside its historical base of expertise—say, artificial intelligence for an auto company or gene stem cell therapy for a pharmaceutical company—it may not know enough about the technology to even develop a reasonable plan of attack. Questions like "What's the probability *this* will work?" or "What's the size of the market if *this* works?" are not only unanswerable, they may not even make sense. The technology itself may not be well enough defined to even assess what is or is not feasible. The set of technology choices may not be clear, and the markets in question may not yet be discovered.

Similar kinds of ambiguity can enshroud business model innovations as well. Like technologies, early versions of business models are often so poorly understood that uncertainty regarding feasibility, customer acceptance, and market size is essentially unbounded. Think about how e-commerce has evolved since its inception in the mid-1990s. In the earliest days, basic economic parameters like "Who will pay for this?" were not even understood. When Larry Page and Sergey Brin started

Google from their PhD thesis work at Stanford, the prevailing view at the time among many "experts" was that there was no money in search. The concept of two-sided markets was in its infancy. Brin and Page were not choosing among "uncertain" options, each with different probabilities and different pay-offs. Early in the life of Google, the options were not clearly defined. Brin and Page had to discover them.

As should be evident, uncertainty and ambiguity make innovation project selection a risky proposition. When it comes to allocating resources, ignorance is not bliss—it is downright scary. You are riding a knife's edge between two types of errors. On the one side, you might erroneously conclude that a project is a winner when in fact it is really a loser. This will lead to an error of commission (say, the Segway or the Supersonic Transport). On the other side, you might mistakenly conclude that the project is a loser when in reality it is a winner. This will lead to errors of omission (say, Xerox passing up on ethernet). The statistical analogy is between type 1 errors (false positives—rejecting null hypotheses that are true) and type 2 errors (false negatives—accepting a null hypothesis that is false). A key principle of statistical theory is that for any given sample there is a trade-off between type 1 and type 2 errors. Reducing the chance of a type 1 error increases the chance of a type 2 error (and vice versa). The same principle applies to selecting projects. As you raise the bar for the level of certainty you require before committing to a project, you will reduce your chances of committing to bad projects; but, at the same time, you will increase the likelihood of mistakenly culling some projects that would have turned out to be winners. And, obviously, the opposite is true. Being very lax on project selection criteria will reduce your chance of killing off a great project too soon, but it also means you waste a lot of resources on loser projects.

Making Better Judgments
About Innovation Project Selection

Judgments are decisions based on limited information or limited understanding of potential outcomes from choices. By definition, these kinds of decisions are not black and white. Decisions about innovation projects are inherently judgmental. We never have enough information or understanding in advance to perfectly predict the technical or financial outcome of a project. But, obviously, there are many shades of gray, and so some types of innovation projects require more complex judgments than others. As discussed earlier, innovation outside an organization's home court typically embodies greater degrees of uncertainty and ambiguity than routine innovation and therefore requires much more complex and subtle judgments.

As decision makers, our goal is to make rational judgments. That is, we want to weigh all the pros and cons, costs and benefits, and risks and rewards in a way that gives us the best chance to get a desired outcome (even if, in the end, things do not turn out as expected). As we can all attest from experience, this is a mentally taxing exercise. We find ourselves thinking through all the possible factors that might be relevant and trying to assess how much weight to give each. We run through alternative scenarios of the future. We bring together information from different sources, and we grapple with the different signals we get from each. We find ourselves asking "what if?" and "what about?" over and over. We desperately want to get the "right" answer when such an answer does not seem particularly anxious to reveal itself. It can be exhausting.

As if our pursuit of a rational decision is not hard enough intellectually, we now know from decades of research in behavioral economics and psychology that our judgments are clouded by any number of cognitive biases and distortions.[8] We do not look at data, information, and "facts" as coldly or objectively as we might hope or think. We tend to stubbornly cling to our initial hypotheses about the correct course of action and weigh evidence more heavily that supports our view (confirmation bias). If we believe a particular project is a winner, we will tend to view data that contradict this view more skeptically than data that support this view. Our initial impressions of projects tend to persist (anchoring). Once we label a project a "winner," we tend to stick with that view. We tend to attribute our past success to our capabilities but our failures to bad luck (attribution bias). This can lead us to be overly optimistic in assessing our capacity to execute a project. For instance, imagine that our last forecast proved to be quite accurate. This will bolster our view that we are good forecasters and therefore should put a lot of confidence in the forecast for the current project. However, if our last forecast proved to be terrible, we will tend to write that off as bad luck. We find more recent experiences more salient (recency effects). If the last risky innovation project failed, we will tend to overestimate the risks of the current project. If it succeeded, however, we will tend to underestimate the risks. These and other cognitive biases systematically work against our capacity to reach rational decisions.

Of course, despite its intellectual demands and psychological hazards, project selection simply cannot be avoided. You may find the process stressful, aggravating, or imperfect, but, at the end of the day, resources must be committed to some projects and not to others. To make the process as rational as possible, organizations deploy various analytical tools and techniques. We examine their uses and limits below.

A (Partial) Defense of Financial Analytical Tools

Within the world of innovation, perhaps no set of management techniques is more maligned than financial analysis. Discounted cash flow, net present value, internal rate of return, and their kin have become the villains in most popular writing on innovation. My Harvard Business School colleagues Clay Christensen, Stephen Kaufman, and Willy Shih refer to financial tools as "innovation killers" in their 2008 *Harvard Business Review* article.[9] The "alleged crimes" (their words) against financial tools include causing managers to underestimate returns on innovation, shackling incumbent firms' responses to attackers, and tilting resource allocation toward projects that pay off in the short term. In essence, opponents of traditional financial analysis argue that these tools exacerbate rather than fix the problems of bias in resource allocation. And, specifically, they are supposed to cause managers to be excessively conservative in their resource allocation decisions. Before convicting financial analysis of these crimes, however, it is worth a bit more investigation.

The general purpose of financial analysis is to help organizations implement the basic principle of allocating scarce resources to their most valuable usage. In this regard, the basic motivation behind financial analysis is hard to argue against. Discounted cash flow, net present value, and internal rate of return analysis are the most common techniques for assessing whether a given investment is a good use of resources relative to the alternatives. Despite differences in specific mechanics, all operate according to a similar logic: they compare the resources you expect to expend on a project with the financial returns (cash flow, profits, etc.) you expect to receive in the future. Because a dollar you *might* earn tomorrow (if the project goes as expected) is worth less than a dollar in your hand today, you reduce the value or "discount" the value of that dollar in your calculations. There are many levels of sophistication one might employ in doing these calculations, but this comparison of resources versus potential future returns is the essence. All these techniques are just ways to structure our logic.

The first thing to recognize is that, like any tool, financial evaluation tools are designed to do some things well, some things less well, and some things not at all. A claw hammer is great at driving nails into wood and prying things open. It would be adequate but not optimal for demolition (a sledge hammer would be better). It would be downright lousy for driving a screw through a metal surface. Whether a tool is helpful—be it a hammer or discounted cash flow analysis—depends on the match between the tool and the problem it is being asked to address. The "flaws" of traditional financial analytical tools are the result of problems in how they are used, rather than the tools themselves. It is not discounted cash flow analysis that might cause companies to make bad project selection decisions; rather, it is the managers using those tools and interpreting them incorrectly.

The inherent uncertainty and ambiguity of innovation projects start to complicate the use of techniques like discounted cash flow and net present value. Uncertainty is often dealt with by estimating probabilities of costs and future revenues, in essence yielding an "expected net present value." Another approach is to increase the discount rate used to value future cash flows. The greater the uncertainty, the less weight we give future cash flows (because of the likelihood we may never see them). Projects perceived to have higher risks get a higher discount rate, which in turn lowers the return on the program. In theory, this is not a bad idea. It says that if you are going to pursue a risky project, it better be worth it in terms of the potential return. You don't want to take high risks without high returns. The problem in practice, though, is really getting your hands around the magnitudes. How much higher should the discount rate be given our uncertainty? How high is the uncertainty? What is the probability of a project hitting certain financial benchmarks in the future? Estimating probabilities of future events—particularly events you have never encountered—is really hard. For routine innovation, it may be possible to use data from similar past projects to create reasonable probability estimates. However, for nonroutine innovation, we typically do not have enough experience or knowledge to estimate probabilities based on data. In practice, the probability estimates used in these analyses are subjective human judgments, and that's fine; it may be the best we can do. But, we should not fool ourselves into thinking that the presence of a "hard" number means we have an objective analysis.

Coming up with probability estimates for future uncertain forecasts or estimating levels of risk are themselves judgments, subject to all the cognitive and behavioral biases I mentioned before. As a result, our analyses just reflect our biases, rather than correcting them.

The limits of financial analytical tools become even more apparent once we consider the impact of ambiguity. Recall that ambiguity implies that we do not even have a handle on the structure of problem. We do not know the options. We do not know the range of alternative scenarios. We do not know how the key drivers of different potential outcomes. The financial models we build are representations of potential future states of the world. With enough ambiguity, our model is completely unrepresentative; it is fiction.

That financial analytical tools have their limits and are not as objective as proponents claim is quite clear. But it is not at all clear why the use of financial analytical tools should create a systematic bias against more innovative (riskier) projects, as critics claim. Remember, we can just as easily be too exuberant as too pessimistic about a project. An overly optimistic forecast is just as likely to lead us to fund a loser project as an overly pessimistic one will lead us to kill a good one. Because judgmental errors can go in either direction, the results of financial analysis based on those judgments can lead to *both* type 1 and type 2 project selection failures. Overreliance on financial analysis can lead to bad project selection decisions, but it does not necessarily lead to more conservative ones.

Proponents of the use of financial analysis will point out correctly that there are more-advanced analytical techniques like real option valuation that are better suited to evaluating R&D projects than basic tools like discounted cash flow and net present value. Because real option analysis takes into account the possibility of abandoning projects as more information becomes available, it avoids overestimating project risks (e.g., if I can walk away from an R&D project after spending just $1 million, it is much less risky than if I have to commit $100 million all up-front). In addition, it helps us quantify the benefits of "upside" that may become apparent only as projects unfold. Risk is not necessarily a bad thing in real option valuation because it increases the potential upside.

I agree that real option valuation can be an improvement over traditional tools, but it is not a panacea either. While it provides a logical structure to incorporate uncertainty and the value of resolving uncertainty through staged investments, real option valuation still requires subjective estimates of all the critical parameters (like future revenues, future costs). In addition, real option valuation does little to blunt the impact of ambiguity. Like its more basic brethren, real option valuation requires the analyst to have a clear understanding of the structure of the problem. The underlying decision tree should be reasonably well understood. If it is not, then applying real option valuation gets tricky. You cannot value options that are not even identified.

Despite the well-known flaws and limits of financial evaluation tools for innovation, many companies slavishly adhere to them in selecting programs to pursue. I have sat through presentations containing lists of projects rank-ordered by net present value and where a red line indicates the cutoff for which projects will be selected and which will not. I have watched project teams calculating and recalculating their financial models in preparation for senior management approval meetings. I've experienced interminable debates about the right terminal value to use in a discounted cash flow analysis as well as intense debate about revenue forecasts for innovative drugs that were at least ten years away from coming to market. And yet something has always bothered me in these settings. I do not think the managers involved are stupid or naïve. The vast majority, I believe, know that these kinds of analytics have limits. They know the numbers are estimates. They all know there are a lot of judgment calls about parameters like probabilities of success, time to market, costs of development, and future revenue streams. They know the number "on the board" may prove to be too optimistic or too pessimistic. When I have asked them why they are still depending on these methods, I get two kinds of responses.

The first is that they value the *rigor* of a quantitative analysis. Quantitative methods may use subjective inputs, but, by boiling everything down to specific numerical values, there is a sense that the output is more precise. A number is, after all, a number. The word "rigor" is often associated with "quantitative." This is as true in academia as it is in companies. *Rigor* means logical, meticulous, and thorough. Rigorous analyses have a healthy appetite for facts and a propensity to subject facts to careful scrutiny. *Rigorous, however, does not necessarily mean quantitative.* And quantitative approaches do not guarantee rigor. Consider a situation where you lack even the most rudimentary information needed to estimate a return on investment. A technology is so new no one really understands whether it will work and for which uses it might be valuable. If you were asked at this point about the expected return on investment, a truly rigorous response would be, "I don't know...but here is what I might do to learn more." It would not be a precise number like 21.576 percent spit out of a spreadsheet containing dozens of arbitrary assumptions. But, too often, we confuse the apparent precision of a number with rigor. The risk with both traditional and more sophisticated analytical tools is that they can create the *illusion* of objectivity and precision. If you are allowing yourself to be fooled by the false sense of security of having an "objective" number (based on highly subjective inputs), then your resource allocation process is anything but rigorous. The adage that it is better to be vaguely right than precisely wrong is worth keeping in mind the next time you ask a project team to "firm up the numbers."

The second common response I hear about relying on analytical tools is, "There is no alternative." Sure, net present value and other techniques have their flaws, I have been told, but they are better than nothing. Without the discipline of financial models, countless managers have explained to me, the whole resource allocation process can degenerate into a free-for-all guided by no more than wild-eyed guesses and gut feelings. And, despite their flaws, financial models provide a common language and standard reference point for comparing different projects. In essence, this argument is akin to saying that if all you have is a hammer, then a hammer is what you use regardless of the job. I have some sympathy for this argument. Gut feelings can lead any of us astray in making complex choices, and models provide a common logic structure for comparison. However, I strongly disagree with the notion that the only alternative to financial modeling is unhinged guesswork. As noted above, rigor does not exclude qualitative analysis of project valuation. Quantitative financial models and structured qualitative approaches are not even alternatives to one another. They can complement each other. We do not need to throw out financial analysis, nor should we. We just need to think about how financial modeling techniques can be used as part of a more integrative process related to exploration, inquiry, and learning. In the section below, we explore such an approach in more detail.

Selection as a Process of Learning

Deciding which projects to fund, which to start, and which to stop when confronted with high degrees of uncertainty and ambiguity requires a very different approach to decision making than is typically practiced.

As my late colleague David Garvin once argued, decision making is too often mismanaged as a discrete event.[10] By this, he meant that although a leader might take some time to gather evidence, muster different opinions, and conduct detailed analyses, the actual decision itself is made in a fairly compressed time frame and generally takes a binary "up/down" or "go/no-go" form. An event-driven approach to decision making can be entirely appropriate, of course, when the alternatives are relatively clear at the outset and most of the relevant data required to decide is available in advance. Buying a new piece of equipment, for instance, has that character. There is generally plenty of data available on the equipment's expected performance and specifications (and if you have operated that type of equipment before, you have the benefit of your own experience with it), and the alternatives are pretty sharply defined: buy it now, buy it later, or don't buy it. Once you buy it, changing your mind might be costly (e.g., you would have to resell it).

An event-driven approach to project selection can also be reasonable when dealing with routine innovation with relatively small changes in technology or market positioning. With an event-driven approach to project selection, questions like "What's the market size?" "What is the return on investment?" "When will this hit the market?" and "What specific customer need does this address?" are fair game. These kinds of questions should be answerable with careful analysis and reflection on the company's past experience. Senior leadership should expect answers to these questions, and, once they have answers, then the decision to fund or not to fund is relatively straightforward.

As I discussed earlier, though, potentially transformative innovation projects do not have this character. The alternatives may be poorly understood. Uncertainty is high, and so forecasts about future technical performance and market potential are likely to be highly variable at best, and ambiguity means that you cannot even discover what you do not know until you dig into the project (somewhat like opening the walls of an old house!). The problem arises when the traditional "event-driven" resource allocation process meets the transformative innovation proposal. Questions like "How big is the market?" and "What is the return on investment?" are unanswerable up front. There are likely too many unknown unknowns. Yet, with the event-driven approach to project selection, answering (honestly), "I don't know" to any of these questions is pretty certain to get you (and your project proposal) sent on your way. In fact, it is this attitude that leads to a bias against transformative innovation proposals, rather than the analytical tools themselves.

Instead of being event driven, selection for transformative innovation needs to be structured and managed as a learning process. There is not one best process for doing this, but there are some principles that research suggests will help you get to better judgments about making decisions in highly uncertain and ambiguous settings. Let's examine some of the concrete ways an organization can do this and what leadership behaviors are required to support such an approach.

Build Proposals Around Working Hypotheses

Project selection proposals are generally developed and presented as an instrument of advocacy. That is, the proposers try to "make the case" for their program. There is nothing nefarious about their intentions. In general, proposers—perhaps a scientist or engineer in the organization—truly believe in their projects and see them as great opportunities for the company; their advocacy is genuine. But the problem with an advocacy approach is that it tends to distort the information available.[11] Advocates try to make their case by highlighting what is known and positive. They view their task as mustering evidence in support of the program. Of course, the senior managers listening to the proposals are not fools (they have likely been successful advocates before!), so they adopt the role of skeptic. R&D and portfolio review committee meetings like this have the feel of a courtroom proceeding with advocates making their case and senior leaders cross-examining them. The process is set up to create winners (those whose projects are selected) and losers (those whose projects get rejected). It is not set up to open deeper exploration of the opportunity.

A good way to orient the process around learning is to frame proposals as a set of working hypotheses about the technology, markets, customers, value streams, and business model and strategy choices.[12] A hypothesis is a proposition that can be tested against data (qualitative or quantitative). Hypotheses are generally based on specific assumptions about technology, customers, economic conditions, and so forth. The statement "Autonomously driven vehicles will open up new markets for ride-sharing services and reduce demand for privately owned vehicles by 30 percent in the next ten years" is a hypothesis (based on an assumption that autonomous vehicle technology progresses to a point where it is safe and on the assumption that necessary regulatory frameworks are in place). If you are in an auto company, framing a proposal for R&D on autonomous vehicles in this fashion would be an explicit way to acknowledge that information and understanding about the program are highly incomplete, but the goal of the process is to fill those gaps as best as possible, rather than to judge the program. Recall the earlier example of Flagship Pioneering. New venture proposals are explicitly framed as *venture hypotheses* containing a specific set of "if-then" questions. As Noubar Afeyan explained, venture hypotheses "draw from asking 'what if?' and 'if only…'" questions pointing to hypothetical solutions that would be valuable to the world "*once discovered.*"

Initial hypotheses do not need to be true for the program to be ultimately valuable. At Honda, the initial hypothesis behind the light jet program was that some of Honda's automobile technologies and engineering capabilities could be applied to the design of light jets— this turned out not to be true. As Honda began to explore aircraft technology, the company learned that there were significant differences between automobile engineering and aeronautical engineering. But having a clear hypothesis up front helps the senior leadership judge the basis on which the program should be initiated and, if information changes, whether to continue. At Honda, they decided to continue the aircraft program even after learning that their initial hypothesis was not valid (automobile technology could not be applied to aircraft design) because in the course of their early research they developed a new hypothesis about the market for light jets.

A hypothesis-driven approach is not an excuse for sloppy thinking or for keeping bad programs alive. Hypotheses should be well thought out and have clear criteria for acceptance or rejection. At Flagship, teams proposing a venture hypothesis must also specify a "killer experiment" designed to rigorously validate the science behind it. There is rigor in developing hypotheses about technology and markets. Senior leaders should ask about the assumptions underlying the hypothesis and demand clarity around the logic. There should be a clear path for how some of the critical hypotheses may be tested (as quickly and cheaply as possible). A hypothesis-driven approach also does not mean every project is approved. Some hypotheses may be untestable within the company's resource constraints or strategy.

To return to the example that opened the chapter, at Vertex, each of the four possible drug development programs entailed varying degrees of uncertainty in both the underlying science and the markets. Each program had accumulated only fairly limited data from small samples of human patients at the time. Anyone familiar with drug R&D knows that preliminary clinical studies are poor predictors of program success. The vast majority of drug R&D programs eventually fail either because of safety concerns or lack of therapeutic efficacy. Additionally, market sizes are notoriously difficult to forecast in pharmaceuticals (because the attractiveness of the drug on the market depends on the data generated from clinical studies that have not yet been conducted). Thus, it was natural for Vertex management to frame their discussions around hypotheses concerning issues like these: Do we understand the underlying biology of the disease? Do we understand how the particular molecule intervenes in the disease process? What are the risks concerning the molecule itself (e.g., safety or side effect issues)? What might be the potential challenges of commercializing this drug? None of these, of course, were answerable up front. There were some preliminary data and some previous scientific literature that provided clues. Different people in the organization had different judgments about which hypotheses were more plausible than others. But being clear about the hypotheses motivating each program helped to focus management's discussion and thinking around critical issues and trade-offs. It enabled the senior leadership to ask relevant questions, consider the risks, and formulate alternatives.

Use Analytics to Drive Questions Rather Than to Provide Answers

In traditional resource allocation processes, financial analytics (and other quantitative analysis) are used to provide answers. They become key tools in the advocacy process. In a learning-centric approach to selection, analytics are not used so much to provide answers ("we estimate the rate of return on the project will be 30 percent") as they are used to suggest questions. The power of quantitative approaches is that they provide a structured and logical way to think through a problem. Putting together a good financial analysis is really hard. You have to think through many details like future prices, future competitive conditions, future customer tastes, future costs, and alternative technologies. Forcing deep thinking about these issues, and forcing management to recognize the uncertainties around these issues, is the valuable part of undertaking structured analyses. That is, good analytics is a process, not an outcome.

Vertex utilized relatively sophisticated analytical tools (real option analysis, combined with Monte Carlo simulation) in its process of evaluating its four candidate programs. However, Vertex did not use these tools—or, more specifically, the numerical outputs of these tools—to decide what to do. The company used financial analytics as a tool for inquiry. Analyses would be conducted and presented, but, rather than triggering a decision, they triggered questions about assumptions and alternatives. The analysis would then be iterated based on more up-to-date views (and with different assumptions). One program for a molecule hypothesized to target the hepatitis C virus initially had significantly lower commercial value than the other three programs being considered. In many organizations I have seen, this would have been enough to terminate further consideration. Economically, the project looked like a loser. But, instead, the senior management team asked more questions. Why was the commercial valuation so low? Was it the size of the market? Was it due to expected competition? Was it due to the potential therapeutic benefits of the drug? Digging into the model they learned that the molecule in question had a very high expected manufacturing cost. Normally, in the drug industry, manufacturing costs are such a small part of the revenue (less than 10 percent) that they are not a major consideration as to whether to undertake a project. But, in this particular case, the molecule was so complex that it was expected to require a very expensive manufacturing process. Based on assumptions about the market and the expected price, the high manufacturing cost would eat up a big chunk of the potential profits. Again, many companies would stop there.

But the team at Vertex asked more questions. Were there alternative processes for making the drug? How much would it cost and how long would it take to find out? Some additional exploration with external experts suggested there *could be* some alternative paths forward (not definite) that *could* lead to lower manufacturing costs (again, not definite). Further analysis ensued that indicated that even moderate reductions in the manufacturing cost would have a large impact on future commercial value. Nothing was definite, but the analysis helped Vertex senior management understand the trade-offs and the risks.

Using financial analytics as a tool of inquiry is an iterative dialogue between quantitative analysis and management judgment. Unlike traditional approaches to financial analysis, the learning-oriented approach does not let the "numbers" drive the decision. But neither does it toss out financial analysis in favor of gut feelings. Analytics are used to focus the conversation, drive deeper investigation into hypotheses and assumptions, simulate alternative scenarios, and structure the project plan to address critical uncertainties.

Foster Vigorous Debate

In an advocacy approach to project selection, debate centers on winning the argument, not on learning. My experience with some companies is that debate is tacitly discouraged for running counter to norms of "teamwork" and "cooperation." This represents a deep misunderstanding about the nature of debate. Debate is a form of conflict (intellectual), and conflict makes some of us uncomfortable. But if properly managed, debate and the associated conflict can be very productive. It can serve as a critical tool of inquiry and learning.

Vigorous debate is essential to a rigorous selection process. Through such debate we scrutinize facts, assumptions, and logic. Vigorous debate also helps to surface additional information and alternative perspectives. For any proposed program of reasonable complexity, lack of debate is actually a worrisome sign. It suggests that either people are not engaged intellectually or they do not feel safe enough to engage in constructive disagreements. Research on decision making suggests that leaders make better judgments when they utilize debate among peers and team members as a means of deepening their own understanding of a problem. A classic example is how President Kennedy handled the Cuban missile crisis in comparison to how he (mis)handled the Bay of Pigs invasion.[13] With the failed Bay of Pigs invasion, a fairly small group of advisors dominated the formulation of plans. There was little debate about the plan or exploration of potential alternatives to invasion. With the Cuban missile crisis, Kennedy insisted on debate among representatives of the State Department, the CIA, the Department of Defense, and the Joint Chiefs of Staff. Subgroups were established to examine various options, and he pushed the group to think through alternatives to solutions that were on the table (e.g., an airstrike).

Creating vigorous debate does not happen naturally in organizations. Leadership must drive the process. There are several steps that leaders can take to help foster healthy debate. The first is *actively and publicly soliciting input* from people and parts of the organization known to have conflicting views. In many organizations, some functions (say R&D or finance) tend to dominate the project selection process. This is not healthy. It shuts out valuable perspectives from others and leads to worse decisions. The leader's job is to make sure the relevant perspectives enter the debate in a serious way. Actively asking for input from groups or people who have tended to be shut out of the process is a good step toward changing the tenor of the discussion. As a leader, you need to make it clear that you sincerely want and need input from different sources, and that reticence to engage in the process is not acceptable. At Vertex, Boger made it clear that input on the R&D programs could come from any source. In my interview with him, he told me that, as companies grow, employees who join later are often considered (and feel) less important than the original founding team. He tried to make Vertex work differently: "We believe the last person in the door is just as important as the first....We want the guy on the loading dock to be thinking about clinical programs."

Good debate also requires a willingness to criticize. Criticism, again, is one of those potential conflict-inducing behaviors that many of us prefer to avoid. It can be particularly difficult for people to criticize ideas or proposals from people more senior to them in the organization. Leaders can counteract this by *demanding criticism* of proposals, even those they put forward themselves. Approximately three weeks before the planned invasion of Normandy (Operation Overlord) during World War II, General Dwight Eisenhower conducted a briefing of the battle plan to the top one hundred officers of the Allied forces. Military organizations are extremely hierarchical, and chains of command are sacred. Failing to follow the orders of a superior can lead to a court martial or other sanctions. And this makes it all the more remarkable how Eisenhower started that meeting:

> I consider it the *duty* of anyone who sees a flaw in the plan *not* to hesitate to say so. I have no sympathy with anyone, whatever his station, who will not brook criticism. We are here to get the best possible results.[14]

Notice here that Eisenhower is not just suggesting that it is okay to criticize the plan. Criticism is not *just* to be tolerated. It is a *duty*. And then he crystalizes the whole reason they are in that room: to get the best possible results. Eisenhower was indeed open to criticism. The plan did evolve and actually changed up until the final hours of the invasion. There were, however, boundaries. The strategic decision itself to invade Normandy was *not* up for discussion. That decision had already been debated, analyzed, and made, and this was not the time to revisit that discussion (Great Britain's prime minister, Winston Churchill, had strong reservations about Operation Overlord). Criticism becomes most productive to learning when it is focused on the relevant issues.

A third characteristic of healthy debate is *transparency*. Debates should be held in forums that enable the relevant parties to hear the others' arguments and perspectives and to respond. However, because of the political climate in many organizations, too often real debate does not happen in the open. In the meeting room, everyone is sufficiently "polite," and there is a lot nodding. Everyone seems to agree. But, once the meeting is over, the real debate—in the hallway, behind closed doors, on the walk to the parking lot—begins. Here, different players pull various leaders aside and begin to make their case. They will point out that "Joe's data was a bit suspect" or that "Mary's analysis was making some questionable assumptions." This sort of behavior is troubling in many respects, but it is particularly damaging for learning. Maybe Joe's data really is suspect. If this were true, then wouldn't it be better for everyone (including Joe) to know? If this issue were surfaced, rather than buried, the team could think about what new data might be needed to make a more informed decision. What if, though, the skeptic is wrong? What if Mary's assumptions are actually quite reasonable? Wouldn't it then be much better for Mary to have a chance to defend her assumptions and allow the management team to feel confidence in them? Of course, for practical reasons, not every discussion can take place at the assigned time in the assigned format. Two people might run into each other in the hall or be having lunch and start to talk about the program. There is no harm in that. Or a senior leader might call someone into her office to ask some additional questions about the project. Side discussions will inevitably happen. It is important, though, that the substance of those discussions be brought into the room or made available to everyone at the appropriate time. Finally, with transparency, the senior leader's task of explaining the rationale behind his decision will be much easier. Everyone—whether they support the final decision or not—will have had access to the same basic facts, analyses, arguments, and counterarguments.

Finally, vigorous debate should be about the ideas, assumptions, hypotheses, data, analyses, and judgments and not about the people who bear them. Debate should never be personal. If debate degenerates into personal attacks on someone's credibility, competence, or motives, the atmosphere will become so poisoned that it will be impossible for productive learning.

Keep Your Mind Open as Long as Possible

If you want to create a learning environment, then you, as the leader, must truly be prepared to learn. Learning, by definition, means evolving your thinking and, at times, changing your mind. We all enter decisions with opinions, sometimes strong ones. You may be really excited about a project and see it as definite winner (or vice versa). This is natural and fine as long as you are willing to keep your mind open to evidence, logic, and perspectives that conflict with your own. If not, you are not setting yourself up to learn. As a side point, others in the organization will quickly sniff out your bias. The pretense of "learning" and "exploration" will correctly be viewed as a farce. Your colleagues will either disengage, or they will simply tell you what they think you already want to hear.

At some point in the process, as you listen to the various arguments about a project, your mind may start to become set. Again, this is natural. But, as a leader, the second you vocalize your point of view, you may begin to distort the process. You may essentially end the debate. This may be warranted if you believe all the available information, arguments, and viewpoints have been presented and opportunities for further learning are small. Then, by all means, decide. There is no point in prolonging a debate beyond the point of diminishing returns. However, you need to be careful that you do not end the debate prematurely. If you believe there is still some information that could cause you to change your mind, there is value in keeping the debate alive. This suggests an exception to the full transparency principle mentioned above. You may not want to "tip your cards" if you want to keep the debate alive. Signal, instead, that you still have questions or are still not completely convinced about a particular option. At Vertex, Boger was so concerned about prematurely shutting down the debate that he would not disclose to the team where he stood. He commented:

> We [Boger and Vertex president Vicki Sato] have talked a lot about which project to select [for the past several months], and I have pretty much made up my mind. However, I want to keep the channels of information open and to keep the discussion going.... I could change my mind tomorrow if someone comes to me with new information.

Keeping your mind open—being willing to change your mind—is difficult in practice. We all take comfort in the certainty of our intentions. Given the choice of knowing what to do and not knowing what to do, I am pretty sure most of us would choose the former. Uncertainty about our decisions makes us anxious. Moreover, leaders often feel pressures to decide *now*. So much of the writing on leadership highlights that leaders are "decisive." They have the psychological stuff to make "courageous decisions" in the face of uncertainty. They are not afraid to commit. All of this sounds wonderful, but, from a quality of decision point of view, it is pretty bad advice. Good leaders make decisions *when* they have to, but not before, and they hold out for as much information as possible, right up until the last minute. As Boger explained to me, he tried not to make premature decisions: "I have an incredible tolerance for ambiguity...not indecision, but openness to contradictory points of view. As a result, it takes Vertex longer to make a decision."

Another leader I interviewed, Sergio Marchionne, the CEO who saved both Fiat and Chrysler from the brink of extinction (and later lead the merger of the two) explained to me, "I have often changed my mind about the changes I want to make to an organization. That's ok. I am willing to wait. Action does not always mean resolution."[15] Changing your mind is not a sign of weakness. It is a sign of an agile mind.

Conclusion: Building a Learning Innovation System

This chapter concludes Part II and its focus on the key components of an innovation system: search, synthesis, and selection. By necessity, the chapters were written in a sequential order. As I warned at the outset, innovation systems do not work in a linear fashion. Search, synthesis, and selection are highly interactive activities. A key theme in this chapter on selection is that it is not a one-shot event. Selecting which projects to fund is not like choosing dishes from a restaurant menu where you are presented with a set of well-defined choices. With the exception of some minor modifications that a good restaurant might make to your dish, you are pretty constrained to choose what they offer. Project selection does not work that way. The menu evolves, and you can actually change the dishes pretty substantially. Selection triggers additional search and synthesis. Organizationally, this implies that the common practice of dedicating groups to project selection (e.g., R&D portfolio committees) is flawed because it isolates selection from other innovation activities. The management involved with selection should also be capable of search and synthesis. They are not "selectors"—they need to be innovators.

Learning was a critical theme echoing throughout the three chapters of Part II. Innovation—particularly transformative innovation—necessarily involves learning. You never have all the right answers formulated in advance. You search in a complex, incomplete, and evolving landscape of opportunities. You conduct small (inexpensive) experiments where you can. You focus on having a high "learn-to-burn" ratio. Selection itself is a learning process. A learning approach to project selection probably feels a lot "messier" than many of the resource allocation processes you may have experienced. It has some familiar elements (financial analysis, review meetings, etc.), but they are implemented in some unfamiliar ways. Financial analyses become input used to generate additional search and experimentation—they are not the arbiters of which projects are good or bad. Decisions may be postponed until better information is available. Projects can be reshaped. There is debate, criticism, and even conflict. Yet the process is not a free-for-all. It can be structured around specific meetings and specific types of information that are expected to be available at different points in the process. Rules of engagement can be set to ensure that debate is focused on the right issues and undertaken in a way that avoids personal attacks. Senior leaders need to signal *their personal willingness* to learn from the process.

Throughout Part II, you may have noticed that the advocated processes and approaches implied certain kinds of behaviors and attitudes by people in the organization. The best-designed innovation system will not perform very well if it is not supported by the right culture. In Part I of this book, I described the leader's innovation strategy task. In Part II, I described the role of leaders as designers of an innovation system. In Part III, the next and final part of the book, I turn to the role of the leaders as creators of an innovation culture.

PART III
BUILDING THE CULTURE

Innovation is deeply a human activity, despite the fact that today it often uses lots of sophisticated equipment like computers and scientific instruments. Ultimately, people make all the critical decisions about innovation. They decide which problems are most interesting and potentially valuable to solve; they decide which technical options to explore and which solutions might be attractive; they decide which design features to include and which customers to target; they decide who works on the teams and which teams get the most resources. People make all the tough calls about which projects to kill and which ones to move forward.

Culture shapes the way people think and more importantly how people behave, and, thus, it profoundly shapes how innovation happens. You cannot really talk about building a capability for innovation without talking about organizational culture. In most large organizations, existing cultural norms have become deeply ingrained over a long history and are thus difficult to change. If you are a young, rapidly growing company, preserving your innovative culture is perhaps equally challenging. Regardless of company size or circumstances, the best strategy and the best system for innovation will amount to nothing if a company does not have the right culture for innovation. But what is the "right" culture for innovation? What does a culture for innovation look like? And is the same culture right for all organizations? (Short answer: no.) And what can leaders do to shape a culture conducive to innovation? These are the issues explored in Part III.

8

THE PARADOX OF INNOVATIVE CULTURES

Why It's Not All Fun and Games

As he stepped into the bright California sunshine, Dennis surveyed the sprawling corporate campus in front of us. "When I started working here, we used to do good science in the hallways," he lamented. "Now, things are much more formal. We have a lot more process and a lot more meetings." Dennis had joined the now very successful biotechnology company about ten years prior when it was a start-up with a handful of scientists housed in one building. Along with the success propelled by the launch of two blockbuster drugs came growth, and with growth came change. Some of the changes were tangible—more people, bigger and better buildings, much larger parking lots (and much nicer cars occupying the spaces!). Other changes were more intangible. The place "felt" and worked differently. The spontaneous brainstorming in the hallways was replaced by more formal, structured modes of operation. There were more procedures to follow and more committees to approve decisions. People behaved differently. In short, the culture had changed.

Culture consists of the shared values and social behaviors of members of an organization. We can think of culture as akin to organizational "software." It shapes how an organization's formal systems—its "hardware"—function. As is true for computers, organizations require both hardware and software to operate. Culture is an extraordinarily powerful driver of organizational behavior and performance. It can either lubricate or block the intentions of formal systems and processes. Let's say that the leaders of an organization take my advice and institute a set of processes for searching for ideas, synthesizing diverse ideas into coherent concepts, and selecting among potential projects. Whether these processes yield transformative innovations will depend heavily on the attitudes and expectations of the people involved in these processes. Are they willing to speak up? Are they willing to challenge each other's ideas? Are they willing to take chances? If not, then the formal system simply will not matter. Culture can be thought of as a "shadow" organizational system. You cannot always see it, but you feel its effects all the time.

A common view among both academics and practitioners is that as organizations grow in size, their cultures change in ways that *inevitably* inhibit their capacity for transformative innovation. Like Dennis's company, they become more formal, less spontaneous; people are afraid to take risks. Therefore, the argument goes, no matter what the large organization tries to do in terms of strategy and systems, its efforts to become a transformative innovator ultimately fail because it is stuck with a "big company culture."

I agree that, as organizations grow, their cultures can change and sometimes need to change. Additionally, I have certainly seen my fair share of cases where those changes in culture have led to behaviors that are antithetical to innovation. Although innovative cultures are actually quite rare, I do not agree that changes antithetical to innovation are inevitable. Organizational cultures, like everything else about organizations, are human creations. As such, they can be shaped through the hand of management. Since nothing is inevitable about organizational culture, let's explore how a large company can create one that is vibrant.

The Paradox of Innovative Cultures

What are the characteristics of an innovative culture? I have posed this question to dozens of management audiences over the past several years. These verbal on-the-fly "surveys" in no way constitute research, of course. They are just a way for me to gauge what audiences *believe* about innovative cultures. Quite comforting, though, is the fact that, in general, the responses correspond remarkably well to the academic research and case studies written on innovative cultures. Let me summarize the major themes I hear:

A Tolerance for Failure: Given that innovation involves exploration of uncertain and unknown terrain, it is not surprising that a tolerance for failure is believed to be an important characteristic of innovative cultures, and for good reason. No one will take risks in an environment where failure is punished and people fear the personal consequences of their own failures. Innovation, which is inherently risky, will be snuffed out.

A Willingness to Experiment: As discussed in earlier chapters, experiments are vehicles for learning and, as such, are essential for innovation. Innovative organizations tend to experiment a lot. Conducting experiments requires more than a system and resources, though. Organizations that embrace experimentation are comfortable with uncertainty and ambiguity. They do not pretend to know all the answers up front or to be able to analyze their way to insight. They experiment to learn rather than to produce an immediately marketable product or service. They accept the fact that many experiments will generate unexpected or even undesirable information (bad news), but they do not view such occurrences as failures. Organizations with an experimental mind-set are always looking for ways to disprove their initial hypothesis so they can switch to more promising paths.

Psychological Safety: Psychological safety is an organizational climate in which individuals feel they can speak truthfully and openly about problems without fear of reprisals. Decades of research on this concept by my colleague Amy Edmondson indicates that psychologically safe environments not only help organizations avoid catastrophic errors, but they also support learning and innovation.[1] For instance, when Edmondson, Richard Bohmer, and I conducted research on how cardiac surgical teams adopted a novel minimally invasive surgical technology, we found that the teams where nurses felt safe to speak up about problems during surgeries were faster at mastering the new technology.[2] Psychological safety promotes innovation because it enables the kind of criticism that General Eisenhower asked for on the eve of

Normandy. If people in an organization are afraid to brook criticism, openly challenge and debate the ideas of others, and raise counterperspectives, then potentially valuable information is lost in all three critical innovation processes—search, synthesis, and selection—that we discussed in Part II.

Collaboration: As discussed in Part II, well-functioning innovation systems need information, input, and significant integration of effort from a diverse array of contributors. The collaboration required for innovation is a behavior, not a process, and it cannot be dictated through processes or systems. People who work in a collaborative culture view seeking help from others as natural, regardless of whether providing such help is within their formal job descriptions. People work together not because they are ordered to do it or paid to do it, but because it is a shared norm of behavior. Collaborative cultures also require people to accommodate one another. This means, in practice, that I might have to do more work or change my design or modify my plan in order to make your job easier or your contribution stronger. In collaborative cultures, the focus is on getting the best overall result, rather than everyone optimizing their own contribution.

Flatness: An organizational chart gives you a pretty good idea of the *structural* flatness of a company, but little about its *cultural* flatness—how people behave and interact regardless of official position. In culturally flat organizations, people throughout the organization are given wide latitude to take actions, make decisions, and voice their opinions. Deference is granted to competence, not title. Channels of communication are fluid and direct (there are no "official channels"). Good ideas can come from anywhere and anyone regardless of position or function (recall Josh Boger's quote in the previous chapter about wanting the person on the loading dock to be thinking about clinical trials).

It is easy to see why flatness facilitates innovation. Culturally flat organization can typically respond more quickly to rapidly changing information because decision making is decentralized and closer to the sources of relevant information. People in flat organizations have less need to "run things up the flagpole" or to check with their bosses (who, in turn, must check with their boss before approving "your" decision);

they have greater freedom to experiment. Flat organizations tend to generate a richer diversity of ideas for innovation than hierarchical ones because they tap the knowledge, expertise, and perspectives of a broader community of contributors.

These cultural attributes complement and reinforce one another. A willingness to experiment requires a tolerance for failure. A tolerance for failure depends on psychological safety.[3] Psychological safety helps support flatness. The benefits of flatness depend on how willing people are to collaborate. We can think of all these attributes together as forming a system of beliefs and behaviors that reinforce innovation. Focusing on just one is not enough. You have to buy the whole package.

A few years ago, I became puzzled by an observation I made consulting for a large health-care company. Like many other organizations, this company wanted to create a more innovative culture. Senior leaders had actually identified many of the attributes listed above as "targets" for the kind of culture they wanted to create. And yet, like leaders of many other organizations, they struggled to make progress to implement this "package" of cultural attributes. This struck me as odd. Hard-to-implement organizational changes are usually associated with practices that garner resistance because they impose some kind of pain. You do not have to be an organizational scholar to know that people resist changes they do not like or changes that impact them personally in negative ways. In these situations, organizational change is akin to taking bad-tasting medicine. Ultimately, it may be good for the organization, but it is tough to swallow.

The cultural attributes most people associate with innovation, though, do not seem so tough to swallow. What is so painful about tolerance for failure, freedom to experiment, willingness to speak up, openness to collaboration, and less hierarchy? All the attributes I described above struck me as not just good for the organization (because they promote innovation) but also as creating a rather pleasant work environment. I asked group after group at this company whether they would want to work for an organization that had such a culture, and virtually everyone said yes. Before reading further, ask yourself the same question: Would you want to work in such a culture?

I have asked this question numerous times at organizations around the world, and I generally get an overwhelmingly positive response. This confirmed my sense that the cultural attributes I described above are not at all like bad-tasting medicine. In fact, the contrary appears to be true. These are practices almost everyone seems eager to embrace.

How could a set of organizational practices that everyone seems to love be so hard to implement? Imagine if the latest research showed that eating ice cream was good for your health. The more ice cream you ate, the longer and healthier you would live. If that were true, my assumption is that everywhere you looked, you would see people eating ice cream. After all, everyone likes ice cream (note—in my fantasy world here, there is no lactose intolerance either). Personally, I would eat more of it if it were not bad for my health. If it were actually good for me, I would probably have it for breakfast, lunch, and dinner (and dessert too!). It would be really puzzling in this scenario if you did not see people eating a lot ice cream. Hard to beat "good for you" *and* "good to eat"!

Tolerance of failure, willingness to experiment, psychological safety, collaboration, and flatness all seem like the ice cream of organizational practices. People seem to like them. And why not? They seem really pleasant. And hence the puzzle: Why don't we see more organizations implementing these practices? How can a set of practices that seem so pleasant—so tasty—be so rare?

Perplexed, I dug a bit deeper at the health-care company and talked to a number of senior executives, asking them why they were struggling to implement this culture. As I listened, I started to hear some reticence. Sure, tolerating failure might stimulate more innovative behavior, but couldn't that same mentality if carried too far lead to costly and risky consequences? And if failure is tolerated too much, couldn't that lead to sloppy thinking? Experimentation sounds fine, but how do you get people focused on execution? Collaboration is wonderful, but some managers thought the organization was already being bogged down by excessive meetings and the need for alignment. Freedom to speak up could certainly help the organization challenge the status quo, but couldn't it also lead to conflict? In principle, they liked the basic precepts of innovative culture but were not sure how they could be implemented "practically."

At first glance, it is easy to dismiss these concerns as senior managers simply feeling threatened by changes that impinge on their power and control. But I did not see it this way. The more I thought about it, the more I realized their concerns were potentially valid. This raised a question in my mind. Perhaps tolerance for failure, willingness to experiment, psychological safety, collaboration, and flatness—while important features of innovative cultures—*alone* are not sufficient for creating an innovative culture.

What I learned in researching this question over the past few years is that these easy-to-swallow practices—tolerance for failure, willingness to experiment, psychological safety, collaboration, and flatness—are just one side of the innovation culture coin. Innovative cultures have a rougher side as well. These less palatable practices, though, are critical complements to the more pleasant ones. It is as if "ice cream" could be healthy *only* if you dipped it in cod liver oil. Innovative cultures consist of pairs of practices that appear to be in tension with each other. However, as explained below, this tension is exactly what is needed to get the delicate balance right. Innovative cultures are a paradox.

Tolerance for Failure **but No Tolerance for Incompetence**: Innovative organizations set exceptionally high performance standards for their people. They recruit the best people they can find and then hold them accountable for high levels of performance. People who do not meet expectations are either fired or moved into roles that better fit their skill sets. Steve Jobs was notorious for firing people at Apple he deemed not up to the task. At Amazon, employees are ranked on a forced curve, and the bottom part of the distribution is culled. Google is known to have a very "employee-friendly culture"—free food, gyms, generous parental leave policies, and the like. It is routinely ranked among the "best places to work." But Google is also one of the hardest places on earth to get a job (each year the company gets more than 2 million applications for about 5,000 positions).[4] Google is not known to fire people, but it does have a rigorous performance management system that moves people into new roles if they are not a good fit for their existing ones. At Pixar, directors who cannot get movie projects on track after extensive feedback are replaced.[5]

How can strong performance standards coexist with a cultural tolerance for failure? Wouldn't the fear of getting fired lead people to take fewer risks? Paradoxically, a tolerance for failure requires having strong individual performance standards. Say you have two employees on your team. One you deem a very high performer. She has demonstrated superb technical judgment and has a track record of delivering. The other team member has struggled. Her technical skills are not what you thought they were when you hired her. She has a mixed track record when it comes to executing projects. Think about how you might interpret a "failure" experienced by each of these employees on a future project. My guess is that if the strong performer fails, you are more likely to see it as the result of thoughtful risk taking than as a result of sloppiness. You are likely to be more tolerant. If the less competent employee fails, you are more likely to see the episode as simply confirming your initial suspicion about her capabilities. In most organizations, you would not even go this far. You probably would hesitate to even let the less competent employee take on a risky project.

Google is able to encourage risk taking and failure because it can be pretty confident that most Google employees are very competent. Really smart and competent people might fail when they try hard things. That is inherent to innovation. However, if you are not confident that you have the "A team," then you cannot be sure if the failure was due to thoughtful risk taking or simply sloppy execution.

*Willingness to Experiment **but Highly Disciplined***: A willingness to experiment does not mean working like some third-rate abstract painter who randomly throws paint at the canvas to see "what sticks." Experiment-oriented organizations—like really accomplished abstract painters (and other artists and scientists)—are highly disciplined in their approach to experimentation. They select experiments carefully based on learning value. They design experiments to yield as much information as possible relative to the costs. They keep the costs of experimentation, particularly at the earliest phases of explorations, as cheap and fast as possible. And they face the facts generated by experiments.

This may mean killing a project that once seemed promising or redirecting it in a significant way. A willingness to experiment does not mean infinite patience with bad ideas.

Recall the example of Flagship Pioneering in an earlier chapter. Experimentation is central to its exploration process. But its experiments are highly focused. It runs "killer experiments" designed to create the clearest possible evidence about the feasibility of the science underlying a venture. The goal of a killer experiment, as the name implies, is to kill ideas quickly, not to confirm initial hypotheses. Venture hypotheses are either killed or reformulated in the face of contradictory experimental data. Bad ideas are not allowed to linger or to come back like Lazarus from the dead. Keeping experiments relatively cheap and fast is another critical dimension of discipline experimentation. At Flagship, venture hypotheses are usually tested with less than $1 million and within a few months.

Discipline should not be confused with sluggishness or bureaucracy. In fact, the opposite is true. Discipline means having a clear sense up front about the criteria for moving forward with, modifying, or killing an idea. Discipline drives speed in decision making. If you are disciplined about killing losing projects, then it is less risky to try new things. Amazon experiments a lot but also kills a lot of projects. Killing projects or reformulating ideas takes discipline because you have to be willing to admit that your initial hypothesis was wrong.

Psychologically Safe **but Brutally Candid**: We all love the freedom to speak our minds without fear—we all want to be heard—but psychological safety is a two-way street. If it is safe for me to criticize your ideas, it must also be safe for you to criticize mine. Most of us feel much more comfortable being on the giving rather than the receiving end of critical feedback. I have experienced the "joys" of tough feedback firsthand. As an academic for the past thirty years, I have presented my work in many seminars and scholarly conferences. The norm in these events is for the audience to poke holes in the presenter's work. Their job is to be skeptical about the data, methods, logic, and conclusions. We all know that such feedback is essential to improving our scholarly work. As academics, we could not succeed without it. But anyone who tells you that they enjoy getting utterly hammered in front of a room full of their peers is either disingenuous or has a warped sense of pleasure. Getting tough feedback is like cod liver oil. Good for you, but not so tasty.

Unvarnished candor is critical to innovation because it is the means by which ideas evolve and improve. Having observed or participated in numerous R&D project team meetings, project review sessions, and board of directors' meetings, I can see that comfort with candor varies dramatically across organizations.

Some years ago, while consulting for Teradyne, a manufacturer of semiconductor testing equipment, I got to see what productive candor looks like. The company had a strong engineering culture. It also had a very healthy learning culture. Engineers debated technical issues in the open, and they were expected to back up their arguments with rigorous technical analyses. In one project team meeting I attended, two engineers got into an extremely heated debate about the design of the cooling system to be used on a new tester (these are very large pieces of equipment packed densely with delicate electronics, so efficient cooling is critical). Their voices rose, and their faces became red as they fired back and forth at one another their different views on the design. They both believed they were right and were not hesitant to explain why the other was completely wrong. I never realized anyone could get so passionate about thermodynamic coefficients. Immediately after the meeting, I saw them in hallway. I was surprised to see they were having coffee together and sharing a laugh. They weren't even talking about cooling systems. I learned that they had worked together for years, had enormous respect for one another, and had a great working relationship.

In other organizations, the climate is more polite. Disagreements are restrained. Words are carefully parsed. Critiques are muffled (at least in the open). To challenge too strongly is to risk looking like you are not a "team player." At one large company I consulted for, one of the managers captured the essence of the culture well when she said, "Our problem is that we are an incredibly 'nice' organization. People are uncomfortable with tough conversations."

When it comes to innovation, the former will outperform the latter type of organization every time. The latter confuses "politeness" and "niceness" with respect. There is nothing inconsistent about being frank *and* highly respectful of individuals. In fact, I would argue that providing and accepting frank criticism is a sign of respect. Listening to the devastating critique of your idea is only possible if you have respect for the opinion of the person providing that feedback. Frankness does not mean berating or belittling, of course (with which it is often confused). The two engineers I described above had the highest respect for one another. Their "fight" was never personal. It was about designs, heat transfer, thermo-efficiency, and other engineering parameters. They challenged (in the open) each other's logic, data, and analyses, but never for a second did either of them imply the other was a bad engineer. Never was it about "winning" the argument, but rather about designing a better cooling system.

Still, with that important caveat aside, these are not necessarily the most comfortable environments in which to work. To outsiders or newcomers, the people in such organizations might appear aggressive or hard edged. No one minces words about data, logic, methods, design philosophies, strategy, assumption, or perceptions of the market. Everything anyone says is scrutinized (regardless of their title). No one lets anything slide. Most of us hold our ideas dearly, and there is a very fine line between attacks on them and attacks on us. Brutally frank feedback is essential to innovation, but it is also tough medicine to swallow.

*Collaborative **but Individually Accountable***: Good teams collaborate and have a sense of collective responsibility. "We are all in this together." (How many times have you heard a coach or professional athlete utter the cliché "it was a team effort"?) However, a sense of collective responsibility does not preclude individual accountability. Collaboration is not the same as consensus. Getting help and input from a broad variety of players is collaborative and, as discussed earlier, critical to innovation. But quick decision making is also essential to innovation, and nothing is worse for speed than consensus decision making, particularly for complex problems where opinions may vary significantly on the right path forward. Consensus, of course, can be comforting. It is good to know that a group of colleagues shares the same view. It can also make implementation a lot easier—no need to "sell" the idea to skeptics after the fact. But, unfortunately, consensus is not always possible, nor does it necessarily reflect the best decision. The overwhelming consensus among the aeronautical engineers at Honda and elsewhere was that engines could not be mounted above the wings of an airplane, but, as Michimasa Fujino demonstrated, the consensus was wrong. At Vertex, the consensus choice for which program to pursue turned out to be wrong (fortunately, the company did not use a consensus-driven approach: Josh Boger and Vertex president Vicki Sato picked which projects to undertake, and they did not go with the consensus).

Innovative cultures blend both collaboration (and the sense of shared objectives that go with that) and individual accountability for decisions. Committees might review decisions or teams might provide input, but, at the end of the day, specific individuals are charged with making critical design choices, deciding which features go (and stay), which suppliers to use, which distribution channel strategy makes most sense, which marketing strategy is best, and so on. Pixar has created several ways to provide candid feedback and help to directors of its films, but, ultimately, directors are entirely responsible for their films. They choose which feedback to take and which to ignore. They "own" the film. And they are ultimately held accountable for how it performs.[6]

In many ways, accountability can drive collaboration. Consider an organization where *you* personally will be held accountable for a specific set of decisions. There is no hiding. You own the decisions you make for better or worse. When the stakes are high personally, you have a lot of incentive to get all the help you need. The last thing you would likely do is to shut yourself off from feedback or from seeking cooperation and collaboration from others inside and outside the organization who can help you. In a fast food chain I studied,[7] all store managers (called "owner operators") were 100 percent accountable for the performance of their individual stores. Their entire personal income depended on the profits of their store (after two years in their position, they were paid no fixed salary). What was striking is how much the store managers collaborated. They met routinely to share best practices or would use some of their days off to help a store that was having trouble (or in a start-up phase), despite the fact they received no compensation for this. Why? Because in this super-high-accountability culture, collaboration was essential to one's own performance. Not collaborating would be suicide. Think about Dwight Eisenhower's position before Normandy. The invasion involved more than 150,000 troops from more than a dozen countries and every branch of the military.[8] It was a massively collaborative effort, and yet, in the final analysis, Dwight Eisenhower, as head of the Allied Expeditionary Forces in Europe, was well aware that history would judge him personally for this extraordinarily risky endeavor. No wonder he *demanded* criticism of the plan a month before the scheduled operation.

There is a fairly simple way to know whether you are in a high-individual-accountability culture. Come up with a list of critical decisions made across various phases of a project and simply ask, "Who made that decision?" for each. If you hear things like "marketing" or "R&D" or "the project governance committee" or "senior management," chances are yours is an environment with low individual accountability. Committees and groups make decisions. In high-individual-accountability environments, decisions can be traced back to specific individuals.

For organizations that have operated in a low-individual-accountability mode, the shift to high accountability can be challenging. If people are not used to making decisions or are simply incapable, then this kind of culture is very risky. They can feel threatened (a feeling that is not wholly unjustified if they have poor decision-making skills). Getting high individual accountability for innovation decisions can be particularly challenging given the inherent risks of innovation. As we have discussed throughout this book, when it comes to innovation, failure is more common than success. This means that in a high-individual-accountability culture, a fair share of *your* decisions will turn out to be wrong. Embracing failure is one of the most common mantras of innovation today. You are supposed to "celebrate failure" (a term quickly ascending the ranks of most overused business clichés). Such exhortations are disingenuous. As individuals, we do not really enjoy failure. We would always prefer to be right. In fact, if you have risen to become a senior executive, you probably have relatively little practice with failure. Let's face it—you do not get to be a senior leader by failing a lot. If you operate in a high-individual-accountability culture, you have to become comfortable with the fact that *you* (not the team) will be the one "celebrating" the failure.

*Flat **but with Strong Leadership***: Lack of hierarchy does not mean lack of strong leadership. Paradoxically, flat organizations require stronger leadership than hierarchical ones. Flat organizations devolve into chaos unless leadership sets clear strategic priorities and directions. Amazon is very flat. Recall that the idea for Amazon Web Services bubbled up from a smaller initiative within the retail group. The project was incubated by a relatively small team lead by (at that time) a relatively young manager (Andy Jassy). Teams at Amazon are kept small and entrepreneurial. The company has a "two pizza rule"—meaning that no team should have more people than can be fed by two pizzas. Yet, Amazon is a company with incredibly strong and visionary leadership. Jeff Bezos has definite ideas about the overall direction of the company and how it (and its culture) should work. Google is another example. Innovation at Google (now Alphabet) is highly decentralized. Engineers are given time to work on their own initiatives. But like Bezos, Google's Larry Page and Sergey Brin are strong leaders. Josh Boger at Vertex wanted the person on the loading dock to be thinking about clinical trials, but at the end of the day, he was going to make the critical call on which program to select.

Legendary founder CEOs aside, the principle of strong leader / flat organization also applies throughout the organization. Strong project leaders (not coordinators or project managers) set the stage for empowered teams by setting priorities, clarifying objectives, and ensuring that the team gets the resources (human and financial) that it needs.

Conclusion

Innovative cultures are rare. Becoming one involves several clear challenges. First of all, innovative cultures are not rooted in one or two practices such as tolerance for failure or willingness to experiment, practices we so often hear about in discussion of "what it takes to be innovative." Innovative cultures are complex organizational systems. They are composed of an array of practices. Second, innovative cultures are paradoxical. They employ practices that push the organization in seemingly inconsistent directions. This can be confusing for both employees and for leaders who are taught that they are supposed to be consistent in their styles. Yet, as discussed above, the "contradictions" are not contradictions. Innovative cultures require a delicate balance between different values. Getting this balance right is the job of leadership. And, finally, not all of the practices of innovative cultures will make everyone comfortable. Innovative cultures are not always pleasant to work in. They require some strong medicine. They are not for everyone. Before you decide to go down the path of creating an innovative culture in your organization, you need to make sure you understand the realities of such cultures and ask whether you and the organization are willing to take your ice cream with a healthy dose of cod liver oil on top!

9

LEADERS AS CULTURAL ARCHITECTS
Reengineering the Cultural DNA
of an Enterprise

The year 1995 was incredible for Pixar. The animation studio had released *Toy Story*, a blockbuster film that won three Academy Awards, and had enjoyed a wildly successful IPO. As CEO of Pixar, Ed Catmull obviously faced a lot of different challenges. But, for him, the most important challenge was how to preserve the innovative culture that lead to *Toy Story*. Throughout his career, he had witnessed other once-successful companies fail, and he wondered what made leaders blind to the forces that threaten them.

> My desire to protect Pixar from the forces that ruin so many businesses gave me renewed focus. I began to see my role as a leader more clearly. I would devote myself to learn how to build not just a successful company, but a sustainable creative culture.[1]

This theme of leaders owning culture shows up time and time again in companies that have striven to preserve innovative cultures or have had to become innovative again. Sergey Brin and Larry Page, cofounders of Google, have been quite public in articulating their views on what Google's culture should be (going back to their first letter to the shareholders, Brin and Page stated the now often repeated mantra, "Google is not a conventional company and has no intention of becoming one"). Steve Jobs created Apple University as a means to preserve the culture he created at Apple. Amazon's Jeff Bezos talks to both employees and shareholders about the importance of keeping Amazon's "Day 1" culture. Satya Nadella, CEO of Microsoft, has written, "The CEO is the curator of an organization's culture. Anything is possible for a company when its culture is about listening, learning, and harnessing the individual passions and talents to the mission of the company. *Creating that kind of culture is my chief job as CEO.*"[2]

Organizational culture is not an accident. It is the product of decisions, behaviors, and attitudes of an organization's most senior leaders. Many leaders think of culture as a "soft" construct because it revolves around intangibles like people's thoughts, feelings, and expectations. But just because culture is intangible does not mean it cannot be actively engineered to support organizational priorities. In this chapter, we examine the concrete steps leaders can take to engineer an innovative culture.

Engineering an Innovative Culture at Scale

Engineering an innovative culture is particularly difficult because, as discussed in the previous chapter, culture results from a complex interaction of fairly diverse values and behaviors. In general, it is easier to create a culture from scratch than to change an existing one, and cultures are generally easier to build with a small group of people. It is much easier to get 10 people to agree on a set of values and norms than 100,000 people. This is why start-ups are generally considered to have more innovative cultures than established companies. The founders of a start-up get to, by definition, start from scratch. There is nothing to be "undone." They can hire people who share their view of what the culture should be. Of course, they do not always get it right. Not all start-up founders focus on culture or know what kind of culture they want to create (remember, most start-ups do fail). But, the task of cultural engineering is easier (not easy, just easier) for the start-up than for larger companies.

Growth creates challenges for innovative cultures in two ways. First, the strategy of the company can become more complex. For most start-ups, the focus is pretty simple: go for the transformational innovation. It is a make-or-break strategy, and everyone who joins pretty much understands that. Now think about that same start-up once it launches a successful product or service. There is now a whole host of new activities like operations, supply chain, technical support and customer service, marketing, and regulatory and legal issues. The company has to exploit opportunities to grow revenues through incremental innovation and to defend its turf from envious rivals. The company may still want to do transformational innovation, of course, but it has to balance the competing needs of exploiting today's profit opportunities from tomorrow's longer-term growth potential. No longer is everyone in the organization focused on transformative innovation. And the company has had to hire a lot more people. As the ranks swell from dozens to hundreds to thousands, it is not automatic that everyone understands or is even aware of the original cultural values. It is one thing to get 10 people on board with your cultural vision of a company—it's another when you have 20,000 or 541,000 (like Amazon!).

The original founders can have a powerful "imprinting effect" on the culture of an organization over a long time. That is, even after founders leave a company, the original cultural values often live on,[3] but there is no guarantee this will happen. Culture is a bit like DNA— it replicates, but sometimes imperfectly. In biology, this type of imperfect replication is called a mutation. In organizations, every time you hire a new person who brings his own values, experiences, and expectations, you introduce a potential mutation.

Of course, as organizations mature and grow, their culture gains a degree of momentum. Think about venerable enterprises like IBM (founded in 1911 and currently employing 380,000 people) or GE (founded in 1892 and currently employing 295,000 people worldwide). Such organizations have deeply rooted cultures, ingrained by decades of operating in specific ways and dealing with specific competitive challenges. Changing long-held norms is challenging enough; now consider the need to change the thinking and behavior of a few hundred thousand employees!

The mutability of cultures is both bad and good news. The bad news is that if you already have a culture conducive to innovation, you have to fight to keep it that way. As noted above, there are a lot of "moving parts" to innovative cultures, and keeping the delicate balance between competing forces is a constant struggle. The good news is that if your organization does not have a culture conducive to innovation, it can change. Deeply ingrained cultures of even the largest corporations can be changed by strong leadership.

In 2003, Sergio Marchionne became CEO of Fiat, the Italian automaker whose market share had been eroding for years because of poor quality and uninspiring cars.[4] The culture Marchionne found there was bureaucratic, hierarchical, status driven, and low on accountability. He knew that the only way to save Fiat was to reengineer the culture. He started by replacing 10 percent of the company's 20,000 managers. He promoted a new generation of talented managers from the company's ranks and gave them unprecedented levels of autonomy (and accountability). He obliterated layers of management and organizational processes that slowed decision making and through his own behavior made it clear that he demanded fast and transparent communication. No more would fiefdoms be tolerated. He moved his office closer to the engineering group and immersed himself in product development planning and reviews. He authorized risky new development programs like the Fiat Cinquecento. After Fiat turned the corner financially, he acquired then-bankrupt American automaker Chrysler in 2009 and engaged in a similar cultural overhaul. Turning around existing cultures is challenging, but it can be done, and has been done, through strong leadership.

How can a leader preserve or create a culture of innovation? As you might expect by this point, I am not going to offer any simple "three-step" magic solutions. There are, however, some principles that can guide you.

Take Direct Ownership of the Cultural Problem. While many senior executives talk about the importance of having a culture conducive to innovation, they often delegate the actual work of cultural change to human resource departments or outside consultants. There are, after all, quarterly financial results to be reviewed, analysts and investors to be communicated with, major customers to be seen, operating reviews of business units to be conducted, board meetings to get ready for, budgets to be prepared and approved, corporate partnerships to be negotiated, and so forth. The agendas of C-suite executives in large corporations *are* packed. So it is easy to see how culture, for all its supposed importance, can get short shrift. But cultural change or preservation *demands* direct intervention from the top. When you look at organizations (of all sizes) that have highly innovative cultures, you tend to find leaders like Ed Catmull, David Kelley, Jeff Bezos, Larry Page, and Sergey Brin, who have an almost maniacal focus on culture. Creating and preserving the innovative culture is their top priority. Is an innovative culture a high priority for you? Ask yourself some hard questions. How much time do you really spend on culture? Of all the meetings on your calendar, how many are focused on culture? How often do you speak about the kind of culture you want to see take hold in your organization? How often do you frankly challenge whether the culture is working the way you want it to? How much of the culture work are you "outsourcing"? How important is cultural fit in your criteria for hiring and promotion?

Model the Behavior You Want. At its roots, an organization's culture is a system of shared values defining expectations and norms of behavior. Behavior is how values are expressed. Values may be abstract, but behaviors are not. Behaviors are the expression of values. While leaders should communicate clearly and consistently the critical values underpinning the culture, the best way to influence behavior is to model it for others. For instance, when Paul Stoffels became chief scientific officer of Johnson & Johnson, he set about creating a significant cultural change in how the corporation conducted innovation. J&J has been an extraordinarily successful corporation over its long life. The company had always been good at introducing new products (or acquiring companies with good products) and then using its operational and marketing expertise and global reach to grow sales. What the company had not done as well in recent years was to launch truly transformative innovations. The problem though was that the culture at J&J had historically discouraged significant risk taking. J&J was known as a company that could hit its quarterly growth targets and never surprise analysts with bad news. Business unit leaders were focused on meeting the short-term demands of their markets. A critical challenge was getting managers throughout J&J comfortable with taking risks and overcoming skepticism that things were really changing—that it really was okay to take thoughtful risks and that failure would not be punished. Stoffels was an excellent role model for encouraging this behavior. An MD by training, Stoffels joined R&D at Janssen Pharmaceuticals (J&J's pharmaceutical division) in 1990 but then left in 1996 to start Tibotec and Virco, two biotechnology firms focused on AIDS treatments and diagnostics. When J&J acquired Tibotec and Virco in 2002, he became a senior executive within J&J pharmaceuticals and eventually rose to the role of worldwide chairman of pharmaceuticals. During his second tenure at J&J pharmaceuticals, Stoffels had a major late-stage clinical program fail. Such failures are costly, and, as he describes it, the senior leadership and the board asked him, "Who is at fault?" Stoffels replied, "I am accountable. If I let this go beyond me, and I point to people who took the risk to start and manage the program, then we create a risk-averse organization and are worse off. This stops with me." Over the years, I have seen Paul retell this story countless times to audiences of managers throughout J&J, and he finishes the story with a simple but powerful line: "You take the risk, I will take the blame." And then he urges his audiences, "Cascade this principle down the organization, and you will create an entrepreneurial organization."

In a corporation where people historically were afraid of the consequences of failure, these were powerful words. They sent a signal. *I have your back.* Even more importantly, they laid out his expectation of leaders throughout the company—*you need to have the backs of your people.* Of course, these words were powerful because they had been backed by consistent actions over the years.

If you are in an organization whose historical cultural norms were antithetical to innovation, then it is important to send strong signals that things have changed. In a medical device company I consulted for, the historical norms put primacy on managers meeting their quarterly sales and profit targets. When the company decided strategically that it needed to undertake longer-term, more transformational innovation efforts, it knew that it also had to change its culture. Many veterans of the company were skeptical. Sure, the company's senior leaders, right up to the CEO, were talking about the importance of innovation, but many believed that "hitting the numbers" still mattered more than anything. The corporation's real emphasis on innovation, however, became quite apparent when the chief operating officer conducted the next round of reviews with business units. Rather than asking to go over the quarterly results, he asked all the business unit managers to explain their long-term innovation strategy and to show him their portfolio of innovation projects. He then peppered them about the balance between their short-term routine innovation and their longer-term outside the home court projects. As one business unit leader mentioned to me, "That's when we knew things were changing."

Incubate and Protect "Revolutionary" Pockets. Cultures compete vigorously for preservation and dominance. Such competition has, of course, led to terrible wars between nations, regions, and ethnic groups. Given how important values are to people, it should come as no surprise that intraorganizational conflict over culture is common. Cultures not only define *what* is important in an organization, but they also define *who* is important in that organization, and specifically who has influence. For instance, in a culture that prioritizes scientific prowess, power and influence are more likely to lie with employees with strong scientific skills and credentials than those with a strong finance background. We are all keenly aware of the culture we work in and, even more importantly, how we fit in.

Being a good fit within the culture is very comforting. It means we are valued. It means we have influence. It means that we tend to behave in ways that are not only accepted by others but also celebrated. It means we not only understand the unwritten "rules of the game" but that we actually play that game exceptionally well. The opposite is equally true. If you have ever been part of an organization where you are not a good cultural fit, you know well that it is usually a lousy experience.

This explains why cultural changes are brutally difficult. They are, in many ways, an act of organizational war. Those who have enjoyed the status, power, influence, and rewards that come with being part of the dominant tribe will usually (and often correctly) view significant cultural changes as threatening. They usually fight back. Not, thankfully, with the instruments of warfare but through various kinds of passive-aggressive behaviors designed to suffocate the new culture. *You* may think it would be wonderful for the company to develop a more innovative culture, but recognize that not everyone inside the company will view themselves as better off under new rules of engagement.

Like any cultural change, creating an innovative culture is a competitive process, pitting old habits and behaviors against emergent ones. In this competition, the status quo usually has the upper hand. There is, after all, strength in numbers. In general, old cultures usually only fall if an organization is going through such an extreme crisis that its very survival is at stake (e.g., IBM in the early 1990s, or Fiat early 2000s, or Chrysler post-bankruptcy 2009). And, even under these circumstances, old cultural habits continue to fight for their own survival. Since waiting for the organization to be on death's doorstep is not a particularly effective leadership strategy, what can leaders do to affect cultural transformation in the face of vigorous competition from the status quo?

To survive and thrive, emergent cultures need protection, access to resources, and an internal network of champions. One potentially effective strategy is to use quasi-autonomous teams or units where new cultural norms can be incubated and isolated from the status quo. Many larger companies today utilize some form of internal venturing to nurture outside the home court innovations. But these internal quasi-independent ventures can also be used as "safe spaces" to incubate new cultures. That is, internal ventures should have two goals: create a transformation innovation and create a template for a new culture (we will return to this second theme later).

Isolating the venture from the parent organization helps, but keeping it "safe" requires direct senior management intervention and protection. Even if they are isolated, internal ventures can be seen as a threat to the prevailing culture. They are often perceived jealously as "spoiled children" who get to enjoy unusual privileges (differences in pay scales, procedures, resources, work environment, etc.). Leaders should be prepared to intervene directly on behalf of new ventures to protect pay scales, processes, systems, work environment, and other perceived privileges. This is substantially important both to protect the emergent culture from threats but also to send a very powerful signal about leadership's intentions. In larger organizations, the new culture requires a network of champions who will act as protective "godfathers."

Note, an alternative means to incubate a new innovative culture is to acquire a company with such a culture. In general, such acquisitions wind up destroying the culture of the target company, but they certainly do not need to. This happens when the leaders do not explicitly manage the cultural tension and do not take concrete steps to protect the culture of the acquired company. When the Swiss pharmaceutical giant Roche acquired biotechnology superstar Genentech in 2009, many observers expected that Genentech's innovative culture would be crushed. But Roche senior leaders, starting with CEO Severin Schwan, were adamant in protecting the Genentech culture because they saw it as critical to Genentech's own innovative success and a potential stimulus for cultural changes within Roche.[5] They took concrete steps to protect Genentech. Only two Roche executives were transferred to Genentech (a CEO and a CFO). Genentech's former CEO and chairman, Art Levinson, joined the Roche board of directors (where he stayed until 2014). A number of Genentech executives were promoted into key leadership positions at Roche. Roche kept Genentech's vaunted research operations completely independent. Genentech employees stayed on their own compensation packages. I am sure not all Roche employees welcomed these decisions. There were likely some feelings of resentment that Genentech was getting "special treatment." But this is the reality of cultural transformation. It is messy, and it is never conflict-free.

Get the Right People. Because cultures are ultimately embodied in people and expressed through their behaviors, cultural transformation cannot happen without the right people. Many writings on culture emphasize the need for persuasion and "getting everyone on board." Certainly, it helps to win over skeptics rather than fight, and, as a leader, you should do everything you can to make the case for cultural change, persuade skeptics, and seek converts. You may be surprised by how many people are willing to embrace a new culture. But, as pointed out above, cultural transformation is ultimately a competitive process yielding winners and losers. And the people who stand to lose are not usually anxious to go along. Hard decisions will have to be made regarding people, particularly people on the senior team. Recall that Marchionne had to replace much of the Fiat senior leadership team when he took over.

We often think of innovative cultures stemming from the vision of charismatic and inspired leaders like Jeff Bezos or Steve Jobs. Certainly, these inspired leaders exert a powerful effect on the cultures of their organizations. But even these leaders do not work alone. They build teams of people who share their values of organizational culture. Cultural transformation requires a team of well-placed supporters throughout the organization who can carry the message, model the behavior, and recruit like-minded people to the effort.

The wrong person in a position of power or the departure of a champion can stop a cultural transformation in its tracks. I have watched this dynamic unfold many times in my career as a researcher and consultant. In one case, a fairly senior member of the management team was the focal point for driving the implementation of a culture for innovation. Given his experience (he had led cultural transformation previously), his position of power (all the business unit heads reported to him), and his status (he was exceptionally well respected for his track record), he was the ideal person to drive the innovative cultural transformation. He engaged both the business unit leaders and various corporate functional groups like R&D in a process of learning about innovative cultures and in developing systems to reinforce new behavioral norms. Progress was excellent for three years until he retired. After that, progress essentially halted. No other leader in the organization stepped forward or felt empowered to step forward to fill the void. There was no other cultural champion. A cultural transformation in a large company is too complex to be the burden of a single individual, no matter how talented or energetic that person is.

If you want to build an innovative culture, then you need to recruit and promote into positions of influence people who not only share these values but also who have the personal capabilities and qualities to thrive in the culture you want to create. For instance, if you want the organization to become more comfortable with risk taking, then you need people in the organization who are willing to take risks (and who follow Stoffels's adage of "You take the risk; I take the blame"). If you want your organization to embrace individual accountability, then you need people who are comfortable being held personally accountable and who don't run for cover when things do not work out as planned. While culture is much more than the sum of the values of the people in the organization, congruence between individuals' values and skills and the culture is essential.

Can You (and Should You) Create a Start-Up Culture in a Large Organization?

In just about every large company I have researched or consulted for, there has been at some point or another an aspiration or even a formal program to create a "start-up" culture inside the organization. Some companies have gone as far as to break up their R&D functions into small "start-up-like" ventures, as did pharmaceutical giant GSK when it reorganized its research group into small disease-focused units called "centers for excellence in early discovery."[6] When IBM decided to enter the personal computer industry in late 1970s, it established an organizationally autonomous and geographically separate unit in Boca Raton, Florida (almost 2,000 miles from the company's Armonk, New York, headquarters), to be able to move unencumbered by the corporate bureaucracy. The early phases of the HondaJet program were carried out by a small team of twenty engineers working from a hangar in Greensboro, North Carolina—quite literally half a world away from Honda corporate headquarters.

There are often very good reasons to create such organizationally autonomous units. They enable a focused team to explore innovative technologies or business models unencumbered by the distractions and pressures of the core business. As noted earlier, they can also be used to incubate (and protect) new cultures. They are sometimes used in an attempt to create a start-up culture inside a larger corporate structure. The hypothesis is that a large enterprise could become as innovative as a start-up if only it could replicate the culture of a start-up. Is this correct? And is it even possible?

Recognize first that start-ups represent a very diverse set of cultures. There are some common characteristics of start-up cultures, but there is no one start-up culture for innovation. Some start-ups have cultures conductive to innovation, but many do not. Remember, the vast majority of start-ups fail. For every Apple, Amazon, Google, or Facebook, there are *thousands* of companies that vanish. Just being a start-up does not guarantee a culture conducive to successful innovation.

Just saying you want to create a "start-up" culture inside your organization, then, is probably not particularly helpful. Instead, it is better to focus on the specific characteristics of start-up cultures that you seek to emulate and then try to understand whether it is possible to achieve those in an established enterprise. Having served as an advisor and board member of many start-ups ventures, as well as cofounding one, I see three salient cultural traits of *healthy* start-up cultures worth emulating. *The first is an obsession with speed.* Because most start-ups are in a race against the clock—or, more specifically, a race against dwindling cash—speed is an all-consuming priority. Every day, they burn cash, and therefore every day they get closer to what is known as the "cash-out date" (the day when cash balances hit zero and the company dies). The tyranny of the cash-out date creates an intense sense of urgency. An instrument in your lab breaks; you try to figure out how to fix it yourself on the weekend, rather than wait a week for a service technician from the manufacturer. Your strategy is flawed; you pivot immediately to a new approach. You see project schedules; you reflexively ask, "Why can't we do that faster?" You face a tough decision; you get the right people in the room to resolve it *today*. The clocks inside start-ups seem to run faster. Start-ups also have the ability to move more quickly because they can operate unencumbered from processes, procedures, and policies that have been designed to support existing businesses.

A second significant difference is the level of *individual account-ability* around companywide objectives. In start-ups, critical tasks are assigned to small teams or to individuals. There is no place to hide. If you cannot perform as expected, the organization can't afford to carry you. There is no tolerance for incompetence. In addition, because the price of failure is borne by everyone, there is no tolerance for priori-tizing functional or departmental subgoals over enterprise objectives. Problems that might delay a launch or lead to a poorly functioning product become *everyone's* problem. The attitude "I did my part fine; the problem is someone else's fault" just doesn't cut it.

The third trait of start-ups cultures is *comfort with extreme risk-reward outcomes*. Many start-ups pursue audacious goals. Achieve those goals, and the company can become worth billions of dollars. Since most start-ups use some kind of equity-based incentive plans, a suc-cessful venture can make founders and early employees extraordinarily wealthy. But most start-ups fail. So most people will not get that big pay-off. In fact, many lose their jobs. And some founders may lose even more if they have borrowed against personal assets to fund their ven-tures. Everyone knows the risks when they join a start-up. This means, almost by definition, start-ups are full of people who embrace risk. Anyone who has a low tolerance for risk is not going to be working there.

Innovation in enterprises of any size can be helped by greater fo-cus on speed, more personal accountability, and greater comfort with high risk-reward pay-offs. The question, though, is whether these traits can really be replicated inside larger corporations. The first thing that should be obvious is that simply breaking up a large organization into smaller units or creating autonomous teams is not sufficient to replicate a start-up culture. Urgency, accountability, and risk tolerance in start-ups are mind-sets. Re-creating these mind-sets inside an established company is challenging because they result partly from the unique pressures and circumstances under which start-ups operate. Consider the impetus for speed driven by the ticking of the cash outflow clock and the risk of bankruptcy. For most large enterprises, the risk of running out of cash and bankruptcy is remote. With more than $143 billion in cash and cash equivalents on its balance sheet as of December 31, 2017, for instance, Microsoft is *not* in any danger of folding this year.[7] Time really is of the essence in a start-up. The same is true for individual accountability. An enterprise with 25,000 employees does not have to practice individual accountability to survive; a start-up with 25 people has *no choice* but to practice it. Likewise, the "all or nothing" pay-off structure of a start-up is very hard to replicate in an established enterprise with much lower underlying volatility of equity value. The upside potential of start-ups dwarfs that of the vast majority of larger enterprises.

Given the structural differences between a start-up and an established enterprise, it is easy to understand why most efforts to "re-create" a start-up culture by organizing into smaller units inside a big company fail. The problem with most of these efforts is that they conflate size and culture. Being small, per se, does not automatically endow an organization with the key cultural attributes of a start-up: speed, accountability, and tolerance of high risk-reward outcomes. The bad news, then, is that re-creating a start-up is a lot harder than just creating small autonomous teams or breaking up your organization into small units. The good news is that being large does not necessarily prevent you from adopting these mind-sets. Because conditions inside a larger enterprise do not usually make these mind-sets necessary for survival, it falls to the leaders to create them through their action, expectations, and policies.

Replicating the Speed of a Start-Up in a Big Company. There is no "law of physics" that says large enterprises cannot move quickly. They often don't because, unlike a start-up, their survival does not depend on it. To re-create the speed and agility of a start-up inside a large enterprise, leaders should take away the luxury of time. Set aggressive time goals for projects, hold project teams accountable for reaching those goals, and provide project teams the autonomy and flexibility to execute in ways that enable them to move quickly. Allow project teams, for instance, to opt out of any corporate policies that are not essential to comply with legal, regulatory, or ethical standards. It is remarkable how fast large organizations have been able to move when they have found themselves in desperate straits (e.g., facing their own cash-out dates) or when external circumstances have demanded speed. After Sergio Marchionne took over Fiat when it was on the brink of bankruptcy, one of the first questions he asked was why it took the company three years to introduce new models. He did not accept the answer, "It always took that long," and he demanded that his development organization figure out a way to cut the time in half. The first major product launched under his tenure came to market in less than eighteen months.[8] When confronted with a major public health crisis, like the AIDS epidemic or the threat of Ebola, some of the world's largest pharmaceutical giants (and regulatory agencies) have moved with record speed to bring life-saving therapies from the lab to market.

Replicating the Accountability Culture of a Start-Up in a Big Company. Like speed, accountability is a mind-set created by expectations and policies. High-accountability cultures establish clear expectations about performance and provide individuals the power (and support) to make decisions in the best interest of the organization. There is nothing about enterprise scale that prevents this. For instance, if you pursue the route of creating small autonomous teams or internal ventures to re-create the start-up environment, then treat the leaders of those teams like CEOs. This starts by appointing people with the requisite leadership skills (not just pure technical skills) and with a deep sense of commitment to the vision of the program. Like all CEOs, they should be held accountable for the venture's success. With accountability, of course, must come room to operate within relatively broad boundaries. This is often the most challenging element of accountability in large enterprises. For senior leaders, it requires giving up some degree of control. Because unless internal venture leaders have significant control over the program they have been asked to run, they cannot have real accountability.

Replicating the Risk-Reward Incentives of a Start-Up in a Big Company. As noted earlier, it is very difficult to replicate the extreme risk-reward incentive of a start-up in a big company for the obvious reason that equity values of bigger companies are less volatile than those of entrepreneurial companies. As a result, the potential for a massive upside gain to an employee paid in stock options is usually lower (but so is the chance of losing your job because the company folded). In theory, it is possible to create high risk-reward incentives inside a large enterprise by shifting compensation away from fixed base salaries toward variable performance-based bonuses. If the variable bonus component is set high enough, then it may even be possible to replicate the financial pay-offs of a start-up. Technically, this is not very hard to do. You could take an internal venture team, pay the members far lower fixed salaries than comparable employees inside the company, but then reward them a bonus based on the performance of the venture (you could even mimic the pay-off structure of an equity option by using external benchmarks of valuation).

The problem with implementing such highly leveraged compensation systems inside established companies is more sociological and psychological than technical. The vast majority of companies employ hierarchical compensation schemes with pay related to position. People at about the same level (usually referred to as "grades") get paid approximately the same. Performance bonuses are typically set within predetermined minimum/maximum bounds. These systems are generally considered "fair" in the sense that people with approximately the same level of responsibility are compensated about the same. The expectation is that high performers will get an opportunity to earn greater compensation through promotion. Highly leveraged compensation systems can create large disparities in pay for people at the same level (in fact, it is entirely possible for "lower-level" employees to earn greater compensation in any given year than senior executives under a true highly leveraged system). There is often a legitimate concern that by creating "haves" and "have-nots" inside the same company, highly leveraged compensation could destroy the shared sense of purpose critical to the functioning of the company.

In the few cases I have witnessed companies trying to create these systems, they have generally gotten bogged down in exactly these kinds of political dynamics. In one large company I consulted for, an internal venture team was established to explore a radical new, but risky, technology. The venture was established very much like a start-up. It was spun outside the company's normal business unit structures and reported directly to a corporate venture group. The venture leader was given all the responsibilities of a CEO. A board of directors of senior corporate leaders was established to oversee the venture. The employees who joined the internal venture had to resign from their positions inside the company and none were guaranteed a job back In the event the venture failed. In return for lower fixed salaries, members of the venture team were promised hefty bonuses upon hitting well-defined milestones.

The problems with this scheme emerged when the team hit its first major milestone. This happened to coincide with a severe recession, which hit the corporation's earnings hard and had triggered salary cuts, a freeze on bonuses, and lay-offs. In such an atmosphere, several corporate leaders thought it would be inappropriate to pay out the promised bonuses. They rightly pointed out that if the venture had truly been independent, the recession would have hit the market value of their equity in any case and they would not have been able to cash in. The team rightly felt betrayed by the reneging (the original agreement did not have a contingency clause, and the bonuses were far less than what they would have received for cashing out of a truly independent start-up). Eventually, a compromise was reached, and the bonus was paid on a deferred basis. Later, the venture was reintegrated back into the regular corporate structure, and the team was placed back on the corporate compensation system.

I am no great fan of rigid hierarchical compensation systems. At some level, they make no sense. Let's take an example from sports. Few would argue that Tom Brady is not one of the best quarterbacks in the NFL. Because he is so important to the performance of his team, the New England Patriots pays him a lot (prior to the 2017 season, he signed a two-year contract for $41 million). It is pretty safe to say that stars like Brady make more than their coaches or even the team presidents. Their pay is based on their performance (and contribution to the team's success), and not on their "grade level." But under a typical corporate compensation system, the Patriots would pay Tom Brady more if he were "promoted" to coach or to a front-office job. In a sports setting, this absurd scenario would never happen. And yet this is exactly the way compensation works in most companies.

Given though how deeply ingrained hierarchical compensation systems are inside companies, I do not think it is practically feasible to replicate the *financial* incentives of a start-up inside them. But this does not mean you cannot use other, very powerful motivating devices. Money is not the sole force motivating many people. We are "compensated" for our work partly by the money we are paid and partly by the other psychological rewards we reap from trying to solve interesting and important problems. Many of the entrepreneurs I meet are motivated by having an impact more than making a ton of money. And the same is true for many of the scientists and engineers I meet inside larger companies. Being part of the team that creates a breakthrough in cancer treatment is a powerful motivator.

Think about Alphabet (the holding company that owns Google) today. At a current market capitalization of about $800 billion, it stands to reason that Alphabet offers new employees far less upside financial potential than employees who joined predecessor Google in 1998.[9] Yet Alphabet continues to attract far more prospective employees per position than just about any company in the world, indeed some of the best technical talent on earth. Certainly, Alphabet compensates employees well and provide nice perks like free food and child care, and if Alphabet stock continues to perform well, the company's stock-based compensation system will yield handsome financial returns for even the newest employees. But what attracts talent to companies like Alphabet is the possibility of doing really interesting and challenging work on important problems. That is exactly why in the past century top talent was flowing to Bell Labs. It was not about the money. It was about the environment, the freedom to explore, and the freedom to pursue projects that excited them. Whether you create an environment like this has little to do with your company size and everything to do with your leadership.

Conclusion: Engineering an Innovative Culture Requires Your Full Leadership Tool Kit

Some years ago, while visiting a large industrial corporation, a group of managers told me that the company was undergoing a cultural transformation to make it more innovative. As evidence of the "new" culture, they pointed out that the dress code was now casual (previously, the dress code was traditional business attire, including ties). As I looked around, I saw that most of the managers—who were mostly men—were all dressed nearly identically (khaki slacks, blue or white button-down shirts, and blue blazers). It struck me that the company had simply replaced one form of conformity with another. This made me suspicious that anything had really changed, and, in fact, upon further investigation, I learned that there were no substantive changes in incentives, roles and responsibilities, reporting relationships, team structures, or decision-making power.

Culture is not superficial, and cultural changes require more than tweaking symbols (like dress codes or physical surroundings). You do not create an innovative culture by putting lava lamps in the lobby or wearing a hoodie. Physical appearance of places and people may be outward manifestations of certain cultural values, but they are not the culture themselves. Symbols, of course, are an important component of culture. They are visible, and thus we cannot ignore them. In a documentary about the design firm IDEO's innovation process, founder David Kelley points to a DC-3 airplane wing sticking out of the ceiling, and he says laughingly, "That's décor. That's ambience. That says 'we are weird and we are proud it.'" But IDEO is not innovative because it has a DC-3 wing sticking out of the wall. It is innovative because of the values, behaviors, and processes its leaders have put in place. Effecting lasting changes in patterns of behavior—the essence of cultural transformation—requires using a broad arsenal of management tools. In addition to communicating clearly the values to which you wish the organization to aspire (e.g., "You take the risk; I take the blame"), leaders need to manipulate systems, reporting relationships, structures, policies, decision-making processes, and incentives. There I have often been asked, "What's more important to do first—change the culture or change the formal systems?" The answer is both: systems and culture are inextricably linked. Each reinforces the other. Finally, cultural transformation is not episodic. The culture of your organization is shaped every day by every action, every decision, and every behavior you model. When should you start engineering your culture? That is easy to answer. You have already been engineering it. The only question you need to ask yourself is whether you are engineering the innovative culture your organization needs.

10

BECOMING A CREATIVE CONSTRUCTIVE LEADER

Imagine you arrive at work today and you are told that your current computer is going to be replaced with a "new" one. You are excited until you see that the new computer is a replica of 1977 Apple II (4KB of memory, audio cassette memory, 40 × 48 sixteen-color monitor, and of course no Internet connection). How would you react? No doubt pretty negatively since computers are a critical tool for a lot of daily work. ("How on earth do you expect me to do my work with this thing?" might be one of your gentler reactions.) If you are a CEO or business leader, you would never dream of instituting a policy where everyone had to go back to using an obsolete technology like the Apple II or to, say, ban mobile phone usage for work or to disconnect your company from the Internet. Obsolete technologies hinder our ability to get our work done, and so organizations tend to be diligent about upgrading them.

But, ironically, we are much less diligent when it comes to upgrading our organizational "technology"—our strategies, our systems, and our cultures—to make them capable of innovation. And yet, as I have tried to point out in this book, our organizational technology is just as important to our capacity for innovation as the physical technological tools that we use in our daily work. No one will tolerate using forty-year-old computer technology, but, unfortunately, many companies not only tolerate obsolete management practices, they actually embrace them.

There are many ingredients to successful innovation. We of course need resources to invest in R&D, and we need smart, highly trained, motivated people. We need the right infrastructure, both physical (like labs and sophisticated tools) and institutional (like patents). But, most of all, *we need organizations capable of innovation.* The brightest, most creative, most motivated individuals will accomplish little in the way of innovation if placed in an organization that does not put a high priority on innovation, does not deploy the right innovation systems, and does not provide a culture that unlocks their potential to question and explore.

A key theme in this book has been that an organization's capacity for innovation is a function of leadership, not of size or age. And, most importantly, it is not immutable. As companies age and grow, their capacity for innovation will only ebb if they allow their organizational capabilities for innovation to become obsolete. But such obsolescence is not inevitable. Companies are not subject to laws of physics or biology that determine their fate. Obsolescence or renewal is determined by leadership.

The Creative Constructive Leader

A creative constructive enterprise is one that, despite its success and its scale, continues to pursue strategies, design systems, and nourish cultures that proactively embrace transformational innovation opportunities. They reject the dogma that "big companies" do not do transformational innovation. Strategically, they manage the trade-offs between the needs of the existing business (the home court) and the opportunities for transformation (outside the home court). They deploy systems for search, synthesis, and selection that increase their odds of finding and exploiting these opportunities. Culturally, they manage the tension between the highly complex and paradoxical behaviors required to foster innovation. It is *hard* to get any one of these elements—strategy, systems, and culture—right. Being a creative constructive enterprise means getting all three right.

Creative constructive enterprises are not born, and they do not happen by accident. They are the product of leaders throughout an organization. In short, creative constructive enterprises require creative constructive leaders who take direct ownership of all three major innovation challenges facing their organization: strategy, systems, and culture. You do not have to be the CEO or a senior executive to be a creative constructive leader. Whatever your position, you have opportunities for value-creating innovation. In fact, while creative constructive enterprises need creative constructive leaders at the top, they also need them throughout the organization, right down to the shop floor or storefront. Creative constructive leadership is a habit of mind, more than a position. These habits of mind include the following:

1. *Outward Looking:* As noted throughout this book, innovation, at its core, is about solving problems. Good innovators are good problem solvers. And good problem solvers are constantly thinking about, talking to, observing, and engaging with customers, suppliers, partners, and other outsiders. Creative constructive leaders have an obsession with what is happening outside their organizations. And they learn about customers, technologies, and trends through firsthand experience, rather than by reading predigested reports or getting "briefed" by staff.

2. *View Innovation as* the *Competitive Weapon:* Creative constructive leaders see things pretty simply: their companies are either winning or losing the battle for customers and the fight for value. For them, innovation is *the* weapon of choice for this fight. Innovation is not a tactic you are forced into by more aggressive competitors or new entrants. For creative constructive leaders, their organization is the *aggressor,* not the defender. Innovation is not an inconvenient option or distraction that takes you away from "running the business." Innovation *is* the business. Innovation strategy is the business strategy. It pervades every serious discussion and decision from the board level down to the shop floor.

3. *Embrace Being Different:* The art of strategy is about finding ways to make yourself different from and better than competitors. This same logic applies to innovation strategy. In a world bloated with messages about *the* most important technology and market trends to follow, creative constructors know that competitive success come from being different. This does not mean ignoring important trends, of course. It just means thinking deeply about how *your* organization can create its *unique* and advantaged position. Many times,

this requires a company to buck trends and even endure public skepticism. Few thought Apple's move into retail stores was a very good move at the time the company made the announcement (a period when vertical "dis-integration" was the strategy de jour and the only computer company that had its own stores, Gateway, had just filed bankruptcy).[1] When Amazon announced it was moving into web services, many analysts scoffed. Good strategists in general, and good innovation strategists in particular, are very comfortable standing out from the crowd.

4. *Disciplined About Tough Trade-Offs Between Short- and Long-Term Innovation Opportunities:* In successful organizations, there are always going to be more opportunities for innovation than there are resources. Many of these opportunities will lie within the company's home court. They will offer fairly certain and attractive returns in the short run. Other opportunities may be longer term. The cold calculus of resource scarcity says that a dollar spent on today's home court opportunity is one less dollar spent on tomorrow's potential transformative innovation. As we discussed in Part I, there is no right answer to this trade-off. Some companies will find it very attractive to focus on the home court opportunities while others will need to tilt their balance to long-term outside-the-home-court explorations. While there is no right answer to the problem, there is one wrong one: not choosing! Creative constructive leaders know they own the tension between the short-term and long-term and develop explicit and transparent strategies about the trade-offs the organization needs to make. They explain (and sell) their strategy both to employees and to investors.

5. *Systems Perspective on Innovation Capabilities:* Creative constructors know that innovation capability is not rooted in a single practice or tool. Like any organizational capability, innovation capabilities stem from a complex interaction of many practices, processes, tools, and behaviors. Creative constructors are organizational "systems architects." They think as much about *how* their organizations innovate—how they search, synthesize, and select—as they do about *what* innovations their organization produces. Creative constructors know that if

they can build the right organizational capabilities, they have a trust-worthy engine that can consistently generate valuable innovations.

6. *Organizational Innovators:* Creative constructors are organizational innovators. They are open to ideas about management practice from anywhere, but they understand the difference between learning from others and blindly imitating. They know that what is best for Apple or any other high-profile company is not necessarily going to be best for their company and its strategy. Creative constructors recognize that they must design and build a customized system of innovation tailored to the unique strategy and circumstances of their company. This is much harder than simply benchmarking others and trying to ape their so-called best practices. It requires deep analysis of the organization and engagement with the people involved in the innovation process. It also means continuously challenging the systems to improve and looking for new ways to innovate. Creative constructors do not let their organizational capabilities become obsolete. Creative constructors know that, to lead an innovative organization, they must be organizational innovators.

7. *Talent Hawks:* Creative constructors recognize that innovation is an intensely human activity. A company can formulate a compelling innovation strategy; it can design and implement fantastic systems and processes; it can arm its scientists and engineers with the most sophisticated instruments and computer algorithms known to the world; it can even lavish money on project teams; but ultimately, these can never make up for a lack of creative, talented, motivated, engaged people. Your B team can never become an A team through technology, systems, and resources alone. Creative constructors make it a priority to recruit, develop, train, and retain the best talent available *at all levels.* They track how the organization is doing and hold managers accountable for getting the best people onboard. They know that smart, talented, innovative people are attracted to organizations with other smart, talented, innovative people. They therefore set high standards. Creative constructors also understand that, when it comes to innovation, a melting pot of backgrounds, experience, training, and perspective is an asset. The "best" talent is not homogenous. Creative

constructors also know that, while financial incentives are important, people are attracted to an organization and motivated by more than money. So creative constructors create an environment where people have the freedom and capacity to explore and experiment with novel ideas and to pursue high-risk projects. Strategy, resources, and systems are designed to enable talent to excel, rather than as a remediating device to address workforce deficiencies.

8. *Culture Warriors:* Creative constructors are obsessed with organizational culture. They know that, without the right culture, their company's capacity for innovation will be stunted. They refuse to yield to the assumption that, as organizations grow and age, they inevitably lose their innovative cultures. Creative constructor leaders do not get trapped in the false dichotomy of "big company" cultures versus "start-up" cultures. For them, it is all about creating an innovative culture. For the creative constructive leader, culture is a potent tool, and they keep their hands firmly on it. Culture is not to be outsourced to consultants or human resource departments. Culture is their job. Creative constructive leaders recognize that every day they are shaping culture through every decision they make, every word they communicate, every behavior they display. Creative constructive leaders know they are being watched and listened to very carefully by employees looking for clues about what's really important. Creative constructive leaders are incredibly diligent in thinking through the cultural ramifications of everything they do. They know that innovative cultures are complex and take time to build. Creative constructive leaders are also keenly aware that innovative cultures can be destroyed very quickly.

Wanted for the Twenty-First Century: Creative Constructive Leaders

The capacity to innovate is one of humanity's distinguishing features. This above all else probably does more to explain our success as a species than anything else. We have been improving our lives by innovating everything around us—daily artifacts, tools, production processes, energy sources, communication methods, services, organizations, and institutions—for nearly our entire existence. Our remarkable capacity to innovate, though, will be sorely tested in future decades. Global warming and water shortages, severe poverty, brutal diseases like cancer and dementia, the economic challenges of aging populations, and growing inequality and the resulting sociopolitical tensions that come with it are just some of the awesome challenges looming over twenty-first-century societies.

Of course, if I were writing this at the beginning of the past century rather than this one, I might have voiced similar concerns. There were good reasons to be pessimistic about society's prospects in 1918. The world had just endured a war that killed more than 16 million people and suffered through a flu pandemic that killed more than 50 million people. And certainly, the twentieth century saw its share of challenges. But what no one could fully foresee was how innovation in products, services, organizations, and institutions—would utterly transform our societies and economies for the better. We thrived in the twentieth century because of innovation. The question is whether we are up to the task of innovation in the current century.

Not everyone is optimistic on this front. The eminent economic historian, Robert Gordon of Northwestern University, has argued in his recent book *The Rise and Fall of American Growth*[2] that the society-transforming innovation of the past century (e.g., electrification, urban sanitation, modern chemicals, the internal combustion engine, and modern communication) are not going to be repeated, and that more recent technological forces (including digitization) are having less impact on our standard of living. This is not the place to debate Gordon's thesis (that could be the subject of an entire book!). I am more optimistic, but with a very important qualification. Innovation does not just "ride to the rescue" like some gift dropped from the heavens. We are not passive actors in this play. As I have stated throughout this book, innovation is an intensely and uniquely human activity. Look around you. Everything you see and experience—physical artifacts like products, buildings, and machines, the services you use like a bank or movie channel, the organizations in which you work, the management practices you are using, even the laws you are following—were created by people working in organizations of some type. Our capacity to rise to the challenges of the twenty-first century depends on the capacity of our organizations to harness the human potential for incredible innovation. And, as I have argued throughout this book, innovative organizations do not just form spontaneously. They are not "natural" in any sense of the word. Innovative organizations are themselves the product of human creativity. Whether we rise to society's great challenges through transformative life-changing innovation depends on us and only us. This is both a refreshing and daunting thought. The need for creative constructive leaders has never been greater.

Notes

Introduction

1 National Science Foundation, "Science & Engineering Indicators, 2016," http://www.nsf.gov/statistics/2016/nsb20161/#/report/chapter-4/recent -trends-in-u-s-r-d-performance; PwC, "Corporate R&D Spending Hits Record High for Top 1000, Despite Concerns of Economic Protectionism," press release, October 24, 2017, https://www.pwc.com/us/en/press -releases/2017/corporate-rd-spending-hits-record-highs-for-the-top-1000 .html; Industrial Research Institute, "2017 Global R&D Forecast," supplement, *R&D Magazine,* 7.

2 KPMG, "2017 Global Venture Capital Investment Hits Decade High of $155 Billion Following a Strong Q4: KPMG Venture Pulse," press release, January 18, 2018, https://home.kpmg.com/sg/en/home/media/press -releases/2018/01/kpmg-venture-pulse-q4-2017.html.

3 Joseph A. Schumpeter, *Capitalism, Socialism and Democracy* (1942; London: Routledge, 1994), 82–83.

4 Joseph A. Schumpeter, *Business Cycles: A Theoretical, Historical, and Statistical Analysis of the Capitalist Process* (New York: McGraw-Hill, 1939).

5 The seminal studies in this literature include William Abernathy and Kim Clark, "Innovation: Mapping the Winds of Creative Destruction," *Research Policy* 14 (1985): 3–22; Michael L. Tushman and Philip Anderson, "Technological Discontinuities and Organizational Environments," *Administrative Science Quarterly* 31, no. 3 (1986): 439–465; Rebecca M. Henderson and Kim B. Clark, "Architectural Innovation: The Reconfiguration of Existing Product Technologies and the Failure of Established Firms," *Administrative Science Quarterly* 35, no. 1 (1990): 9–30; Clayton Christensen, *The Innovator's Dilemma* (Boston: Harvard Business School Press, 1997).

6 Andrew Baum, Peter Verdult, C. C. Chugbo, et al., "Pharmaceuticals: Exit Research and Create Value," Morgan Stanley Research, January 20, 2010.

7 For a comprehensive review of the statistical studies on this topic, see Wesley Cohen, "Fifty Years of Empirical Studies of Innovative Activity and Performance," in *Handbook of the Economics of Innovation,* ed. B. H. Hall and N. Rosenberg, 129–213 (Amsterdam: North Holland Elsevier, 2010).

8 For a description of this study, see Gary Pisano, *Science Business: The Promise, Reality, and Future of Biotech* (Boston: Harvard Business Review Press, 2006).

9 See for instance the seminal work of Tushman and Anderson, "Technological Discontinuities and Organizational Environments"; Abernathy and Clark "Innovation"; and later Christensen, *Innovator's Dilemma.*

10 There are many excellent histories of the IBM 360. See, for instance, Carliss Baldwin and Kim Clark, *Design Rules: The Power of Modularity—Volume* (Boston: MIT Press, 1990). See also IBM Archives, https://www-03.ibm .com/ibm/history/exhibits/mainframe/mainframe_PR360.html.

11 "Fortune 500 Archive, 1964 Full List," *Fortune,* http://archive.fortune.com /magazines/fortune/fortune500_archive/full/1964/.

12 "Fortune 500 2007," *Fortune,* http://fortune.com/fortune500/2007/.

13 "Fortune 500 Archive, 2004 Full List," *Fortune,* http://archive.fortune .com/magazines/fortune/fortune500_archive/full/2004/301.html.

14 "Amazon: Financials," Yahoo Finance, accessed April 4, 2018, https://finance .yahoo.com/quote/AMZN/financials?p=AMZN.

15 "Alphabet," Fortune 500, April 6, 2018, http://fortune.com/fortune500 /alphabet/.

16 Trefis.com, "Total Revenue of Johnson & Johnson Worldwide from 2012 to 2024 (in Billion U.S. Dollars)," accessed March 29, 2018, www .statista.com/statistics/258392/total-revenue-of-johnson-und-johnson -worldwide/.

17 "Top Companies Globally by Revenue," April 6, 2018, Capital IQ, Inc., a division of Standard & Poor's; "Johnson & Johnson," Fortune 500, *Fortune,* April 2, 2018, http://fortune.com/fortune500/johnson-johnson/; PwC, "Global Top 100 Companies by Market Capitalization," March 31, 2017, https://www.pwc.com/gx/en/audit-services/assets/pdf/global-top-100 -companies-2017-final.pdf.

18 Johnson & Johnson, Form 10-K 2017, p. 1, accessed March 2018, http://files .shareholder.com/downloads/JNJ/6058290261x0xS200406%2D18%2D5 /200406/filing.pdf.

19 Johnson & Johnson, Form 10-K 2017, p. 14. Johnson & Johnson's expenditure on research and development from 2005 to 2017, www.statista .com/statistics/266407/research-and-development-expenditure-of-johnson -and-johnson-since-2006/ (accessed March 29, 2018).

20 Johnson & Johnson, Form 10-K 2017, p. 1.

21 Based on the author's analysis of 4,012 companies with more than $1 billion in revenues. April 2, 2018, Capital IQ, Inc., a division of Standard & Poor's. A database called the Global 5000, which tracks the world's largest companies by revenue, claims 4,455 companies have more than $1 billion in annual revenues. The Global 5000, April 2, 2018, http://theglobal5000 .com/about/.

22 Jeff Bezos, letter to the shareholders, 2015, Amazon.com, p. 2.

23 Nitin Noria and Michael Beer, "Cracking the Code of Change," *Harvard Business Review,* May/June 2000.

24 James G. March, "Exploration Versus Exploitation in Organizational Learning," *Organization Science* 2, no. 1 (February 1991): 71–87.

25 On the dilemma of exploration vs. exploitation in innovation, see the excellent work of Charles O'Reilly and Michael Tushman, *Lead and Disrupt: How to Solve the Innovator's Dilemma* (Palo Alto, CA: Stanford Business Books, 2016).

26 For an analysis, see Sara Moeller, Frederick Schlingemann, and Rene Stulz, "Do Shareholders of Acquiring Firms Gain from Acquisitions," NBER working paper no. 9523; Boston Consulting Group, "A Brave New World of M&A: How to Create Value from Mergers and Acquisitions," July 2007.

Part I: Creating an Innovation Strategy

1 The organizational dilemma between exploitation and exploration was first highlighted by March, "Exploration in Organizational Learning."

Chapter 1: Beginning the Journey

1 Parts of this chapter are adapted from my article "You Need an Innovation Strategy," *Harvard Business Review*, June 2015, reprint R1506B.

2 I am grateful to my colleague Stefan Thomke of Harvard University for bringing this example to my attention.

3 "The Salad Is in the Bag," *Wall Street Journal*, July 27, 2011, http://www.wsj.com/articles/SB10001424053111903999904576469973559258778.

4 William Abernathy and James Utterback, "Patterns of Industrial Innovation," *Technology Review* 80, no. 7 (1978): 40–47; Abernathy and Clark, "Innovation"; Tushman and Anderson, "Technological Discontinuities and Organizational Environments"; Henderson and Clark, "Architectural Innovation"; Christensen, *Innovator's Dilemma*; Pisano, "You Need an Innovation Strategy."

5 "Audi on Demand, Frequently Asked Questions," 2018, https://www.us.audiondemand.com/us/service/en_ondemand/nav/faq.html.

Chapter 2: Navigating the Route

1 Jack Nicas, "Google Reorganization Isn't About Cutting Costs, Alphabet CFO Says," *Wall Street Journal*, October 7, 2015, https://www.wsj.com/articles/google-reorganization-isnt-about-cutting-costs-alphabet-cfo-says-1444258203.

2 Corning's strategy and capital allocation framework is described in the company's 2016 annual report, https://investor.corning.com/investor-relations/our-strategy/our-corporate-strategy/strategy-and-capital-allocation-framework/default.aspx.

3 Data source: S&P Capital IQ, Intel, public company profile, Capital IQ, Inc., a division of Standard & Poor's.

4 Data source: S&P Capital IQ, Microsoft, public company profile, Capital IQ, Inc., a division of Standard & Poor's.

5 Data source: S&P Capital IQ, Apple, public company profile, Capital IQ, Inc., a division of Standard & Poor's.

6 On the EMI CAT scanner case, see David J. Teece, "Profiting from Technological Innovation: Implications for Integration, Collaboration, Licensing and Public Policy," *Research Policy* 15 (1986): 285–305.

7 comScore, "Share of Search Queries Handled by Leading U.S. Search Engine Providers as of January 2018," accessed April 4, 2018, www.statista.com /statistics/267161/market-share-of-search-engines-in-the-united-states/.

8 Alphabet, "Google's Ad Revenue from 2001 to 2017," https://www.statista.com /statistics/266249/advertising-revenue-of-google/; GroupM, "Global Advertising Spending from 2010 to 2018 (in Billion U.S. Dollars)," accessed April 4, 2018, www.statista.com/statistics/236943/global-advertising-spending/.

9 Data source: S&P Capital IQ, Goodyear, public company profile, Capital IQ, Inc., a division of Standard & Poor's.

10 The first authors to make this argument and demonstrate it through case work were William Abernathy, Kim Clark, and Alan Kantrow, *Industrial Renaissance: Producing a Competitive Future for America* (New York: Basic Books, 1983).

11 Mike Isaac and Michael de la Merced, "Dollar Shave Club Sells to Unilever for $1 Billion," *New York Times,* July 20, 2016, https://www.nytimes.com /2016/07/20/business/dealbook/unilever-dollar-shave-club.html.

12 Christensen, *Innovator's Dilemma.*

13 The concept of technological paradigms was first introduced by Giovanni Dosi, "Technological Paradigms and Trajectories: A Suggested Interpretation of the Determinants and Directions of Technical Change," *Research Policy* 11, no. 3 (1982): 147–162; Thomas Kuhn, *The Structure of Scientific Revolutions* (Chicago: University of Chicago Press, 1962).

14 There is an entire stream of literature on the concept of punctuated equilibrium, which demonstrates this point with extensive case study evidence. See, for example, Elaine Romanelli and Michael L. Tushman, "Organizational Transformation as Punctuated Equilibrium: An Empirical Test," *Academy of Management Journal* 37, no. 5 (1994): 1141–1166; Kim Clark, The Interaction of Design Hierarchies and Market Concepts in Technological Evolution," *Research Policy* 14, no. 5 (October 1985): 235–251; Daniel A. Levinthal, "The Slow Pace of Rapid Technological Change: Gradualism and Punctuation in Technological Change," *Industrial and Corporate Change* 7, no. 2 (1998): 217–247.

15 M. Mitchel Waldrop, "More Than Moore," *Nature* 530, no. 11 (February 2016): 145–147.

16 See, e.g., Tushman and Anderson, "Technological Discontinuities and Organizational Environments"; Henderson and Clark, "Architectural Innovation."

17 Richard Levin, Alvin Klevorick, Richard Nelson, and Sidney Winter, "Appropriating the Returns from Industrial Research," *Brooking Papers on Economic Activity* 3 (1987): 783–820; Teece, "Profiting from Innovation"; Gary Pisano and David Teece, "How to Capture Value from Innovation: Shaping Intellectual Property and Industry Architecture," *California Management Review* 50, no. 1 (Fall 2007): 278–296.

18 Trefis Team, "Gigafactory Will Cost Tesla $5 Billion but Offers Significant Cost Reductions," *Forbes,* March 11, 2014, https://www.forbes.com /sites/greatspeculations/2014/03/11/gigafactory-will-cost-tesla-5-billion -but-offers-significant-cost-reductions/.

19 Jan W. Rivkin, "Imitation of Complex Strategies," *Management Science* 46, no. 6 (June 2000): 824–844; Jan W. Rivkin and Nicolaj Siggelkow, "Balancing Search and Stability: Interdependencies Among Elements of Organizational Design," *Management Science* 49, no. 3 (March 2003): 290–311.

Chapter 3: Whatever Happened to Blockbuster?

1 Christensen, *Innovator's Dilemma.*

2 Ellen Huet, "Uber Tests Taking Even More from Its Drivers with 30% Commission," *Forbes,* May 18, 2015, www.forbes.com/sites/ellenhuet/2015/05/18 /uber-new-uberx-tiered-commission-30-percent/#3bfaa1a643f6.

3 Theodore Schleifer, "Uber's Latest Valuation: $72 Billion," recode, February 2, 2018, https://www.recode.net/2018/2/9/16996834/uber-latest-valuation -72-billion-waymo-lawsuit-settlement.

4 Willy Shih and Stephen Kaufman, "Netflix in 2011," Harvard Business Publishing, August 19, 2014.

5 Anthony Ramirez, "Blockbuster's Investing Led to Merger," *New York Times,* January 1, 1994, https://www.nytimes.com/1994/01/08/business /blockbuster-s-investing-led-to-merger.html; Joe Flint, "Blockbuster Will Pay Dividend Before Viacom Sheds Its Stake," *Wall Street Journal,* June 21, 2004, https://www.wsj.com/articles/SB108756739175941492.

6 Shih and Kaufman, "Netflix in 2011."

7 "Netflix Plans to Spend $6 Billion on New Shows, Blowing Away All but One of Its Rivals," CNBC.com, October 17, 2016, https://www.cnbc .com/2016/10/17/netflixs-6-billion-content-budget-in-2017-makes -it-one-of-the-top-spenders.html.

8 Bastian Halecker, Rene Bickmann, Katherine Holzle, "Failed Business Model Innovation—A Theoretical and Practical Illumination on a Feared Phenomenon," paper presented at the R&D Management Conference 2014, "Management of Applied R&D: Connecting High Valued Solutions with Future Markets," Stuttgart, Germany, June 3–4, 2014.

9 There is a long literature on reasoning by analogy. See, for example, Dedre Gentner and Keith J. Holyoak, "Reasoning and Learning by Analogy: Introduction," *American Psychologist* 52, no. 1 (1997): 32; Richard A. Posner,

"Legal Reason: The Use of Analogy in Legal Argument," *Cornell Law Review* 91 (2006): 761; and Giovanni Gavetti, Daniel A. Levinthal, and Jan W. Rivkin, "Strategy Making in Novel and Complex Worlds: The Power of Analogy," *Strategic Management Journal* 26, no. 8 (2005): 691–712; Giovanni Gavetti and Jan W. Rivkin, "How Strategists Really Think," *Harvard Business Review* 83, no. 4 (2005): 54–63.

10 See in particular, Gavetti, Levinthal, and Rivkin, "Strategy Making in Novel and Complex Worlds."

11 Daniel Schorn, "The Brain Behind Netflix: Lesley Stahl Profiles Company Founder Reed Hastings," *60 Minutes,* December 1, 2006, https://www.cbsnews.com/news/the-brain-behind-netflix/.

12 "EasyJet Annual Report 2016," http://corporate.easyjet.com/~/media/Files/E/Easyjet/pdf/investors/result-center-investor/annual-report-2016.pdf.

13 "EasyJet Annual Report 2016"; "Occupancy Rates," European Environment Agency, April 19, 2016, https://www.eea.europa.eu/publications/ENVISSUENo12/page029.html.

14 Tom Padwell, Pascal Courty, and Michael Jacobides, "easyCar (B)," London Business School case study, May 2003.

15 Padwell, Courty, and Jacobides, "easyCar (B)," 1.

16 "Model," *Wikipedia,* https://en.wikipedia.org/wiki/Model.

17 Rivkin, "Imitation of Complex Strategies."

18 "Alphabet (GOOG)," February 23, 2018, https://ycharts.com/companies/GOOG/market_cap.

19 See for instance Henry Chesbrough, *Open Innovation: The New Imperative for Creating and Profiting from Technology* (Boston: Harvard Business School Press, 2006).

20 Andrea Ovans, "Can You Patent Your Business Model?" *Harvard Business Review,* July/August 2000, https://hbr.org/2000/07/can-you-patent-your-business-model.

21 Gene Quinn, "Patenting Business Methods and Software Still Requires Concrete and Tangible Descriptions," IP Watchdog, August 29, 2015, www.ipwatchdog.com/2015/08/29/patenting-business-methods-and-software/id=54576/; Miku Mehta and Laura Moskowitz, "Business Method Patents in the United States: A Judicial History & Prosecution Practice," Sughrue Mion, PLLC, 2004.

22 Felix Gillette, "The Rise and Inglorious Fall of MySpace," *Bloomberg BusinessWeek,* June 22, 2011, https://bloomberg.com/news/articles/2011-06-22/the-rise-and-inglorious-fall-of-myspace; Pete Cashmore, "MySpace, America's Number One," Mashable.com, July 11, 2006, https://mashable.com/2006/07/11/myspace-americas-number-one/#lIaCagigG5qq.

23 Nicholas Jackson, "As MySpace Sells for $35 Million, a History of the Network's Valuation," *Atlantic,* June 29, 2011, https://www.theatlantic.com

/technology/archive/2011/06/as-myspace-sells-for-35-million-a-history
-of-the-networks-valuation/241224/.

24 Rani Molla, "Closing the Books on Microsoft's Windows Phone," July 17, 2017, recode, www.recode.net/2017/7/17/15984222/microsoft-windows -phone-mobile-operating-system-android-iphone-ios.

25 Robert Huckman, Gary Pisano, and Liz Kind, "Amazon Web Services," Harvard Business Publishing, case no. 609-048, February 3, 2012.

Chapter 4: Is the Party Really Over?

1 Liu Chuanzhi, "The Man Who Bought IBM," *Fortune,* December 27, 2004, http://archive.fortune.com/magazines/fortune/fortune_archive/2004/12 /27/8217968/index.htm.

2 Timothy Green, "IBMs New Mainframe Is a Security Powerhouse," *Motley Fool,* July 17, 2017, https://www.fool.com/investing/2017/07/17/ibms-new -mainframe-is-a-security-powerhouse.aspx.

3 Dan Strohl, "Ford, Edison and the Cheap EV That Almost Was," *Wired,* https://www.wired.com/2010/06/henry-ford-thomas-edison-ev/.

4 Strohl, "Ford, Edison and the Cheap EV That Almost Was."

5 "Another Wonder of the Age on the Threshold," Proquest Historical Newspapers, *The Wall Street Journal (1889–1922),* April 24, 1917.

6 "Electric Vehicles Increase," Proquest Historical Newspapers, *The Wall Street Journal (1889–1922),* July 17, 1917.

7 "This Day in History: August 17," History.com, accessed April 4, 2018, https://www.history.com/this-day-in-history/charles-kettering-receives -patent-for-electric-self-starter.

8 "Model T Facts," History.com, accessed April 4, 2018, https://www.history .com/topics/model-t.

9 Between 1900 and 1910, annual US field crude oil production tripled from 63,621,000 barrels to 183,171,000, passing 1 billion barrels in 1929. US Energy Information Administration, US Department of Energy, "U.S. Field Oil Production," Washington, DC, https://www.eia.gov/dnav/pet/hist /LeafHandler.ashx?n=PET&s=MCRFPUS1&f=A.

10 Forney Museum of Transportation, "1916 Detroit Electric Opera Coupe," accessed January 2018, http://www.forneymuseum.org/FE_Detroit_Electric .html.

11 Chinhui Juhn, Aimee Chin, and Peter Thompson, "Technical Change and the Wage Structure During the Second Industrial Revolution: Evidence from the Merchant Marine, 1865–1912," no. 2004-03, 2004, NBER working paper no. 10728, https://www.nber.org/papers/w10728, 5–7.

12 Bosch, "Gasoline Direct Injection: Key Technology for Greater Efficiency and Dynamics," accessed April 4, 2018, http://www.bosch.co.jp/tms2015/en /products/pdf/Bosch_di_folder.pdf; Daniel Snow, "Extraordinary Efficiency

Growth in Response to New Technology Entries: The Carburetor's Last Gasp," *Academy of Management Proceedings,* no. 1 (2004): 9–11.

13 Tony Long, "May 2, 1952: First Commercial Jet Flies from London to Johannesburg," *Wired,* April 2, 2012, https://www.wired.com/2012/05 /may-2-1952-first-commercial-jet-flies-from-london-to-johannesburg/.

14 IDC, "Shipment Forecast of Tablets, Laptops and Desktop PCs Worldwide from 2010 to 2022 (in Million Units)," accessed April 3, 2018, www.statista .com/statistics/272595/global-shipments-forecast-for-tablets-laptops-and -desktop-pcs/.

15 IDC, "Shipment Forecast."

16 World Bank, "Number of Bank Branches for United States," Federal Reserve Bank of St. Louis, accessed February 23, 2018, https://fred.stlouisfed .org/series/DDAI02USA643NWDB.

17 Pew Research Center, "State of the News Media 2016," June 2016, http:// www.journalism.org/2016/06/15/newspapers-fact-sheet/.

18 Juan Alcacer, Tarun Khanna, and Christine Snively, "The Rise and Fall of Nokia," Harvard Business School, case no. 714428, January 2014.

19 The remaining share was held by Microsoft (2.9 percent) and RIM (3 percent). See https://www.statista.com/statistics/266136/global-market-share-held-by -smartphone-operating-systems/.

20 Based on the CDC's biannual National Health Interview Survey of approximately 20,000 US households: "Landline Phones Are a Dying Breed," Statista, https://infographic.statista.com/normal/chartoftheday_2072_Landline _phones_in_the_United_States_n.jpg.

21 Gary Pisano, David Collis, and Peter Botticelli, "Intel Corporation: 1968–1997," Harvard Business School, case no. 797-137, May 1997.

22 Collis and Pisano, "Intel Corporation."

23 Ron Adner and Daniel C. Snow, "Old Technology Responses to New Technology Threats: Demand Heterogeneity and Technology Retreats," *Industrial and Corporate Change* 19, no. 5 (2010): 1655–1675.

24 Willy Shih, "The Real Lessons of Kodak's Decline," *Sloan Management Review,* Summer 2016, 11–13.

25 Shih's account is also consistent with the work of external observers. See, for example, Giovanni Gavetti, Rebecca Henderson, and Simona Giorgi, "Kodak and the Digital Revolution (A)," Harvard Business School, case no. 705-448.

26 Shih, "Real Lessons of Kodak's Decline," 11.

27 Michael Porter, *Competitive Strategy* (New York: The Free Press, 1980).

28 A comprehensive study in 2016 of fifty-one US newspapers from 2007 to 2015 shows that revenues from online readership have not increased enough to offset declines in print revenue. As the authors describe it, "The result of newspaper firms' transitions from print to online is, in the business sense, 'exchanging analog dollars for digital dimes.'" Brad Dick, "Spending

Analog Dollars to Get Digital Pennies," *TV Technology,* January 14, 2009, http://www.tvtechnology.com/default.aspx?tabid=204&entryid=1097), cited in Chyi Hsiang Iris and Ori Teneboim, "Reality Check: Multiplatform Newspaper Readership in the United States, 2007–2015," *Journalism Practice* (July 2016): 1–22, http://www.tandfonline.com/doi/full/10.1080/17512786.2016.1208056.

29 Data source: S&P Capital IQ, Walmart, public company profile, Capital IQ, Inc., a division of Standard & Poor's.

30 Amazon, "2016 Annual Report," http://www.annualreports.com/Hosted Data/AnnualReports/PDF/NASDAQ_AMZN_2016.pdf.

31 James Temperton, "Uber's 2016 Losses to Top $3bn According to Leaked Financials," *Wired,* December 20, 2016, http://www.wired.co.uk/article/uber -finances-losses-driverless-cars.

32 Biz Carson, "Lyft Promises Not to Lose More Than $600 Million a Year," *Business Insider,* April 14, 2016, http://www.businessinsider.com/lyft-promises -investors-to-cap-losses-2016-4.

33 Shih, "Real Lessons of Kodak's Decline."

34 Erwin Danneels, "Trying to Become a Different Type of Company: Dynamic Capability at Smith Corona," *Strategic Management Journal 32,* no. 1 (2011): 1–31; Mary Tripsas, "Technology, Identity, and Inertia Through the Lens of 'The Digital Photography Company,'" *Organization Science* 20, no. 2 (2009): 443.

35 Albert J. Churella, *From Steam to Diesel* (Princeton, NJ: Princeton University Press, 1998), 65–66.

Chapter 5: Venturing Outside Your Home Court

1 This section of the chapter draws from my case study on Honda Aircraft Corporation. Gary Pisano and Jesse Shulman, "Flying into the Future: Honda Aircraft Corporation," Harvard Business School, case no. 9-618-012.

2 Ashley Burns, "HondaJet Is Most Delivered Jet in First Half of 2017," *Flying,* August 17, 2017, https://www.flyingmag.com/hondajet-is-most-delivered -light-jet-2017s-first-half.

3 This section draws from information contained in "Du Pont Kevlar® Aramid Industrial Fiber," Harvard Business School, case no. 391-146, written by David A. Hounshell, Marvin Bower Fellow, and Richard S. Rosenbloom, and later abridged by Clayton Christensen and published as "DuPont Kevlar Aramid Industrial Fiber (Abridged)," Harvard Business School, case no. 9-698-079. Information is also drawn from Laura Hayes, "Tough Fiber: DuPont Difficulties Selling Kevlar Show Hurdles of Innovation," *Wall Street Journal,* September 29, 1987, 1.

4 "Going Up?" *Site Selection,* September 2011, https://siteselection.com/online Insider/Going-Up.cfm.

5 See Christensen, *Innovator's Dilemma.*

6 On this issue, see Clark, "Interaction of Design Hierarchies and Market Concepts."

7 Jordan Ellenberg, *How Not to Be Wrong: The Power of Mathematical Thinking* (New York: Penguin, 2015).

8 See for example, Christian R. Østergaard, Bram Timmermans, Kari Kristinsson, "Does a Different View Create Something New? The Effect of Employee Diversity on Innovation," *Research Policy* 40, no. 3 (2011): 500–509, https://doi.org/10.1016/j.respol.2010.11.004; Claudio Dell'Era and Roberto Verganti, "Collaborative Strategies in Design-Intensive Industries: Knowledge Diversity and Innovation," *Long Range Planning* 43, no. 1 (2010): 123–141, https://doi.org/10.1016/j.lrp.2009.10.006.

9 John Gertner, *The Idea Factory: Bell Labs and the Great Age of American Innovation* (New York: Penguin, 2012).

10 On the concept of learning from analogies more broadly, see Gentner and Holyoak, "Reasoning and Learning by Analogy," 32; Posner, "Legal Reason," 761; Gavetti, Levinthal, and Rivkin, "Strategy Making in Novel and Complex Worlds"; Gavetti, Giovanni, and Rivkin, "How Strategists Really Think."

11 "1973 Honda Civic," archived road test, *Road and Track Magazine,* March 1973, https://www.caranddriver.com/reviews/1973-honda-civic-test-review.

12 Hong Luo, Gary Pisano, and Yu Huafang, "Institutionalized Entrepreneurship: Flagship Pioneering," Harvard Business School, case no. 9-718-484, March 23, 2018.

13 Noubar Afeyan, interview by Gary Pisano, 2017.

14 Gertner, *Idea Factory.*

15 David M. Upton and Joshua D. Margolis, "McDonald's Corporation," Harvard Business School, case no. 693-028, October 1992, revised September 1996.

16 Eric von Hippel, *Free Innovation* (Cambridge, MA: MIT Press, 2016).

17 Andrew King and Karim R. Lakhani, "Using Open Innovation to Identify the Best Ideas," *MIT Sloan Management Review,* 55, no. 1 (Fall 2013): 41–48. See also Kevin Boudreau and Karim Lakhani, "How to Manage Outside Innovation," *MIT Sloan Management Review* 50, no. 4 (Summer 2009): 69–76.

18 "InnoCentive Solver Develops Solution to Help Clean Up Remaining Oil from the 1989 *Exxon Valdez* Disaster," November 7, 2007, https://www.innocentive.com/innocentive-solver-develops-solution-to-help-clean-up-remaining-oil-from-the-1989-exxon-valdez-disaster/.

Chapter 6: Synthesis

1 Joseph Schumpeter (translated by Ursula Backhaus), "The Theory of Economic Development," in *Joseph Alois Schumpeter: Entrepreneurship, Style and Vision,* ed. Jurgen Backhause, 61–116 (New York: Kluwer Academic, 2003).

2 Lee Fleming and Olaf Sorenson, "Technology as a Complex Adaptive System: Evidence from Patent Data," *Research Policy* 30 (2001): 1019–1039. They measured "technology components" by the number of technology subclasses assigned to each patent.

3 Rebecca Henderson and Ian Cockburn, "Scale, Scope and Spillovers: The Determinants of Research Productivity in the Drug Industry," *Rand Journal of Economics* 27, no. 1 (Spring 1996): 32–59.

4 Brian Uzzi, Satyam Mukherjee, Michael Stringer, and Ben Jones, "Atypical Combinations and Scientific Impact," *Science* 342, no. 6157 (2013): 468–472.

5 Walter Isaacson, *Steve Jobs* (New York: Simon & Schuster, 2011), 492. The quote is from Jimmy Iovine, CEO of Interscope-Geffen-A&M.

6 Fazioli company website, www.fazioli.com/en/.

7 Ed Catmull and Amy Wallace, *Creativity, Inc.: Overcoming the Unseen Forces That Stand in the Way of True Inspiration* (New York: Random House, 2014), 90.

8 Lee Fleming, "Finding the Organizational Sources of Technological Breakthroughs: The Story of Hewlett-Packard's Thermal Ink-Jet," *Industrial and Corporate Change* 11, no 5 (2002): 1059–1084.

9 Bezos, letter to the shareholders.

10 See, for example, Melvin Conway, "How Do Committees Invent?" 1968, www.melconway.com/Home/Committees_Paper.html; Henderson and Clark, "Architectural Innovation"; Stefano Brusoni, Andrea Prencipe, and Keith Pavitt, "Knowledge Specialization, Organizational Coupling, and the Boundaries of the Firm: Why Do Firms Know More Than They Make?" *Administrative Science Quarterly* 46, no. 4 (2001): 597–621; and Alan MacCormack, John Rusnak, and Carliss Baldwin, "The Impact of Component Modularity on Design Evolution: Evidence from the Software Industry," 2007.

11 Gertner, *Idea Factory*.

12 As John Gertner describes it in his detailed history of Bell Labs, *The Idea Factory:*

> By intention, everyone would be in one another's way. Members of the technical staff would have both laboratories and small offices—but these might be in different corridors, therefore making it necessary to walk between the two, and all but assuring a chance encounter or two with a colleague during the commute. By the same token, the long corridor for the wing that would house many of the physics researchers was intentionally made to be seven hundred feet in length.... Traveling its length without encountering a number of acquaintances, problems, diversions, and ideas would be almost impossible. Then again, that was the point.

13 Gertner, *Idea Factory*, 79.

14 Gertner, *Idea Factory,* 81–91.

15 The notion that organizational designs involve trade-off and that therefore the choice of design is contingent on strategic objectives goes back to Paul R. Lawrence and Jay W. Lorsch, "Differentiation and Integration in Complex Organizations," *Administrative Science Quarterly* (1967): 1–47.

16 The section that follows is based on the case study on Amazon Web Services that I coauthored with Robert Huckman and Liz Kind ("Amazon Web Services"). All quotes and company specific information originate from that case.

17 Amazon, "2016 Annual Report."

18 Huckman, Pisano, and Kind, "Amazon Web Services."

19 Information drawn from Regina Dugan and Kaigham Gabriel, "Special Forces Innovation: How DARPA Attacks Problems," *Harvard Business Review,* October 2013, reprint R1310C.

20 Dugan and Gabriel, "Special Forces Innovation," 8.

Chapter 7: When to Hold 'Em and When to Fold 'Em

1 Information regarding Vertex events are sourced from Harvard Business School case, "Vertex Pharmaceuticals (A)," no. 9-604-101 written by Gary Pisano, Lee Fleming, and Eli Strick.

2 Todd R. Weiss, "Timeline: PARC Milestones," *Computerworld,* September 20, 2010, accessed November 6, 2017, computerworld.com; Douglas K. Smith and Robert C. Alexander, *Fumbling the Future: How Xerox Invented Then Ignored the First Personal Computer* (Lincoln, NE: iUniverse, 1999).

3 "Cutting the Cord," *Economist,* October 7, 1999, http://www.economist.com/node/246152.

4 Harry McCracken, "Shocker: In 1980, Motorola Had No Idea Where the Phone Market Would Be in 2000," *Time,* April 15, 2014, http://time.com/63718/shocker-in-1980-motorola-had-no-idea-where-the-phone-market-would-be-in-2000/.

5 Andrew Kupfer and Kathleen Smyth, "AT&T'S $12 Billion Cellular Dream," *Fortune,* December 12, 1994, http://archive.fortune.com/magazines/fortune/fortune_archive/1994/12/12/80051/index.htm.

6 Mary Tripsas and Giovanni Gavetti, "Capabilities, Cognition, and Inertia: Evidence from Digital Imaging," *Strategic Management Journal* 21, nos. 10–11 (2000): 1147–1161.

7 The term "unknown unknowns" came into popular discourse in the early 2000s when Secretary of Defense Donald Rumsfeld used it to describe the challenges of assessing whether Iraq possessed weapons of mass destruction (February 12, 2002). He later wrote a book with the term in the title: Donald Rumsfeld, *Known and Unknown: A Memoir* (New York: Penguin Group, 2011), xiv.

However, the basic concept of unknown unknowns goes back to economist Franklin Knight in the early 1920s. In his book *Risk, Uncertainty and Profit*, published in 1921 (Mineola, NY: Dover), Wright distinguished between "primary uncertainty" and "secondary uncertainty."

8 The literature on this topic has exploded over the past few decades. I refer interested readers to: Daniel Kahneman, Paul Slovic, and Amos Tversky, eds., *Judgment Under Uncertainty: Heuristics and Biases* (Cambridge: Cambridge University Press, 1982); Max Bazerman and Don Moore, *Judgment in Managerial Decision Making* (New York: Wiley, 2008); Daniel Ariely, *Predictably Irrational: The Hidden Forces That Shape Our Decisions* (New York: HarperCollins, 2008); Francesca Gino, *Sidetracked: Why Our Decisions Get Derailed, and How We Can Stick to the Plan* (Boston: Harvard Business Review Press, 2013).

9 Clay Christensen, Stephen Kaufman, and Willy Shih, "Innovation Killers: How Financial Tools Destroy Your Capacity to Do New Things," *Harvard Business Review,* January 2008.

10 David Garvin and Michael Roberto, "What You Don't Know About Making Decisions," *Harvard Business Review,* September 2001, reprint R0108G.

11 Here again on this point, see Garvin and Roberto, "What You Don't Know About Making Decisions."

12 Rita Gunther McGrath and Ian MacMillan propose a similar approach to resource allocation they call "discovery-driven planning," which also focuses heavily on identifying and testing critical assumptions. Rita Gunther McGrath and Ian C. MacMillan, *Discovery-Driven Planning* (Philadelphia: Wharton School, Snider Entrepreneurial Center, 1995). There are two differences between their approach and the approach I describe. In discovery-driven planning, financial analysis is reduced to identifying critical assumptions. In the approach I describe, financial analysis remains an integral part of the selection process and is used to drive the development and testing of critical program assumptions and hypotheses. Second, the focus of discovery-driven planning is to force identification of buried assumptions. In the approach I described, the hypotheses themselves represent the main rationale for undertaking the project. Their development and articulation are essential to the proposal.

13 Graham Allison, *The Essence of Decision: Explaining the Cuban Missile Crisis* (New York: Little Brown, 1971); Stephen Bates, Richard Neustadt, Joshua Rosenbloom, and Ernest May, "Kennedy and the Bay of Pigs," Harvard Kennedy School, case no. KHS009-PDF-ENG, January 1, 1980.

14 Geoffrey Perret, *Eisenhower* (New York: Random House, 2000).

15 Gary Pisano, Phillip Andrews, and Alessandro Di Fiore, "Fiat-Chrysler Alliance: Launching the Cinquecento in North America," Harvard Business School, case no. 9-611-037, 2011.

Chapter 8: The Paradox of Innovative Cultures

1 Amy C. Edmondson, "Psychological Safety and Learning Behavior in Work Teams," *Administrative Science Quarterly* 44, no. 2 (1999): 350–383.
2 Amy Edmondson, Richard Bohmer, and Gary Pisano, "Disrupted Routines: Team Learning and New Technology Implementation in Hospitals," *Administrative Science Quarterly* 46, no. 6 (2001): 685–716.
3 On this point, see Mark Cannon and Amy Edmondson, "Failing to Learn and Learning to Fail (Intelligently)," *Long Range Planning* 38 (2005): 299–319.
4 Tom Lamont, "How Get a Job at Google: Meet the Man Who Hires and Fires," *Guardian,* April 6, 2015, https://www.theguardian.com/technology/2015/apr/04/how-to-get-job-at-google-meet-man-hires-fires.
5 Catmull and Wallace, *Creativity, Inc.*
6 Catmull and Wallace, *Creativity, Inc.*
7 Francesca Gino, Gary Pisano, and Brad Staats, "Pal's Sudden Service: Scaling an Organizational Model to Drive Growth," Harvard Business School, case no. 916-052.
8 "Fact Sheet: Normandy Landings," White House, Office of the Press Secretary, June 6, 2014, https://obamawhitehouse.archives.gov/the-press-office/2014/06/06/fact-sheet-normandy-landings.

Chapter 9: Leaders as Cultural Architects

1 Catmull and Wallace, *Creativity, Inc.,* 5.
2 Satya Nadella, *Hit Refresh: The Quest to Rediscover Microsoft's Soul and Imagine a Better Future for Everyone* (New York: HarperCollins, 2017), 100, emphasis mine.
3 On imprinting, see A. L. Stinchcombe, "Social Structure and Organizations," in *Handbook of Organizations,* ed. J. G. March, 142–193 (Chicago: Rand McNally, 1965); M. T. Hannan and J. Freeman, *Organizational Ecology* (Cambridge, MA: Harvard University Press, 1989); A. Swaminathan, "Environmental Conditions at Founding and Organizational Mortality: A Trial-by-Fire Model," *Academy of Management Journal* 39 (1996): 1350–1377.
4 Pisano, Andrews, and di Fiore, "Fiat-Chrysler Alliance."
5 C. Copley, "Analysis: After Roche Merger, Biotech Tail Wags Big Pharma Dog," Thomson Reuters (Zurich, 2012); Erika Check Hayden, "Roche Vows to Keep Genentech Culture" (2009): 270; Marne Arthaud-Day, Frank T. Rothaermel, and Wei Zhang, "Genentech (in 2011): After the Acquisition by Roche," McGraw-Hill Education, case study no. MH0014, 2012.
6 Robert Huckman and Eli Strick, "GlaxoSmithKline: Reorganizing Drug Discovery (A)," Harvard Business School, case no. 9-605-074.
7 Microsoft Corporation, "Earnings Release FY18 Q2," https://www.microsoft.com/en-us/Investor/earnings/FY-2018-Q2/balance-sheets.

8 Pisano, Andrews, and di Fiore, "Fiat-Chrysler Alliance."

9 "Alphabet," Yahoo Finance, March 9, 2018, https://finance.yahoo.com /quote/GOOG/.

Chapter 10: Becoming a Creative Constructive Leader

1 James Niccolai, "Gateway to Close All Retail Shops," *PCWorld,* April 1, 2004, https://www.pcworld.com/article/115507/article.html.

2 Robert J. Gordon, *The Rise and Fall of American Growth: The U.S. Standard of Living Since the Civil War,* The Princeton Economic History of the Western World (Princeton, NJ: Princeton University Press, 2017).

Bibliography

Abernathy, William, and Kim Clark. "Innovation: Mapping the Winds of Creative Destruction." *Research Policy* 14 (1985): 3–22.

Abernathy, William, Kim Clark, and Alan Kantrow. *Industrial Renaissance: Producing a Competitive Future for America*. New York: Basic Books, 1983.

Abernathy, William, and James Utterback. "Patterns of Industrial Innovation." *Technology Review* 80, no. 7 (1978): 40–47.

Adner, Ron, and Daniel C. Snow. "Old Technology Responses to New Technology Threats: Demand Heterogeneity and Technology Retreats." *Industrial and Corporate Change* 19, no. 5 (2010): 1655–1675.

Alcacer, Juan, Tarun Khanna, and Christine Snively. "The Rise and Fall of Nokia." Harvard Business School, case no. 714428.

Allison, Graham, and Philip Zelikow. *The Essence of Decision: Explaining the Cuban Missile Crisis*. New York: Little, Brown, 1971.

"Alphabet." Fortune 500. *Fortune*, April 6, 2018. fortune.com/fortune500 /alphabet/.

Alphabet. "Google's Ad Revenue from 2001 to 2017 (in Billion U.S. Dollars)." Accessed April 4, 2018. www.statista.com/statistics/266249/advertising -revenue-of-google/.

"Alphabet." Yahoo Finance, March 9, 2018. finance.yahoo.com/quote/GOOG/.

"Alphabet (GOOG)." February 23, 2018. ycharts.com/companies/GOOG /market_cap.

Amazon. "2016 Annual Report." www.annualreports.com/HostedData/Annual Reports/PDF/NASDAQ_AMZN_2016.pdf.

"Amazon: Financials." Yahoo Finance. finance.yahoo.com/quote/AMZN /financials?p=AMZN.

"Another Wonder of the Age on the Threshold." Proquest Historical Newspapers, *The Wall Street Journal (1889–1922)*, April 24, 1917.

Ariely, Dan. *Predictably Irrational: The Hidden Forces That Shape Our Decisions*. New York: HarperCollins, 2004.

Arthaud-Day, Marne, Frank T. Rothaermel, and Wei Zhang. "Genentech in 2011: After the Acquisition by Roche." McGraw-Hill Education, case study no. MH0014. 2012.

"Audi on Demand, Frequently Asked Questions." 2018. www.us.audiondemand .com/us/service/en_ondemand/nav/faq.html.

Baldwin, Carliss, and Kim Clark. *Design Rules: The Power of Modularity—Volume.* Boston: MIT Press, 1990. See also IBM Archives, www-03.ibm.com /ibm/history/exhibits/mainframe/mainframe_PR360.html.

Bates, Stephen, Richard Neustadt, Joshua Rosenbloom, and Ernest May. "Kennedy and the Bay of Pigs." Harvard Kennedy School, case no. KHS009-PDF-ENG, January 1, 1980.

Baum, Andrew, Peter Verdult, C. C. Chugbo, et al. "Pharmaceuticals: Exit Research and Create Value." Morgan Stanley Research, January 20, 2010.

Bazerman, Max, and Don Moore. *Judgment in Managerial Decision Making.* New York: Wiley, 2012.

Bezos, Jeff. Letter to the shareholders, 2015. Amazon.com. drive.google.com /file/d/0BzVmPBUYS4gaVE9Cc2tualVLMjA/view.

Bosch. "Gasoline Direct Injection: Key Technology for Greater Efficiency and Dynamics." Accessed April 4, 2018. www.bosch.co.jp/tms2015/en/products /pdf/Bosch_di_folder.pdf.

Boston Consulting Group. "A Brave New World of M&A: How to Create Value from Mergers and Acquisitions." July 2007.

Boudreau, Kevin, and Karim Lakhani. "How to Manage Outside Innovation." *MIT Sloan Management Review* 50, no. 4 (Summer 2009): 69–76.

Brusoni, Stefano, Andrea Prencipe, and Keith Pavitt. "Knowledge Specialization, Organizational Coupling, and the Boundaries of the Firm: Why Do Firms Know More Than They Make?" *Administrative Science Quarterly* 46, no. 4 (2001): 597–621.

Burns, Ashley. "HondaJet Is Most Delivered Jet in First Half of 2017." *Flying,* August 17, 2017. www.flyingmag.com/hondajet-is-most-delivered-light-jet -2017s-first-half.

Cannon, Mark, and Amy Edmondson. "Failing to Learn and Learning to Fail Intelligently." *Long Range Planning* 38 (2005): 299–319.

Carson, Biz. "Lyft Promises Not to Lose More Than $600 Million a Year." *Business Insider,* April 14, 2016. www.businessinsider.com/lyft-promises-investors -to-cap-losses-2016-4.

Cashmore, Pete. "MySpace, America's Number One." Mashable.com, July 11, 2006. mashable.com/2006/07/11/myspace-americas-number-one/#lIaCagigG5qq.

Catmull, Ed, and Amy Wallace. *Creativity, Inc.: Overcoming the Unseen Forces That Stand in the Way of True Inspiration.* New York: Random House, 2014.

Chesbrough, Henry. *Open Innovation: The New Imperative for Creating and Profiting from Technology.* Boston: Harvard Business School Press, 2006.

Chin, Aimee, Chinhui Juhn, and Peter Thompson. "Technical Change and the Demand for Skills During the Second Industrial Revolution: Evidence from the Merchant Marine, 1891–1912." *Review of Economics and Statistics* 88 (August 3, 2008): 572–578.

Christensen, Clayton. "DuPont Kevlar Aramid Industrial Fiber (Abridged)." Harvard Business School, case no. 9-698-079.

Christensen, Clayton. *The Innovator's Dilemma*. Boston: Harvard Business Review Press, 1997.

Christensen, Clay, Stephen Kaufman, and Willy Shih. "Innovation Killers: How Financial Tools Destroy Your Capacity to Do New Things." *Harvard Business Review,* January 2008.

Chuanzhi, Liu. "The Man Who Bought IBM." *Fortune,* December 27, 2004. archive.fortune.com/magazines/fortune/fortune_archive/2004/12/27/8217968 /index.htm.

Churella, Albert J. *From Steam to Diesel.* Princeton, NJ: Princeton University Press, 1998.

Chyi Hsiang Iris and Ori Teneboim. "Reality Check: Multiplatform Newspaper Readership in the United States, 2007–2015." *Journalism Practice* (July 2016): 1–22. www.tandfonline.com/doi/full/10.1080/17512786.2016.1208056.

Clark, Kim. "The Interaction of Design Hierarchies and Market Concepts in Technological Evolution." *Research Policy* 14, no. 5 (October 1985): 235–251.

Cohen, Wesley. "Fifty Years of Empirical Studies of Innovative Activity and Performance." In *Handbook of the Economics of Innovation,* edited by B. H. Hall and N. Rosenberg, 129–213. Amsterdam: North Holland Elsevier, 2010.

Collis, David, and Gary Pisano. "Intel Corporation: 1968–1997." Harvard Business School, case no. 9-797-137.

comScore. "Share of Search Queries Handled by Leading U.S. Search Engine Providers as of January 2018." Accessed April 4, 2018. www.statista.com /statistics/267161/market-share-of-search-engines-in-the-united-states/.

Conway, Melvin. "How Do Committees Invent?" 1968. www.melconway .com/Home/Committees_Paper.html.

Copley, C. "Analysis: After Roche Merger, Biotech Tail Wags Big Pharma Dog." Thomson Reuters. Zurich, 2012.

"Corning 2016 Annual Report." investor.corning.com/investor-relations/our -strategy/our-corporate-strategy/strategy-and-capital-allocation-framework /default.aspx.

"Cutting the Chord." *Economist,* October 7, 1999. www.economist.com /node/246152.

Danneels, Erwin. "Trying to Become a Different Type of Company: Dynamic Capability at Smith Corona." *Strategic Management Journal* 32, no. 1 (2011): 1–31.

Dell'Era, Claudio, and Roberto Verganti. "Collaborative Strategies in Design-Intensive Industries: Knowledge Diversity and Innovation." *Long Range Planning* 43, no. 1 (2010): 123–141. https://doi.org/10.1016/j.lrp.2009.10.006.

Dick, Brad. "Spending Analog Dollars to Get Digital Pennies." *TV Technology,* January 14, 2009. https://www.tvtechnology.com/be-blogs/1097.

Dosi, Giovanni. "Technological Paradigms and Technological Trajectories: A Suggested Interpretation of the Determinants and Directions of Technical Change." *Research Policy* 11, no. 3 (1982): 147–162.

Dugan, Regin, and Kaigham Gabriel. "Special Forces Innovation: How DARPA Attacks Problems." *Harvard Business Review,* October 2013. Reprint R1310C.

"EasyJet Annual Report 2016." corporate.easyjet.com/~/media/Files/E/Easyjet /pdf/investors/result-center-investor/annual-report-2016.pdf.

Edmondson, Amy C. "Psychological Safety and Learning Behavior in Work Teams." *Administrative Science Quarterly* 44, no. 2 (1999): 350–383.

Edmondson, Amy, Richard Bohmer, and Gary Pisano. "Disrupted Routines: Team Learning and New Technology Implementation in Hospitals." *Administrative Science Quarterly* 46, no. 6 (2001): 685–716.

"Electric Vehicles Increase: Taxicabs Run by Electricity Fast Taking the Place of Gasoline Cars in Large Cities." ProQuest Historical Newspapers, *The Wall Street Journal (1889–1922),* July 17, 1917.

Ellenberg, Jordan. *How Not to Be Wrong: The Power of Mathematical Thinking.* New York: Penguin, 2015.

"Fact Sheet: Normandy Landings." White House, Office of the Press Secretary, June 06, 2014, obamawhitehouse.archives.gov/the-press-office/2014/06/06 /fact-sheet-normandy-landings.

Fleming, Lee. "Finding the Organizational Sources of Technological Breakthroughs: The Story of Hewlett-Packard's Thermal Ink-Jet." *Industrial and Corporate Change* 11, no. 5 (2002): 1059–1084.

Fleming, Lee, and Olaf Sorenson. "Technology as a Complex Adaptive System: Evidence from Patent Data." *Research Policy* 30 (2001): 1019–1039.

Flint, Joe. "Blockbuster Will Pay Dividend Before Viacom Sheds Its Stake." *Wall Street Journal,* June 21, 2004. www.wsj.com/articles/SB108756739175941492.

Forney Museum of Transportation. "1916 Detroit Electric Opera Coupe." Accessed January 2018. www.forneymuseum.org/FE_Detroit_Electric.html.

"Fortune 500 Archive, 1964 Full List." *Fortune.* archive.fortune.com/magazines /fortune/fortune500_archive/full/1964/.

"Fortune 500 Archive, 2004 Full List." *Fortune.* archive.fortune.com/magazines /fortune/fortune500_archive/full/2004/301.html.

"Fortune 500 2007." *Fortune.* fortune.com/fortune500/2007/.

Garvin, David, and Michael Roberto. "What You Don't Know About Making Decisions." *Harvard Business Review,* September 2001. Reprint R0108G.

Gavetti, Giovanni, Rebecca Henderson, and Simona Giorgi. "Kodak and the Digital Revolution A." Harvard Business School, case no. 705-448.

Gavetti, Giovanni, Daniel A. Levinthal, and Jan W. Rivkin. "Strategy Making in Novel and Complex Worlds: The Power of Analogy." *Strategic Management Journal* 26, no. 8 (2005): 691–712.

Gavetti, Giovanni, and Jan W. Rivkin. "How Strategists Really Think." *Harvard Business Review* 83, no. 4 (2005): 54–63.

Gentner, Dedre, and Keith J. Holyoak. "Reasoning and Learning by Analogy: Introduction." *American Psychologist* 52, no. 1 (1997): 32.

Gertner, John. *The Idea Factory: Bell Labs and the Great Age of American Innovation.* New York: Penguin, 2012.

Gillette, Felix. "The Rise and Inglorious Fall of MySpace." *Bloomberg BusinessWeek,* June 22, 2011. bloomberg.com/news/articles/2011-06-22/the-rise-and-inglorious-fall-of-myspace.

Gino, Francesca. *Sidetracked: Why Our Decisions Get Derailed, and How We Can Stick to the Plan.* Boston: Harvard Business Review Press, 2013.

Gino, Francesca, Gary Pisano, and Brad Staats. "Pal's Sudden Service: Scaling an Organizational Model to Drive Growth." Harvard Business School, case no. 916-052.

"Going Up?" *Site Selection,* September 2011. siteselection.com/onlineInsider/Going-Up.cfm.

Google. "Google's Revenue Worldwide from 2002 to 2017 (in Billion U.S. Dollars)." Accessed April 4, 2018. www.statista.com/statistics/266206/googles-annual-global-revenue/.

Gordon, Robert J. *The Rise and Fall of American Growth: The U.S. Standard of Living Since the Civil War.* The Princeton Economic History of the Western World. Princeton, NJ: Princeton University Press, 2017.

Green, Timothy. "IBMs New Mainframe Is a Security Powerhouse." *Motley Fool,* July 17, 2017. www.fool.com/investing/2017/07/17/ibms-new-mainframe-is-a-security-powerhouse.aspx.

GroupM. "Global Advertising Spending from 2010 to 2018 (in Billion U.S. Dollars)." Accessed April 4, 2018. www.statista.com/statistics/236943/global-advertising-spending/.

Halecker, Bastian, Rene Bickmann, and Katherine Holzle. "Failed Business Model Innovation—A Theoretical and Practical Illumination on a Feared Phenomenon." Paper presented at the R&D Management Conference, "Management of Applied R&D: Connecting High Valued Solutions with Future Markets." Stuttgart, Germany, June 3–4, 2014.

Hannan, M. T., and J. Freeman. *Organizational Ecology.* Cambridge, MA: Harvard University Press, 1989.

Hayden, Erika Check. "Roche Vows to Keep Genentech Culture." *Nature* 458 (2009): 270. https://www.nature.com/news/2009/090318/full/458270a.html.

Hayes, Laura. "Tough Fiber: DuPont Difficulties Selling Kevlar Show Hurdles of Innovation." *Wall Street Journal,* September 29, 1987.

Henderson, Rebecca M., and Kim B. Clark. "Architectural Innovation: The Reconfiguration of Existing Product Technologies and the Failure of Established Firms." *Administrative Science Quarterly* 35, no. 1 (1990): 9–30.

Henderson, Rebecca, and Ian Cockburn. "Scale, Scope and Spillovers: The Determinants of Research Productivity in the Drug Industry." *Rand Journal of Economics* 27, no. 1 (Spring 1996): 32–59.

Huckman, Robert, Gary Pisano, and Liz Kind. "Amazon Web Services." Harvard Business School, case no. 609-048, February 3, 2012.

Huckman, Robert, and Eli Strick. "GlaxoSmithKline: Reorganizing Drug Discovery (A)." Harvard Business School, case no. 9-605-074.

Huet, Ellen. "Uber Tests Taking Even More from Its Drivers with 30% Commission." *Forbes,* May 18, 2015. www.forbes.com/sites/ellenhuet/2015/05/18/uber-new-uberx-tiered-commission-30-percent/#3bfaa1a643f6.

IDC. "Shipment Forecast of Tablets, Laptops and Desktop PCs Worldwide from 2010 to 2022 (in Million Units)." Accessed April 3, 2018. www.statista.com/statistics/272595/global-shipments-forecast-for-tablets-laptops-and-desktop-pcs/.

Industrial Research Institute. "2017 Global R&D Funding Forecast." Supplement, *R&D Magazine,* Winter 2017, 7.

"InnoCentive Solver Develops Solution to Help Clean Up Remaining Oil from the 1989 Exxon Valdez Disaster." November 7, 2007. www.innocentive.com/innocentive-solver-develops-solution-to-help-clean-up-remaining-oil-from-the-1989-exxon-valdez-disaster/.

Isaac, Mike, and Michael de la Merced. "Dollar Shave Club Sells to Unilever for $1 Billion." *New York Times,* July 20, 2016. www.nytimes.com/2016/07/20/business/dealbook/unilever-dollar-shave-club.html.

Isaacson, Walter. *Steve Jobs.* New York: Simon & Schuster, 2011.

Jackson, Nicholas. "As MySpace Sells for $35 Million, a History of the Network's Valuation." *Atlantic,* June 29, 2011. www.theatlantic.com/technology/archive/2011/06/as-myspace-sells-for-35-million-a-history-of-the-networks-valuation/241224/.

Johnson & Johnson. Form 10-K 2017. Accessed March 2018. files.shareholder.com/downloads/JNJ/6058290261x0xS200406%2D18%2D5/200406/filing.pdf.

"Johnson & Johnson." Fortune 500. *Fortune,* April 2, 2018. fortune.com/fortune500/johnson-johnson/.

Johnson & Johnson. "Johnson & Johnson's Expenditure on Research and Development from 2005 to 2017 in Million U.S. dollars." Accessed March 29, 2018. www.statista.com/statistics/266407/research-and-development-expenditure-of-johnson-und-johnson-since-2006/.

Juhn, Chinhui, Aimee Chin, and Peter Thompson. "Technical Change and the Wage Structure During the Second Industrial Revolution: Evidence from the Merchant Marine, 1865–1912." No. 2004-03. 2004. NBER working paper no. 10728. https://www.nber.org/papers/w10728.

Kahneman, Daniel, Paul Slovic, and Amos Tversky, eds. *Judgment Under Uncertainty: Heuristics and Biases.* Cambridge: Cambridge University Press, 1982.

King, Andrew, and Karim R. Lakhani. "Using Open Innovation to Identify the Best Ideas." *MIT Sloan Management Review* 55, no. 1 (Fall 2013): 41–48.

Knight, Frank H. *Risk, Uncertainty and Profit.* Mineola, NY: Dover, 1921.

KPMG. "2017 Global Venture Capital Investment Hits Decade High of $155 Billion Following a Strong Q4: KPMG Venture Pulse." Press release, January 18,

2018. home.kpmg.com/sg/en/home/media/press-releases/2018/01/kpmg-venture
-pulse-q4-2017.html.

Kuhn, Thomas. *The Structure of Scientific Revolutions.* Chicago: University
of Chicago Press, 1962.

Kupfer, Andrew, and Kathleen Smyth. "AT&T's $12 Billion Cellular
Dream." *Fortune,* December 12, 1994. archive.fortune.com/magazines/fortune
/fortune_archive/1994/12/12/80051/index.htm.

Lamont, Tom. "How to Get a Job at Google: Meet the Man Who Hires
and Fires." *Guardian,* April 6, 2015. www.theguardian.com/technology/2015
/apr/04/how-to-get-job-at-google-meet-man-hires-fires.

"Landline Phones Are a Dying Breed." Statista. infographic.statista.com
/normal/chartoftheday_2072_Landline_phones_in_the_United_States_n.jpg.

Lawrence, Paul R., and Jay W. Lorsch. "Differentiation and Integration in
Complex Organizations." *Administrative Science Quarterly* (1967): 1–47.

Levin, Richard, Alvin Klevorick, Richard Nelson, and Sidney Winter. "Appropriating the Returns from Industrial Research." *Brooking Papers on Economic
Activity* 3 (1987): 783–820.

Levinthal, Daniel A. "The Slow Pace of Rapid Technological Change: Gradualism and Punctuation in Technological Change." *Industrial and Corporate
Change* 7, no. 2 (1998): 217–247.

Long, Tony. "May 2, 1952: First Commercial Jet Flies from London to
Johannesburg." *Wired,* April 2, 2012. www.wired.com/2012/05/may-2-1952
-first-commercial-jet-flies-from-london-to-johannesburg/.

Luo, Hong, Gary Pisano, and Yu Huafang. "Institutionalized Entrepreneurship: Flagship Pioneering." Harvard Business School, case no. 9-718-484,
March 23, 2018.

MacCormack, Alan, John Rusnak, and Carliss Y. Baldwin. "The Impact of
Component Modularity on Design Evolution: Evidence from the Software Industry." Harvard Business School Working Paper, No. 08-038, December 2007.

March, James G. "Exploration Versus Exploitation in Organizational Learning." *Organization Science* 2, no. 1 (February 1991): 71–87.

McCracken, Harry. "Shocker: In 1980, Motorola Had No Idea Where the
Phone Market Would Be in 2000." *Time,* April 15, 2014. time.com/63718/shocker
-in-1980-motorola-had-no-idea-where-the-phone-market-would-be-in-2000/.

McGrath, Rita Gunther, and Ian C. MacMillan. *Discovery-Driven Planning.*
Philadelphia: Wharton School, Snider Entrepreneurial Center, 1995.

Mehta, Miku, and Laura Moskowitz. "Business Method Patents in the
United States: A Judicial History & Prosecution Practice." Sughrue Mion,
PLLC, 2004.

Microsoft Corporation. "Earnings Release FY18 Q2." www.microsoft.com
/en-us/Investor/earnings/FY-2018-Q2/balance-sheets.

"Model T Facts." History.com. Accessed April 4, 2018. www.history.com
/topics/model-t.

Moeller, Sara, Frederick Schlingemann, and Rene Stulz. "Do Shareholders of Acquiring Firms Gain from Acquisitions?" NBER working paper no. 9523, March 2003.

Molla, Rani. "Closing the Books on Microsoft's Windows Phone." recode, July 17, 2017. www.recode.net/2017/7/17/15984222/microsoft-windows-phone -mobile-operating-system-android-iphone-ios.

Nadella, Satya. *Hit Refresh: The Quest to Rediscover Microsoft's Soul and Imagine a Better Future for Everyone.* New York: HarperCollins, 2017.

National Science Foundation. "Science & Engineering Indicators, 2016." www.nsf.gov/statistics/2016/nsb20161/#/report/chapter-4/recent-trends-in-u -s-r-d-performance.

"Netflix Plans to Spend $6 Billion on New Shows, Blowing Away All but One of Its Rivals." CNBC.com, October 17, 2016. https://www.cnbc .com/2016/10/17/netflixs-6-billion-content-budget-in-2017-makes-it-one-of-the -top-spenders.html.

Nicas, Jack. "Google Reorganization Isn't About Cutting Costs, Alphabet CFO Says." *Wall Street Journal,* October 7, 2015. www.wsj.com/articles/google -reorganization-isnt-about-cutting-costs-alphabet-cfo-says-1444258203.

Niccolai, James. "Gateway to Close All Retail Shops." *PCWorld,* April 1, 2004. www.pcworld.com/article/115507/article.html.

"1973 Honda Civic." Archived road test. *Road and Track Magazine,* March 1973. www.caranddriver.com/reviews/1973-honda-civic-test-review.

Noria, Nitin, and Michael Beer. "Cracking the Code of Change." *Harvard Business Review,* May/June 2000. https://hbr.org/2000/05/cracking-the-code-of-change.

"Occupancy Rates." European Environment Agency, April 19, 2016. www .eea.europa.eu/publications/ENVISSUENo12/page029.html.

O'Reilly, Charles, and Michael Tushman. *Lead and Disrupt: How to Solve the Innovator's Dilemma.* Palo Alto, CA: Stanford Business Books, 2016.

Østergaard, Christian R., Bram Timmermans, and Kari Kristinsson. "Does a Different View Create Something New? The Effect of Employee Diversity on Innovation." *Research Policy* 40, no. 3 (2011): 500–509. https://doi.org/10.1016/j .respol.2010.11.004.

Ovans, Andrea. "Can You Patent Your Business Model?" *Harvard Business Review,* July/August 2000. hbr.org/2000/07/can-you-patent-your-business-model.

Padwell, Tom, Pascal Courty, and Michael Jacobides. "easyCar (B)." London Business School, case study, May 2003.

Pisano, Gary. *Science Business: The Promise, Reality, and Future of Biotech.* Boston: Harvard Business Review Press, 2006.

Pisano, Gary. "You Need an Innovation Strategy." *Harvard Business Review,* June 2015. Reprint R1506B.

Pisano, Gary, Philip Andrews, and Alessandro di Fiore. "Fiat-Chrysler Alliance: Launching the Cinquecento in North America." Harvard Business School, case no. 9-611-037.

Pisano, Gary, Lee Fleming, and Eli Strick. "Vertex Pharmaceuticals (A)." 2006. Harvard Business School, case no. 9-604-101.

Pisano, Gary, and Jesse Shulman. "Flying into the Future: Honda Aircraft Corporation." January 2018. Harvard Business School, case no. 9-618-012.

Pisano, Gary, and David Teece. "How to Capture Value from Innovation: Shaping Intellectual Property and Industry Architecture." *California Management Review* 50, no. 1 (Fall 2007): 278–296.

Quinn, Gene. "Patenting Business Methods and Software Still Requires Concrete and Tangible Descriptions." IP Watchdog, August 29, 2015. www .ipwatchdog.com/2015/08/29/patenting-business-methods-and-software /id=54576/.

Ramirez, Anthony. "Blockbuster's Investing Led to Merger." *New York Times,* January 1, 1994. www.nytimes.com/1994/01/08/business/blockbuster-s -investing-led-to-merger.html.

Rivkin, Jan W. "Imitation of Complex Strategies." *Management Science* 46, no. 6 (June 2000): 824–844.

Rivkin, Jan W., and Nicolaj Siggelkow. "Balancing Search and Stability· Interdependencies Among Elements of Organizational Design." *Management Science* 49, no. 3 (March 2003): 290–311.

Romanelli, Elaine, and Michael L. Tushman. "Organizational Transformation as Punctuated Equilibrium: An Empirical Test." *Academy of Management Journal* 37, no. 5 (1994): 1141–1166.

Rumsfeld, Donald. *Known and Unknown: A Memoir.* New York: Penguin Group, 2011.

Perret, Geoffrey. *Eisenhower.* New York: Random House, 2000.

Pew Research Center. "State of the News Media 2016." June 2016. www .journalism.org/2016/06/15/newspapers-fact-sheet/.

Porter, Michael. *Competitive Strategy.* New York: The Free Press, 1980.

Posner, Richard A. "Legal Reason: The Use of Analogy in Legal Argument." *Cornell Law Review* 91 (2006): 761.

PwC. "Corporate R&D Spending Hits Record High for Top 1000, Despite Concerns of Economic Protectionism." Press release, October 24, 2017. www .pwc.com/us/en/press-releases/2017/corporate-rd-spending-hits-record-highs -for-the-top 1000.html.

PwC. "Global Top 100 Companies by Market Capitalization." March 31, 2017. www.pwc.com/gx/en/audit-services/assets/pdf/global-top-100-companies -2017-final.pdf

"The Salad Is in the Bag." *Wall Street Journal,* July 27, 2011. www.wsj.com /articles/SB10001424053111903999904576469973559258778.

S&P Capital IQ. Apple Inc. Public company profile. 2018. Retrieved April 2018, from S&P Capital IQ database. https://www.capitaliq.com.

S&P Capital IQ. Goodyear. Public company profile. 2018. Retrieved April 2018, from S&P Capital IQ database. https://www.capitaliq.com.

S&P Capital IQ. Intel. Public company profile. 2018. Retrieved April 2018, from S&P Capital IQ database. https://www.capitaliq.com.

S&P Capital IQ. Microsoft. Public company profile. 2018. Retrieved April 2018, from S&P Capital IQ database. https://www.capitaliq.com.

S&P Capital IQ. Walmart. 2018. Public company profile. Retrieved April 2018, from S&P Capital IQ database. https://www.capitaliq.com.

Schleifer, Theodore. "Uber's Latest Valuation: $72 Billion." recode, February 2, 2018. www.recode.net/2018/2/9/16996834/uber-latest-valuation-72-billion -waymo-lawsuit-settlement.

Schorn, Daniel. "The Brain Behind Netflix: Lesley Stahl Profiles Company Founder Reed Hastings." *60 Minutes,* December 1, 2006. www.cbsnews.com /news/the-brain-behind-netflix/.

Schumpeter, Joseph A. *Business Cycles: A Theoretical, Historical, and Statistical Analysis of the Capitalist Process.* New York: McGraw-Hill, 1939.

Schumpeter, Joseph A. *Capitalism, Socialism and Democracy.* London: Routledge, 1994 [1942].

Schumpeter, Joseph, and Ursula Backhaus. "The Theory of Economic Development." In Joseph Alois Schumpeter, *Entrepreneurship, Style and Vision,* edited by Jürgen Backhaus, 61–116. New York: Kluwer Academic, 2003.

Shih, Willy. "The Real Lessons of Kodak's Decline." *Sloan Management Review,* Summer 2016, 11–13.

Shih, Willy, and Stephen Kaufman. "Netflix in 2011." Harvard Business Publishing, August 19, 2014.

Smith, Douglas K., and Robert C. Alexander. *Fumbling the Future: How Xerox Invented Then Ignored the First Personal Computer.* Lincoln, NE: iUniverse, 1999.

Snow, Daniel. "Extraordinary Efficiency Growth in Response to New Technology Entries: The Carburetor's Last Gasp." *Academy of Management Proceedings,* no. 1 (2004): 9–11.

Stinchcombe, A. L. "Social Structure and Organizations." In *Handbook of Organizations,* edited by J. G. March, 142–193. Chicago: Rand McNally, 1965.

Strohl, Dan. "Ford, Edison and the Cheap EV That Almost Was." *Wired,* June 18, 2010. www.wired.com/2010/06/henry-ford-thomas-edison-ev/.

Swaminathan, A. "Environmental Conditions at Founding and Organizational Mortality: A Trial-by-Fire Model." *Academy of Management Journal* 39 (1996): 1350–1377.

Teece, David. "Profiting from Technological Innovation: Implications for Integration, Collaboration, Licensing and Public Policy." *Research Policy* 15 (1986): 285–305.

Temperton, James. "Uber's 2016 Losses to Top $3bn According to Leaked Financials." *Wired,* December 20, 2016. www.wired.co.uk/article/uber-finances -losses-driverless-cars.

"This Day in History: August 17." History.com. Accessed April 4, 2018. www.history.com/this-day-in-history/charles-kettering-receives-patent-for-electric-self-starter.

Trefis.com. "Total Revenue of Johnson & Johnson Worldwide from 2012 to 2024 (in Billion U.S. Dollars)." Accessed March 29, 2018. www.statista.com/statistics/258392/total-revenue-of-johnson-und-johnson-worldwide/.

Trefis Team. "Gigafactory Will Cost Tesla $5 Billion but Offers Significant Cost Reductions." *Forbes,* March 11, 2014. www.forbes.com/sites/greatspeculations/2014/03/11/gigafactory-will-cost-tesla-5-billion-but-offers-significant-cost-reductions/.

Tripsas, Mary. "Technology, Identity, and Inertia Through the Lens of 'The Digital Photography Company.'" *Organization Science* 20, no. 2 (2009): 443.

Tripsas, Mary, and Giovanni Gavetti. "Capabilities, Cognition, and Inertia: Evidence from Digital Imaging." *Strategic Management Journal* 21, nos. 10–11 (2000): 1147–1161.

Tushman, Michael L., and Philip Anderson. "Technological Discontinuities and Organizational Environments." *Administrative Science Quarterly* 31, no. 3 (1986): 439–465.

Upton, David M., and Joshua D. Margolis. "McDonald's Corporation." Harvard Business School, case no. 693-028, October 1992. Revised September 1996.

US Energy Information Administration, US Department of Energy. "U.S. Field Oil Production." Washington, DC, April 30, 2018. www.eia.gov/dnav/pet/hist/LeafHandler.ashx?n=PET&s=MCRFPUS1&f=A.

Uzzi, Brian, Satyam Mukherjee, Michael Stringer, and Ben Jones. "Atypical Combinations and Scientific Impact." *Science* 342, no. 6157 (2013): 468–472.

Von Hippel, Eric. *Free Innovation.* Cambridge, MA: MIT Press, 2016.

Waldrop, M. Mitchel, "More Than Moore." *Nature* 530 (February 11, 2016): 145–147.

Weiss, Todd R. "Timeline: PARC Milestones." *Computerworld,* September 20, 2010. Accessed November 6, 2017. https://www.computerworld.com/article/2515874/computer-hardware/timeline--parc-milestones.html.

World Bank. "Number of Bank Branches for United States." Federal Reserve Bank of St. Louis. Accessed February 23, 2018. fred.stlouisfed.org/series/DDAI02USA643NWDB.

Index

accountability, 191–194, 207, 209, 211–212

acquisition of innovative companies, 3, 16

Adobe, 155

advocacy approach to decision making, 167, 171

Afeyan, Noubar, 124–125, 143, 168

Airbnb, 47

ALCO, 105

Alice's Adventures in Wonderland (Carroll), 21

Alphabet. *See* Google

Amazon
  Amazon Web Services, 84, 146, 194
  book-selling success, 92
  business model experimentation, 84
  continued innovation, 8
  creation of value for ecosystem, 77
  creative construction, 8
  experimentation, 8, 84, 189
  as flat organization, 194
  increasing returns to scale, 81
  initial third-party seller markets, 144
  innovations to benefit shopper's experience, 26
  as innovator, 1, 4
  letter from Bezos to shareholders, 11
  number of employees, 199
  opening web infrastructure to third-party developers, 147
  ranking of employees, 187
  retail business profitability, 97
  reviews of products, 79
  success at transformative innovation, 8
  as transformative business model, 131
  "two-pizza rule," 194
  use of quasi-autonomous teams, 148
  in VoD market, 72, 103

ambiguity, 156–158, 162

AMD, 53

analogic reasoning, 73, 75, 123–124

analytics. *See* financial analytical tools

anchoring of initial impressions, 159

Annie Hall (film), 103

Apple
  Apple II, 130
  Apple TV, 103
  Apple University, 197
  business model innovation, 54
  creation of value for ecosystem, 77–78
  creative construction, 7–8
  as innovator, 1, 4
  iPod, 136
  Macintosh, 155
  proprietary operating system, 97
  routine innovation by, 32, 38, 53, 157
  use of crowdsourcing by, 127
  value proposition themes of innovations, 26
  in VoD market, 72, 103
  See also iPhone

architectural innovation
  Alphabet's exploration of opportunities for, 41
  comparison to routine innovation, 38–39
  digital photography, 32–33
  explanation of, 32–34
  Google as example of, 33

architectural innovation *(continued)*
  Innovation Landscape Map, 31 (figure)
  Netflix VoD, 71
  when to use, 55–56
Arrow, Ken, 79
Arrow's paradox, 79
AT&T, 2, 155
attribution bias, 159
Audi, 98
Audi on Demand, 34
automobile industry
  autonomous vehicles, 33–34, 41
  potential for paradigm shifts in, 46
  threats from transformative
    innovations, 41

Baldwin Locomotive, 104–105
Bardeen, John, 137, 145
Barnes and Noble, 92
Bay of Pigs invasion, 172
Becton Dickinson (BD), 25–26
Bell Labs
  attraction of talent to, 123, 215
  diversity of talent at, 123
  no constraints on imagination, 125
  structured to drive cross-discipline
    integration, 145
  suspension of belief, 125
  transformative inventions of, 7
Bezos, Jeff, 11, 144, 194, 197, 201
BlackSocks, 43
Blockbuster
  critical resources of, 65
  data on customers' preferences,
    65–66
  failure to anticipate success of DVD
    rental market, 68
  late fees, 69–70
  value capture, 66
  value creation, 66, 68
  value distribution, 66–67, 70
Boeing, 32, 99, 112
Boger, Joshua, 153–154, 173, 175–176,
    192, 194
Bohmer, Richard, 183

Boston Beer Company, 30
Brady, Tom, 213–214
Brattain, Walter, 145
Brin, Sergey
  ambiguity of original options,
    157–158, 194
  as cofounder of Google, 144
  leadership, 194
  preservation of innovative culture,
    197, 201
broadband speeds, 103
bullet hole example, 118–119
business, navigating threats to
  assessment of profits if disruption is
    adopted, 100
  changes in customer behavior and
    tastes, 99
  defend and extend strategy, 104
  estimating time horizon, 99
  facing uncertainty, 104–105
  improvement potential in existing
    technologies, 99
  Mapping Responses to Potential
    Disruptions, 101 (figure)
  pivoting around capabilities, 103–104
  survival-enhancing behaviors, 106
  technological and economic analyses,
    99
business model design
  Business Model Framework (RV³),
    59 (figure)
  exploitation of interdependencies
    among components, 60
  resource choice decisions, 59 (figure)
  using RV³ framework, 59–60
  See also design principles
Business Model Framework (RV³), 59
    (figure), 70 (figure)
business model innovation
  Blockbuster, 65–67
  comparing business models of
    Blockbuster and Netflix, 70
    (figure)
  as competitive weapon, 65
  experimentation and learning, 83

failure of, 73
Netflix, 67–70
as priority, 83
reason for, 46–47
throughout history, 57
transformative, 131
business model innovators
Airbnb, 47
Apple, 54
Boston Beer Company, 30
Flagship Pioneering, 124–125
IKEA, 29
Kodak, 32
Lyft, 30, 47
Netflix, 29
Polaroid, 32
ready-to-eat salad producers, 28–29
Ryanair, 29–30
Tommy John, 47
Uber, 30, 47, 131
Warby Parker, 47
business models
business strategy and business model
    relationship, 62–65
company-owned store, 64
comparison of Blockbuster and
    Netflix business models, 70 (figure)
dangers of imitation, 73–75
design principles, 75–83
evolution through iteration, 143
evolving, 40
franchising, 64
Internet-based, 64
transformative, 131
venture creation, 64
Bussicom, 93

carbon-fiber technology, 49
carburetor improvement, 94
Carroll, Lewis, 21
cash-out date, 208
Catch-22 (film), 1
Catmull, Ed, 138, 143, 197, 201
cell phone telephone service user
    percentage, 92

Chick-fil-A, 64
Christensen, Clay, 32, 44, 58, 160
Chrysler, 176, 200
Churchill, Winston, 174
cloud-based computing, 8, 84, 87, 146
Cockburn, Ian, 132
collaboration, 183–184
Columbia, 49
Compaq, 87
Comparing the Business Models of
    Blockbuster and Netflix using the
    RV³ Framework, 70 (figure)
compensation systems, 214
competition, dynamic quality of, 1
complementarities
    advantages of, 77
    as barrier to imitation, 50–52, 82
    Netflix as example, 75–77
    in Netflix DVD rental business
        model, 76 (figure)
    Tesla's production of batteries for
        electric cars, 52
    use of by iPhone, 82
confirmation bias, 159
consensus, 192
consumer electronics, 41
contact lens company, innovation
    decisions by, 22–24
contest platforms, 127
cooking analogy, 141
Corning
    invention of fiber-optic cable and
        glass manufacturing processes, 7
    strategy and capital allocation
        framework, 37
corporate innovators, list of, 1
creative construction
    at Apple, 7–8
    complexity, 10
    friction, mobility and, 10
    iPhone as example, 7
    at Johnson & Johnson, 9–11
    paradox of, 9
    trade-offs in, 218
    See also innovation; leadership

creative destruction
   defined, 2
   reasons for, 2–3
   victims of, 88–89
   vulnerability of established
      businesses, 2, 35
   waves of, 6
Creativity, Inc (Catmull), 143
Crick, Francis, 132, 137
crowdsourcing
   Apple, 127
   Google, 127
   Microsoft, 127
   as part of innovation process,
      126–127
   as possible strategy, 109
   review sites, 79–80
   Samsung, 127
Cuban missile crisis, 172
culture, defined, 181
cultures. *See* innovative cultures;
      start-up cultures
customers
   changes in behavior and tastes, 44
   customer need satiation, 44
   endogenous preferences of, 93
   hidden customer, 114–118
   unmet needs of, 41–44
   value creation for, 25, 29, 30

da Vinci, Leonardo, 137
DARPA
   ability to alter portfolio of projects,
      150
   fixed timeframe, 149
   program leaders control programs,
      149, 150
   temporary project teams, 149
   transformative technologies seeded
      by, 149
debate, fostering
   absence of personal attacks, 175
   demanding criticism, 173–174
   solicitation of input, 172–173
   transparency, 174

DEC, 2, 88
decentralization, 132–135
decision making
   event-driven approach, 166–167
   hypothesis-driven approach, 167–170
   leadership, characteristics of, 176
defend and extend strategy, 104
Defense Applied Research Projects
      Agency. *See* DARPA
Dell
   business model innovation, 52–53
   in personal computer business, 87
   profitability of personal computers, 97
design principles
   build upon hard-to-imitate resources,
      80–83
   create value for ecosystem, 77–78
   exploit "free" resources, 78–80
   search for complementarities, 75–77
diesel engines, locomotive, 104
digital imaging
   as architectural innovation, 32–33
   Kodak, 96–97
   Polaroid, 155
   profit potential of, 96
   Sony, 136
discounted cash flow, 155–156, 161
disk drive industry, 44
Disney, 1
disruptive innovation, 32, 34, 54
diverse workforce, advantages of,
      122–123
DNA, human, 129, 132
DNA, organizational, 3–4, 199
Dollar Shave Club, 43
drug hunters, 138
drug industry
   drug discovery, 59
   drug hunters, 138
   genetically engineered drugs, 131
   molecular-biology-based approaches,
      48
   new paradigms for, 46
   pharmaceutical R&D programs, 153,
      169

radical innovation in, 32
use of synthesis, 131
Dugan, Regina, 149
DuPont
as innovator, 1
search for replacement for polyester
in tires, 114–115
search for uses for Kevlar, 115–117

easyCar, 74–75
easyGroup, 74
easyJet, 73–74
"eat your own lunch before someone
else does," 85, 88–89, 95–97,
101–103, 106
eBay, transformative business model
of, 131
ecosystem, creating value for
Amazon, 77
Apple, 77–78
Intel, 77–78
Microsoft, 77–78
Toyota, 78
Uber, 77
Eddie Merckx, 49
Edison, Thomas, 89, 137
Edmondson, Amy, 183
Einstein, Albert, 137
Eisenhower, Dwight, 173, 193
electric starter for automobiles, 90
electric vehicles
critical problems of, 117
history of, 89–90
market for, 51–52
use of lithium-ion batteries in, 118
entrepreneurial firms, as source of
transformative innovation, 4
ESPN, 72
event-driven approach to decision
making, 166–167
experimentation
Amazon as example, 8, 84
in business model innovation, 83–84
Hewlett Packard as example, 143
iteration and, 125, 143

project, 189
synthesis and, 141–144
testing and, 125–126
as vehicle for learning, 183
Exxon Valdez oil spill, 127

Facebook
as collector of information about
customers, 79
exploitation of inherent positive
network economies, 97
as innovator, 1
routine innovations of, 39
value creation for customers, 81
failure, tolerance of, 12–13, 143–144,
183, 185–188, 209
fast food chains
collaboration among owner
operators, 192–193
individual-accountability, 192–193
similar strategy, different business
models, 64
Fazioli Pianoforte S.p.A., 138
Fiat, 176, 200, 206, 211
financial analytical tools
"alleged crimes" against, 160
effect of uncertainty and ambiguity
of innovation projects, 161–162
"flaws" of, 161
as "innovation killers," 160
limits of, 162–163
purpose of, 161
reasons for reliance on, 164–165
as tool of inquiry, 170–171
financial services company, as example
of unused potential, 133–135
Flagship Pioneering, 124–125, 168,
169, 189
flat organizations, 194
Fleming, Lee, 131, 142, 143
Ford, Henry, 89, 137
Ford Motor Company, 1
Fortune 500 rankings, 6, 7, 8
franchising, 64
Franklin, Rosalind, 132

Friendster, 82
fuel injection, electronic, 91
Fuji, 103
Fujino, Michimasa, 111–112, 122, 124, 192
futurists, 91

Gabriel, Kaigham, 149
Garvin, David, 165
GE (General Electric)
  aircraft engines business unit, 60
  domination of diesel locomotive industry, 105
  as innovator, 1
  number of employees, 199
GE Medical Systems, 39
Genentech, 4, 205
genetic components of DNA, as example of innovation through combination, 129
genetically engineered drugs, 131
Gillette razors, evolution of, 42–43
GM, 98
GMOs, economic significance of, 7
Goodyear, 40–41
Google (now Alphabet)
  advertising based on customer information, 78–79
  allocation of resources, 37
  Android operating system, 92
  attraction of talent to, 214
  business model evolution, 144
  crowdsourcing by, 127
  decentralized innovation, 194
  disruptive innovation, 32
  as employee-friendly culture, 187
  encouragement of risk taking and failure, 188
  exploration of radical and architectural innovation opportunities, 41
  as innovator, 1, 4
  job applications for, 187
  market demand growth potential, 40

  performance management system, 187–188
  revenues, 40
  routine innovation, 40, 42
  search engine, convenience of, 113
  stock-based compensation plan, 214
  strong increasing returns to scale, 97
  transformative innovation, 8
  in VoD market, 72, 103
GoPro, 96
Gordon, Robert, 223
grocery businesses
  similar strategy, different business models, 63–64
  Stop & Shop, 62–63
  threats from transformative innovations, 85
  Whole Foods, 62–64
GSK, 207

Haji-Ioannu, Stelios, 73–74
Harry's, 43
Harvard Business Review
  on design prowess of Sony, 136
  on financial analytical tools, 160
Harvard University, joint research symposium at, 120–121
Hastings, Reed, 65, 73
Heller, Joseph, 1
Henderson, Rebecca, 132
Hewlett Packard, 87, 143
Hoff, Ted, 93
home court
  advantage, 35
  bias, 35
  routine innovation, 34
  trade-offs between home court and outside opportunities, 218, 220
  venturing outside of, 111–113, 121–128, 158–160, 204–205
Honda
  Honda Aircraft Company, 111
  light jet program hypotheses, 168
  transformative innovation, 8, 111–112

HondaJet program
  Civic design analogy, 123–124
  in Greensboro, North Carolina, 207
  over-the-wing-engine design, 111, 124
  success in light business jet market, 112
hotel chains, threats from transformative innovations, 85
Hulu, 72, 103
human genome mapping, 132
hypothesis-driven approach to decision making, 167–170

IBM
  dominance of mainframe computer business, 86–87
  eating own lunch, 86, 101–102
  entry into personal computer market, 86
  as innovator, 1
  number of employees, 199
  outsourcing of operating system and microprocessor, 87
  personal computer unit in Florida, 207
  revolution of computer architecture by, 6–7
  sale of PC division to Lenovo, 87
  switch to Linux by, 102
  System Z mainframe, 87
IDEO, 215–216
IKEA, 29
imitation, barriers to
  building complementary technologies, 51–52
  business model innovation, 52–53
  continual evolution, 82
  hard-to-replicate resources, 81
  inherent complexity, 52
  patents, 50–52, 80–81
  rapid routine innovation, 53–54
  specialized ecosystem, 82
information, paradox of, 79
ink-jet printer creation, 143

InnoCentive, 127
innovation
  after acquisition of new firm, 16
  alignment with business strategy, 25
  balancing types of, 39, 54–56
  combination of existing ideas and components, 129–130
  competitive advantage of, 15–16
  in complex organizations, 10
  disruptive threat prediction, 88–95
  diversity of talent base, 122
  fear of seeming stupid, 120
  as human activity, 179
  Innovation Landscape Map, 31 (figure)
  involvement of learning in, 177–178
  judging merits of, 38
  leadership tasks, 17
  outside home court, 34–35, 118–120
  paradox of, 1, 15
  profit potential, 95–98
  purpose of, 25
  rapid disruption, 92
  slow disruption, 91
  society-transforming, 223
  solutions in search of problems, 114–118
  as solutions to social problems, 113
  transformative, 6–8
  types of, 28–30
  value creation and, 25–30, 35
  See also architectural innovation; innovation initiatives; innovation strategy; innovative cultures; routine innovation; synthesis; transformative innovation
innovation initiatives
  choices of management practices, 14–15
  cultural changes, 15
  obstacles, 14
  pattern of, 12–13
  percent of failures, 13
  time horizon, 14
  trade-offs, 14

The Innovation Landscape Map, 31
(figure)
innovation strategy
alignment of organizational parts
around common priorities, 19,
25–27
clarification of trade-offs, 19, 21–24,
27
creation of value for customers, 25,
29, 30
focus of resources and energy on
building capabilities, 27–28
framework for different options,
30–34, 31 (figure)
mapping innovation opportunities,
28–30
Moore's Law, 47
organization's capabilities in
alignment with, 109
understanding of objectives, 21
value capture for company, 25, 30
See also resources
innovation systems, 27, 110
innovative cultures
acquisition of innovative company, 205
Apple, as example, 136
beliefs about, 182–185
building, 198, 204
challenges created by growth,
198–200
as complexity of, 195
Google, as example, 32, 37, 187–188,
194
guiding principles of, 200–207
implementation difficulties, 186–187
importance of team of supporters, 206
imprinting effect of original
founders, 199
in large organizations, 207–215
mutation of, 199–200
paradox of, 187–194
as places to work, 191, 195
preservation of, 197–201
requirement of balance between
different values, 195

safe spaces in, 204
See also leadership, role of
innovative cultures, characteristics of
candid feedback, 189–191
collaboration, 183, 184
discipline, 188–189
individual accountability, 191–194
intolerance of incompetence,
187–188
psychological safety, 183–184
shared values, 181, 195, 198, 201, 206
strong leadership, 194
structural flatness, 184–185
tolerance of failure, 183
willingness to experiment, 183
innovative organizations, as products of
human creativity, 224
innovators, list of, 1
Intel
buying back rights to microprocessor,
93–94
creating value for ecosystem, 77–78
exploration of alternative paradigms,
47–48
as innovator, 1, 4
invention of microprocessor, 93,
117–118
outsourcing of IBM's microprocessor
to, 87
profits from personal computers, 97
routine innovation, 32, 38, 42, 53
intellectual arbitrage, 137
internal combustion engine, 45–46,
90, 117
internal rate of return, 156, 161
Internet-based banking, 91
Internet-only vendors, 43–44
Internet purchases, as example of
innovation by synthesis, 130
Internet service providers, domination
of VoD market by, 72
iPad, 38, 91
iPhone
appearance, 113
as example of creative construction, 7

keeping ahead of imitators, 53
as synthesis of known technologies, 130
use of specialized complementary resources, 82
iPod, 136
Isaacson, Walter, 136
iteration
    experimentation and, 125
    at Pixar, 143
    in problem solving, 117
    role of in evolution of business models, 143–144
    suppression of, 144
    as theme in innovative organizations, 143

Jassy, Andy, 147–149, 194
Jobs, Steve
    ability to see connections across fields, 137
    biography by Walter Isaacson, 136
    creation of Apple University, 197
    intolerance for incompetence, 187
    prediction about tablets, 91
Johnson & Johnson
    creative construction of, 9–11
    discouragement of risk-taking, 201–202
    as innovator, 1
joint research symposium at Harvard University, 120–121
Joy, Bill, 126
Joy's Law, 126
judgments, 158–160

Kaufman, Stephen, 160
Kelley, David, 201, 215
Kelly, Mervin, 145
Kettering, Charles, 90
Kevlar
    initial use for, 114–115
    as reinforcement for police vests, 115
    search for more applications and markets for, 115–117

Key Complementarities in Netflix DVD Rental Business Model, 76 (figure)
Kodak
    architectural innovation, 32–33
    digital imaging, effect on profit potential, 96
    dire situation of, 103
    as innovator, 1
    predictions of failure of, 2
Kwoleck, Stephanie, 114

Lakhani, Karim, 127
land line telephone service user percentage, 92
large established enterprises
    acquisitions by, 3
    advantages of, 11, 128
    decentralization, 132–133
    freight train characterization, 5
    learning, 128, 143
    organizational pathologies of, 2–3
    R&D productivity compared to smaller companies, 5
    replicating accountability culture of a start-up, 211–212
    replicating risk-rewards incentives of a start-up, 212–215
    replicating speed of a start-up, 210–211
    scale, innovation and, 5
    transformative innovation, view of, 3
    See also transformative innovations of large firms
"last gasps" of old technologies, 94
latent demand, 113
leaders, characteristics of, 176
leadership, constructive
    becoming different from competitors, 219–220
    discipline about tough trade-offs, 220
    obsession with organizational culture, 222
    as organizational innovators, 221
    problem solving outlook, 219
    systems perspective on innovation, 220–221

leadership *(continued)*
as talent hawks, 221–222
view of innovation as competitive
weapon, 219
leadership, role of in cultural change
arsenal of management tools
required, 216
getting the right people, 205–207
incubating and protecting
"Revolutionary" pockets, 203–205
modeling desired behavior, 201–203
taking ownership of cultural
problem, 200–201
learning
from analogies, 123
in business model innovation, 83
debate and, 171–175
experimentation as vehicle for, 183
in innovative cultures, 177–178,
182–198, 221
keeping mind open, 175–176
orienting R&D proposals around,
167–170
selection as process of, 165–170
as survival enhancing behavior, 106
synthesis and, 151
in transformative innovation, 128, 143
use of analytics in, 170–172
use of criticism, 174
Lego Design byME, 72–73
Lenovo, purchase of IBM PC division
by, 87
Levinson, Art, 205
Linux software, 101–102
lithium-ion batteries, 118
Lyft
business model innovation, 30, 47
financial losses of, 98
imitators of, 80

Macintosh, 155
mainframe computers, 86–87
Mapping Responses to Potential
Disruptions, 101 (figure)
March, James, 15

Marchionne, Sergio, 176, 200, 206, 211
Marconi, Guglielmo, 137
matrix teams, 148
McCaw Cellular, 155
McDonald's
business models, 64
imitators of, 80
as innovator, 1
source of new menu ideas, 126
microprocessors, 93–94, 117–118
Microsoft
balance sheet of, 210
creating value for ecosystem, 77–78
as innovator, 1, 4
mobile operating system of, 83
outsourcing of IBM's operating
system to, 87
profits from personal computers, 97
routine innovation, 38
use of crowdsourcing by, 127
mobility, friction and, 10
model, defined, 75
Model T Ford, 90
Monsanto Corporation, agricultural
seed industry and, 7
Monte Carlo simulation, 170
Moore, Gordon, 94
Moore's Law, 47, 48, 86, 94
Morgan Stanley, 3
Motorola, 7
music, as example of innovation
through combination, 129
Musk, Elon, 89
mutation within cultures, 199–200
MySpace, 39, 82

Nadella, Satya, 197–198
net present value, 161
Netflix
advantages of scale, 72
business model innovation, 29, 30
convenience, 67, 69, 71
domination of VoD market, 72
eating own lunch, 102–103
elimination of stores, 67

evolution of business model, 84
film library, 67
focus on content creation, 72
imitators of, 80
impact of video storage technology on, 93
as innovator, 4
lower cost structure of, 69
move from DVD rental to VoD, 102
strategy-business model coherence, 62–65, 71
value distribution, 68
video on demand (VoD), 71
viewer recommendation system, 67
Netscape, 4
New England Patriots, 214
newspapers, print, 91, 97
Newton, Isaac, 137
Nobel Prize winners, 145
Nokia
creative destruction of, 7, 82, 88
predictions of failure of, 2
sale to Microsoft, 82
Symbian operating system of, 92
Normandy invasion (Operation Overlord), 173–174

oil field analogy, 39–40, 47
online shopping, 8
organizational DNA, 3–4, 199
organizational systems, 128, 182, 195, 217–218
organizationally autonomous units, 207–208
"overshooting the market," 44

Page, Larry
ambiguity of original options, 157–158, 194
as cofounder of Google, 144
leadership, 194
preservation of innovative culture, 197, 201
Palo Alto Research Center, 154
Pal's, 64

paradigm shifts
autonomous vehicles, 33–34, 41, 46, 48
digital photography, 32–33
high-end bicycle frame industry, 48–50
pharmaceutical industry, 46
patents, 50–51, 80–81
Pearson, Gerald, 145
Penn Station, 64
personal computers
as competitive business, 87
as example of innovation by synthesis, 130
impact on IBM, 86–88
low profits for sellers of, 97
as market for microprocessors, 118
unpredictable popularity of, 94
pharmaceutical innovation, 32, 46
phase-gate models, 142
Pinarello, 49–50
Pixar
candid feedback for directors, 192
central role of iteration at, 143
diverse workforce of, 138
preservation of innovative culture, 197
replacement of incompetent directors, 188
routine innovation by, 32
success of, 197
Polaroid
architectural innovation, 31 (figure), 32–33
digital photography and, 155
as example of poor project-selection decisions, 155
predictions of failure of, 2, 88
predicting threats
endogenous customer preferences, 93
system interdependencies, 92
timing of reaction to disruptive innovations, 94–95
product reviews, 79
profit impact, 100–101, 101 (figure)

profit potential, 96–97
project selection. *See* selection decisions
project teams
 Amazon Web Services as example,
  146–148
 DARPA as example, 149–150
 focus on specific innovation
  opportunities, 146
 in innovative cultures, 183, 190–194
 quasi-autonomous, 148, 204–205, 208
propeller aircraft engines, 91

quantum computing, 48

radical innovation, 32, 55
RCA, 1, 2
R&D
 career paths in, 140
 evaluating projects, 163
 expenditures, 2, 9
 homogeneity in organizations, 122
 orienting proposals around learning,
  167–170
 pharmaceutical, 5, 32, 132, 144, 153,
  169
 R&D productivity of large *versus*
  smaller companies, 5
 at Vertex, 173
real option valuation, 163, 170
recency effects, 160
resource allocation principles
 core market growth capability,
  39–41
 creation of barriers to imitation,
  50–51
 customer needs, 41–44
 examples of, 37–38
 optimal, 38
 technological paradigm improvement
  potential, 44–50
resources
 allocation of, 53, 155, 160, 170 (*See
  also* resource allocation principles)
 Alphabet's allocation policy, 37
 Corning's allocation policy, 37

defined, 58
"free," 78–80
hard-to-replicate, 81
making choices, 59–60, 59 (figure)
review sites, 79–80
reviews of products, 79
Reynolds Cycling, 49
ride-sharing business, 98
RIM, 2, 7, 88
The Rise and Fall of American Growth
 (Gordon), 223
road system expansion in US, 90
Roche, 205
routine innovation
 addressing customers' unmet needs,
  42
 anchoring with well-defined
  problems, 117
 denigration of, 38
 rapid, 53–54
 as winning strategy, 54
routine innovation examples
 Amazon, 32
 Apple, 32, 38, 53, 157
 Boeing, 32
 EMI, 39
 Facebook, 39
 GE Medical Systems, 39
 Goodyear, 40–41
 Google, 40, 42
 Intel, 32, 38, 42, 53
 Microsoft, 38
 MySpace, 39
 Pixar, 32
 RV³ business model framework, 59–60,
  68
Ryanair, 29–30, 73

safe spaces, 204
salad, ready-to-eat, 28–29
Samsung, use of crowdsourcing by, 127
Sato, Vicki, 176, 192
Scapin, 49
Schumpeter, Joseph, 2, 131
Schwan, Severin, 205

searches, broadening
  challenging sacred assumptions, 124–126
  creation of forcing mechanisms, 121
  diverse workforce, 122–123
  experimentation and testing, 125–126
  moving people away from home courts, 121–122
  opening up innovative processes, 126–127
  scale, advantages of, 128
  use of analogies, 123–124
searches for problems and solutions
  expanding search arc, 118–127
  hidden customer, 114–118
  outside home court, 112–113
  problem-solving perspective, 113–114
selection decisions
  advocacy approach, 167, 171
  ambiguity, 156–158, 162
  AT&T, as example of poor project-selection decisions, 155
  building a learning innovation system, 176–178
  errors in, 155–158
  event-driven approach, 166–167
  financial analytical tools, 160–165
  fostering vigorous debate, 171–175
  hypothesis-driven approach, 167–170
  judgments, 158–160
  keeping an open mind, 175–176
  managers as innovators, 177
  over- or underestimation of project risk, 160
  Polaroid, as example of poor project-selection decisions, 155
  as process of learning, 165–170
  trade-off between type 1 and type 2 errors, 158
  uncertainty, 105–106, 127, 156, 162–163, 183
  using analytics as tool for inquiry, 170–171

Xerox, as example of poor project-selection decisions, 154–155
semiconductors, 47, 113
Serotta, 49
Shieber, Stuart, 120–121
Shih, Willy, 96, 160
Shimano, 49
Shockley, William, 145
Smith Corona, 100, 103–104
Snow, Dan, 94
Sony, 136
Sorenson, Olaf, 131
Southwest Airlines, 24–25
start-up cultures
  characterization of, 5
  comfort with extreme risk-reward outcomes, 209
  individual accountability, 209
  no tolerance for incompetence, 209
  obsession with speed, 208
statin drugs, 113
Stoffels, Paul, 201, 202
Stop & Shop, 62–63
Stradivari, Antonio, 139
strategy, defined, 24, 37
subscription services, 43
Sun Microsystems, 2, 126
synthesis
  across disease areas, 132
  application of knowledge across fields, 132
  building capability for, 151
  cooking analogy, 141
  creating permeable boundaries, 144–150
  decentralization as problem, 134
  deep cultural divides as challenge, 134–135
  defined, 130, 131
  DNA discovery, 132
  exploration and experimentation, 141–144
  fluidity, 142–143, 146, 148–149, 184
  as a function of management, 151
  having all the pieces, 133–136

synthesis *(continued)*
  innovation and, 130–133
  Internet purchases as example of, 130
  iPhone as synthesis of known
    technologies, 130
  rapid experimentation, iteration, and
    learning, 143, 151
  recruiting synthesizers, 137–141
  transformative innovation and, 151
  unpredictability of, 141
  variety of ingredients, 131
synthesizers
  Catmull, Ed, 138, 143
  characteristics of, 140
  cultivation of within organizations,
    140
  drug hunters, 138
  Fazioli, Paolo, 138–139
  Israeli systems biologist, 139
  list of, 137
  people from "non-conforming"
    backgrounds, 140
  at Pixar, 138
System Z mainframe, 87

talent
  attracting, 78, 214–215, 221
  Bell Labs, attracting talent, 123, 215
  diversity of, 122, 123
  Google, attracting talent, 214
  harnessing talents to mission of
    company, 198
  hiring right talent, 146, 221–222
  investment in, 50
  large enterprises' advantages in
    recruiting, 11, 128
  meshing talents together, 146
taxis, traditional
  company ownership of vehicles, 60
  concern about underutilized cars, 61
  dividends or profit sharing for
    owners, 62
  employment of dispatchers, 60
  licenses, 61, 62
  revenue streams, 62

  seen as safer alternative to private
    rides, 61
  value creation, 61
technological innovation, 32, 45–46, 55
technological paradigm, defined, 44
technological paradigm shifts, 32–33,
    41, 46, 48–50
technologies, obsolete, 217
Teradyne, 190
Tesla, Inc., 52
Tesla, Nikola, 137
3Com, 155
Tibotec, 202
Tommy John, 44, 47
Torvalds, Linus, 102
Toy Story (film), 197
Toyota, 78
trade-offs
  clarification of, 19, 21–24, 27
  in creative constructive enterprises, 218
  in innovation practices, 14, 109
  navigating tough choices, 24, 27, 35,
    37, 220
  in organizational design, 146
  between type 1 and type 2 errors,
    158, 170
  using working hypotheses, 170
transformative innovations
  barriers to achieving, 133–136
  of business models, 131
  decision making, 166–167
  encouraging new ideas, 128
  entrepreneurial firms as source of, 4
  large firms and, 6
  mature slow-growing industries and,
    41
  prediction, 88–89
  threats from, 85
transformative innovations of large
    firms
  Amazon, 8, 131
  Bell Labs, 7
  Corning, 7
  DARPA, 149
  Google, 8

IBM, 6–7
   Monsanto, 7
transistors, 131
TripAdvisor reviews, 79
type 1 and 2 errors in selection, 158

Uber
   automated dispatch system, 61
   business model innovation, 30, 47, 131
   convenience, 61
   extra benefits for customers, 61
   financial losses of, 98
   imitators of, 80
   as innovator, 4
   investment in brand, 61
   low cost, 61
   network of independent drivers, 61
   ownership of cars, 61
   potential capital appreciation, 62
   twenty percent share of fares to
      company, 62
   value creation, 61, 77
   venture funding, 62
   See also taxis, traditional
uncertainty, 104–106, 127, 156,
      162–163, 183
Unilever, 43
Unix, 102, 123

valuation, real option, 163, 170
value capture
   Blockbuster, 69
   choices, 60
   comparison of Blockbuster and
      Netflix, 70 (figure)
   comparison of Uber to traditional
      taxi companies, 61–62
   defined, 59
   by grocery retailers, 63
   from innovation, 25
   by Netflix, 76, 76 (figure)
   as part of fundamental task of
      businesses, 58
value creation
   Amazon, 77

Apple, 77–78
Becton Dickinson (BD), 25–26
Blockbuster, 66, 68, 70 (figure)
business model framework, 59 (figure)
   for customers, 25, 29, 30
   declining, 83
   defined, 58
   easyCar, 74
   easyJet, 74
   for ecosystem, 77–80
   in high-end bicycle market, 49–50
   innovation and, 25–30, 35
   Lego's Design byME, 73
   Netflix, 67–68, 70–71
   as part of fundamental task of
      businesses, 58–59
   routine innovation, 42
   source of for VoD, 72
   by taxi companies, 61
   traditional supermarkets, 63
   Uber, 61
   Whole Foods, 63
value distribution
   of Blockbuster, 66–67
   choices, 60
   comparison of Blockbuster and
      Netflix, 70 (figure)
   comparison of Uber and traditional
      taxi companies, 62
   defined, 59
   of Netflix, 68, 76, 76 (figure)
   as part of fundamental task of
      businesses, 59
value proposition, 26
Vauclain, Samuel, 105
venture creation, 124
venture hypotheses, 168, 189
Vertex Pharmaceuticals
   analytical tools, 170
   consensus choice, 192
   decision dilemma, 153–154
   keeping open mind during decision
      making, 176
   R&D, 173
   use of venture hypotheses, 168

video on demand. *See* VoD
Virco, 202
VoD (video on demand)
 Amazon, 72, 103
 Apple, 72, 103
 defined, 71
 as example of rapid disruption, 92
 Google, 72, 103
 Hulu, 72, 103
 implications for business model
  design, 71–72
 Netflix's move to, 102–103
von Hippel, Eric, 126

Wald, Abraham, 119
Wall Street Journal, on electric cars, 90

Walmart, 1, 97–98
Wang, 2, 88
Warby Parker, 47
waterfall process, 142
Watson, James, 132, 137
Whole Foods, 62–64
Wilkins, Maurice, 132
working hypotheses, 170

Xerox, 2, 154–155, 158
Yahoo, 2
Yelp reviews, 79

zShops, 144

GARY P. PISANO is one of the world's leading scholars in the fields of innovation, strategy, manufacturing, and competitiveness. He is the Harry E. Figgie Professor of Business Administration and senior associate dean for faculty development at Harvard Business School. He is the author of five previous books including *Science Business* and *Producing Prosperity*. Dr. Pisano has served as an advisor to major corporations and start-up companies throughout the world. His many awards include the prestigious McKinsey Award for the best article published in the *Harvard Business Review*.

For more information, visit www.gpisano.com.

PublicAffairs is a publishing house founded in 1997. It is a tribute to the standards, values, and flair of three persons who have served as mentors to countless reporters, writers, editors, and book people of all kinds, including me.

I. F. Stone, proprietor of *I. F. Stone's Weekly*, combined a commitment to the First Amendment with entrepreneurial zeal and reporting skill and became one of the great independent journalists in American history. At the age of eighty, Izzy published *The Trial of Socrates*, which was a national bestseller. He wrote the book after he taught himself ancient Greek.

Benjamin C. Bradlee was for nearly thirty years the charismatic editorial leader of *The Washington Post*. It was Ben who gave the *Post* the range and courage to pursue such historic issues as Watergate. He supported his reporters with a tenacity that made them fearless and it is no accident that so many became authors of influential, best-selling books.

Robert L. Bernstein, the chief executive of Random House for more than a quarter century, guided one of the nation's premier publishing houses. Bob was personally responsible for many books of political dissent and argument that challenged tyranny around the globe. He is also the founder and longtime chair of Human Rights Watch, one of the most respected human rights organizations in the world.

•   •   •

For fifty years, the banner of Public Affairs Press was carried by its owner Morris B. Schnapper, who published Gandhi, Nasser, Toynbee, Truman, and about 1,500 other authors. In 1983, Schnapper was described by *The Washington Post* as "a redoubtable gadfly." His legacy will endure in the books to come.

Peter Osnos, *Founder*